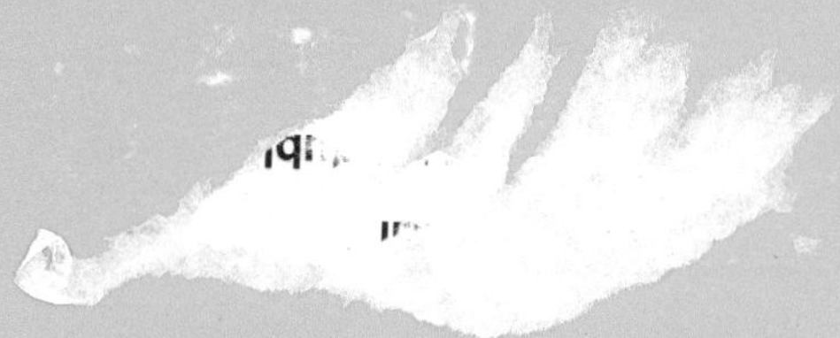

KU-236-799

THE COMPLETE RUNNING & MARATHON BOOK

THE COMPLETE RUNNING & MARATHON BOOK

LONDON, NEW YORK, MUNICH, MELBOURNE, DELHI

Senior Art Editor Michael Duffy
Senior Editor Catherine Saunders
Project Art Editors Phil Gamble, Paul Drislane, Katie Cavanagh
Project Editor Hannah Bowen
Editors Hugo Wilkinson, Jemima Dunne, Georgina Palffy, Alison Sturgeon, Satu Fox
Designers Saffron Stocker, Stephen Bere
Producer Adam Stoneham
Production Controller Mandy Inness
Studio Photography Ruth Jenkinson
Managing Editor Stephanie Farrow
Jackets Team Mark Cavanagh, Sophia M.T.T, Manisha Majithia
Managing Art Editor Lee Griffiths

Illustrators
Rajeev Doshi, Phil Gamble, Adam Brackenbury
Medi-Mation

SAFETY NOTICE
Before attempting the exercises and training in this book, please see p.38 for instructions on having a full health check beforehand, and p.192 for general safety advice.

First published in Great Britain in 2014 by
Dorling Kindersley Limited
80 Strand
London WC2R 0RL

Penguin Group (UK)
10 9 8 7 6 5 4
002-187515-May/2015-

A CIP catalogue record of this title is available from the British Library.

ISBN 978-14093-3763-8

Printed and bound in China

Discover more at
www.dk.com

CONTENTS

ABOUT THIS BOOK

Each chapter of this book tackles a different area of knowledge for anyone wanting to start running, or to take their training up a level. It starts by showing the muscles and biomechanics you can harness to power your performance, and then takes you through the process of preparing to run, beginning and developing your training, all the way to reaching the pinnacle of your performance. It also gives advice and tips on competing in races – and on how to recover. Below is a selection of the book's main features.

Inside the runner's body

Anatomical diagrams show the vital muscles, bones, and ligaments for running to give you knowledge to run better and avoid injury.

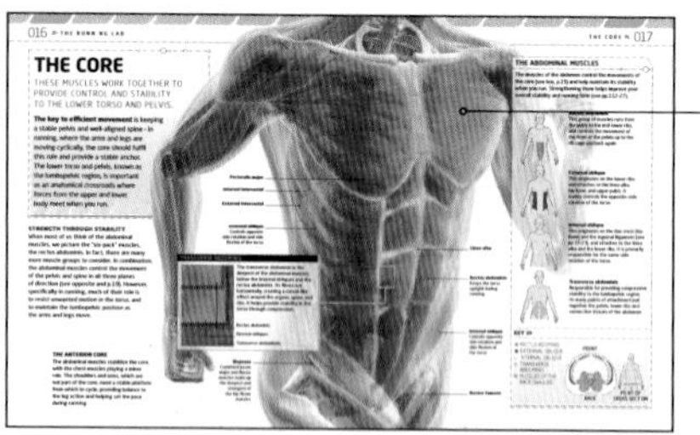

Stunning anatomical models give you a unique view of runners' physiology

The biomechanics of running

Biomechanical analyses of the movements of running show how to improve your form and avoid common mistakes.

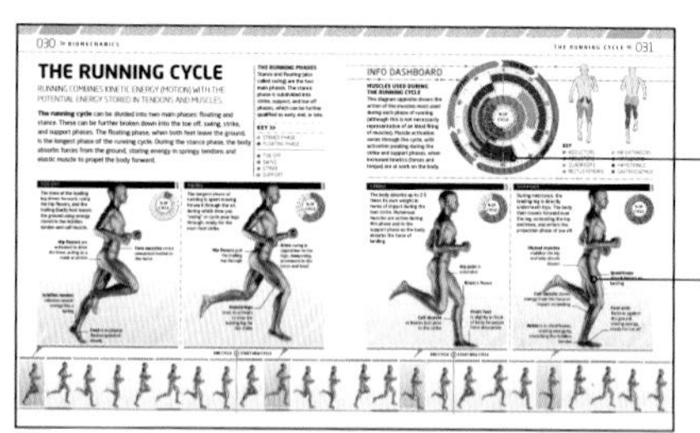

Charts and graphics throughout the book illustrate key information

3-D computer models demonstrate good running technique

Exercises for strength and stability

A selection of exercises gives you the tools to build your overall strength, stability, and mobility for running.

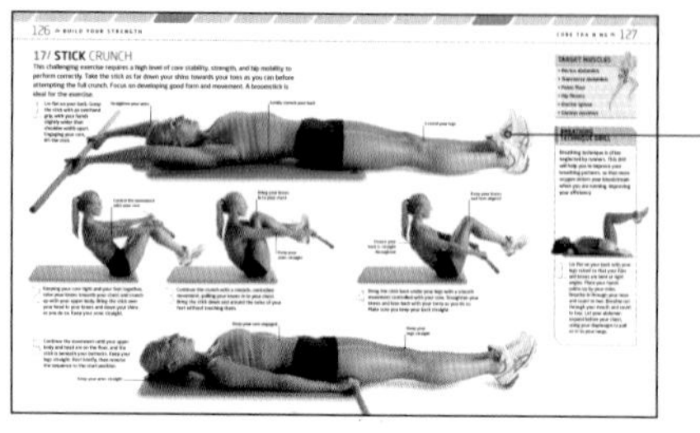

Step-by-step photography leads you through training exercises and technique drills

Tips and advice

Training plans, expert advice, and graphics give you the detailed information you need to maximize your performance.

Q&As, guides to successful training and racing, and insider information aim to give you the best start

Sample training programmes

Plan your training to perfection with sample programmes to prepare you for a range of races, from 5km (3.1 miles) to a full marathon.

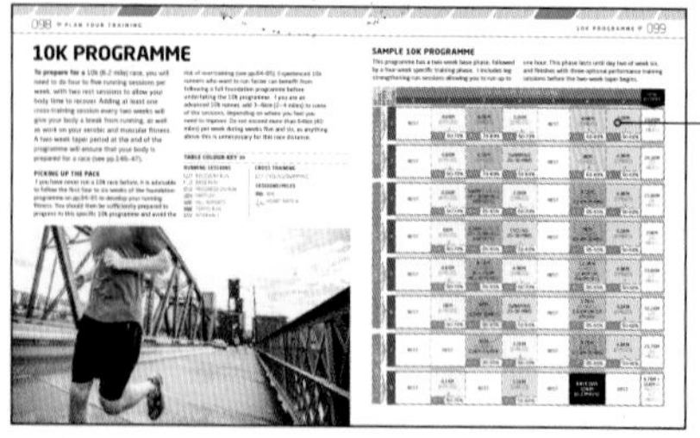

Colour-coded training programmes show you how to prepare for your race or event

Dealing with injury

Learn how to identify, deal with, and recover from a variety of common runners' injuries and health complaints.

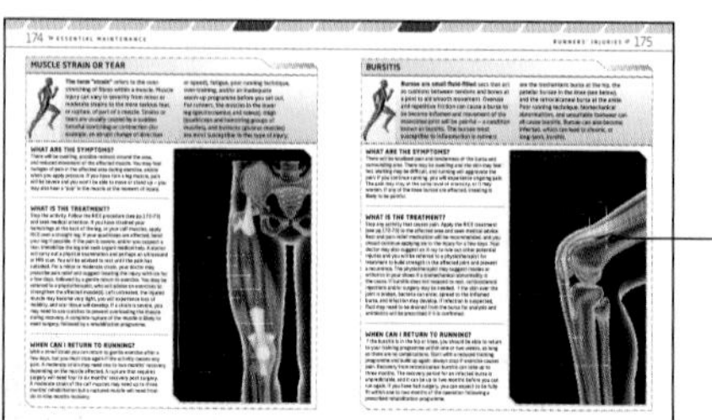

Medical illustrations help identify and treat injuries

INTRODUCTION

Why should I run? You might well ask yourself this. All too often, runners start with plenty of enthusiasm and run with maximum effort, pushing themselves through unnecessary pain barriers, and consequently do more damage than good.

However, it doesn't have to be like that, and this book will show you why and how. With the right approach, running is unbeatable for getting fit and for your general health and well-being – and with the correct training and a little planning, you can soon set yourself on the road to your first race, or to hitting new and better goals.

Whether you're new to running or a seasoned athlete, this book will make the sport more rewarding by developing you into a more efficient and intelligent runner. It will help you to focus on smart, enjoyable goals, and set out structured and achievable training programmes. It will guide you through building a proper fitness base with the expert strength and core programmes that will also benefit your general strength and mobility in day-to-day life. It covers everything from your typical running injuries and ways to prevent them, to what to wear, and nutrition and hydration tips for everyday training. For those who really want to test themselves, it also provides advice and strategies for optimizing your race day preparation, performance, and recovery, whether you are taking on your first short race, or braving a full marathon.

So, what are you waiting for? Start reading, lace up your trainers and enter the world of running one step ahead of the pack.

Good luck!

THE RUNNING LAB

YOUR BODY IS THE MOST IMPORTANT PIECE OF RUNNING KIT YOU HAVE, AND KNOWING THE BASICS OF HOW IT WORKS WILL ENABLE YOU TO BECOME A BETTER, SMARTER, AND MORE EFFICIENT RUNNER. THIS CHAPTER IS DESIGNED TO GIVE YOU THE TOOLS TO UNDERSTAND YOUR BODY'S MOVEMENTS AND TO ASSESS YOUR RUNNING STYLE, SO THAT YOU CAN GET STARTED ON THE RIGHT FOOT.

THE BODY

RUNNING IS AN ALL-BODY, LOAD-BEARING EXERCISE THAT DEMANDS STRENGTH, POWER, COORDINATION, AND GOOD CARDIOVASCULAR FITNESS.

It is generally considered that there are five main groups of muscles that are used during running – quads, hamstrings, gluteals, hip flexors, and the calf muscles. However, there are more than 640 skeletal muscles in the body, and many of these, in particular your core muscles, contribute to your performance. Having a strong, well-coordinated body is essential for perfecting your technique. The following pages take a more detailed look at the structure and function of key body systems and the major muscles and joints.

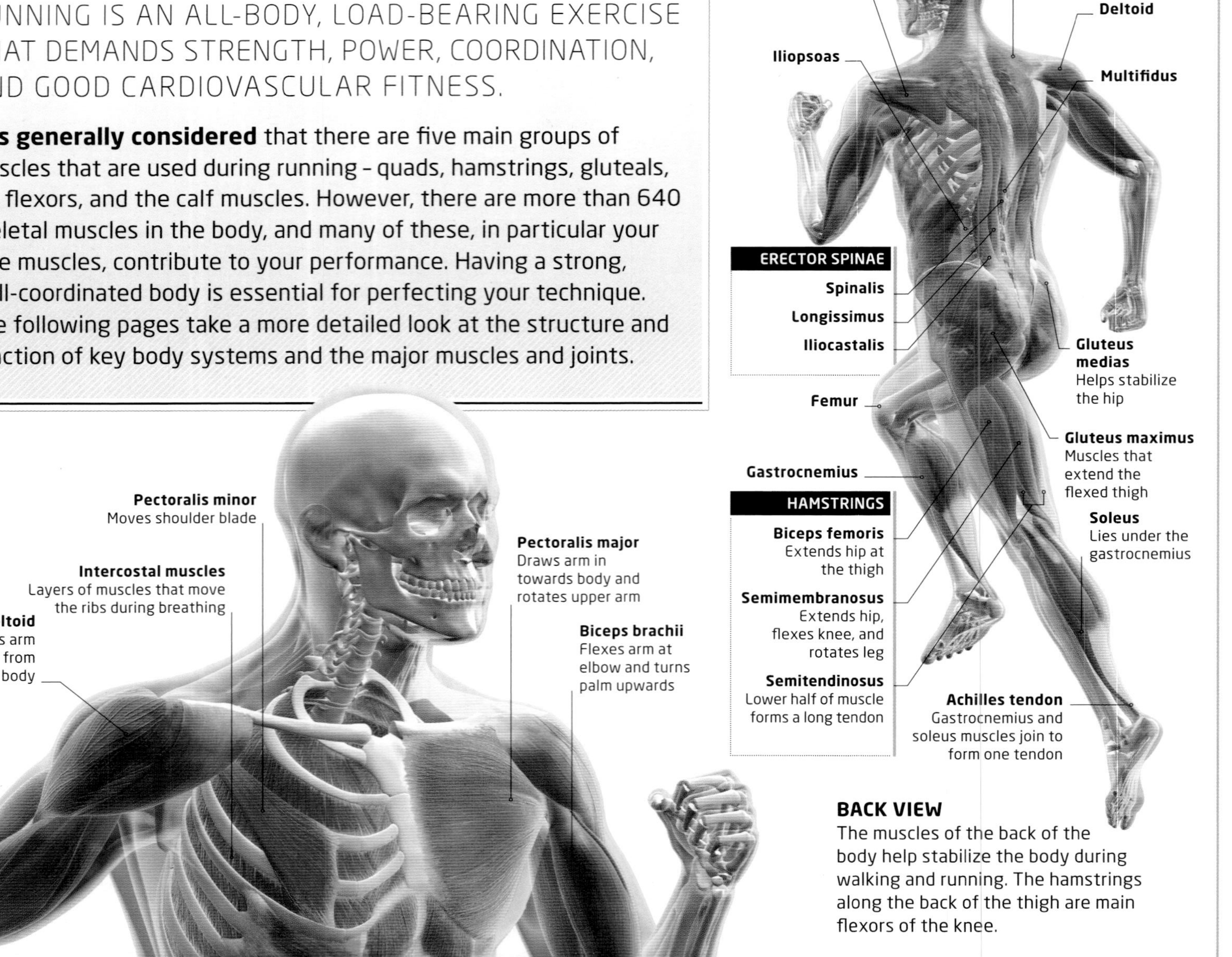

BACK VIEW
The muscles of the back of the body help stabilize the body during walking and running. The hamstrings along the back of the thigh are main flexors of the knee.

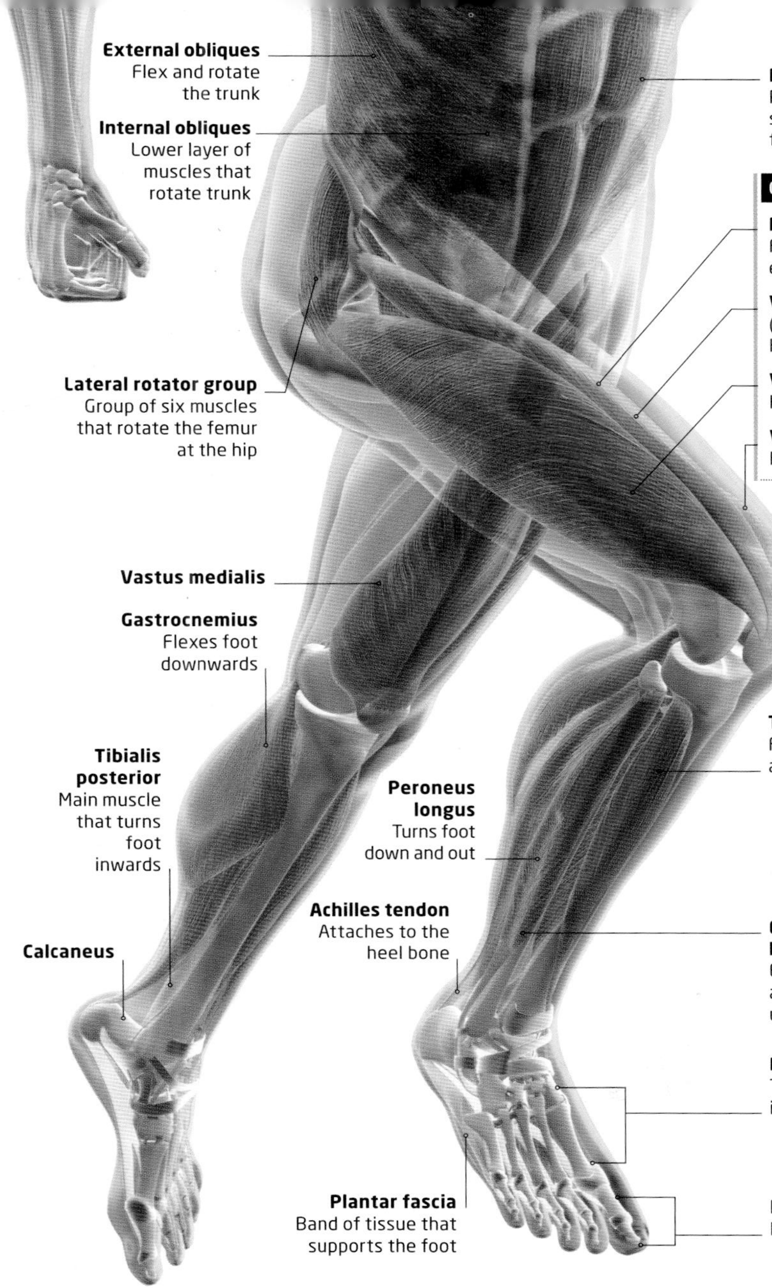

External obliques
Flex and rotate the trunk
Internal obliques
Lower layer of muscles that rotate trunk
Lateral rotator group
Group of six muscles that rotate the femur at the hip
Vastus medialis
Gastrocnemius
Flexes foot downwards
Tibialis posterior
Main muscle that turns foot inwards
Calcaneus
Peroneus longus
Turns foot down and out
Achilles tendon
Attaches to the heel bone
Plantar fascia
Band of tissue that supports the foot
Rectus abdominis
Pair of muscles that flex spine and draw pelvis forwards
QUADRICEPS
Rectis femoris
Flexes hip and extends knee
Vastus intermedius
(Behind rectis femoris) Helps extend knee
Vastus lateralis
Helps extend knee
Vastus medialis
Helps extend knee
Tibialis anterior
Flexes foot upwards and inwards
Extensor digitorum longus
Extends outer toes and helps flex foot upwards
Metatarsals
The long bones in the foot
Phalanges
Bones of the toes

FRONT VIEW
A series of layered muscles help provide core strength and help breathing. The large muscles of the thigh and calves support the hips, knees, and ankles.

THE KINETIC CHAIN

Made up of myofascial (muscular), articular (joints) and neural (motor) components, the kinetic chain is best described as the body's movement system. Each component in the kinetic chain is dependent on the next for optimum running performance. Poor coordination or lack of strength as a result of weak muscles or joints will affect your optimal running technique.

Cervical spine
Thoracic spine
Lumbar spine
Hip
Knee
Ankle
Ankle

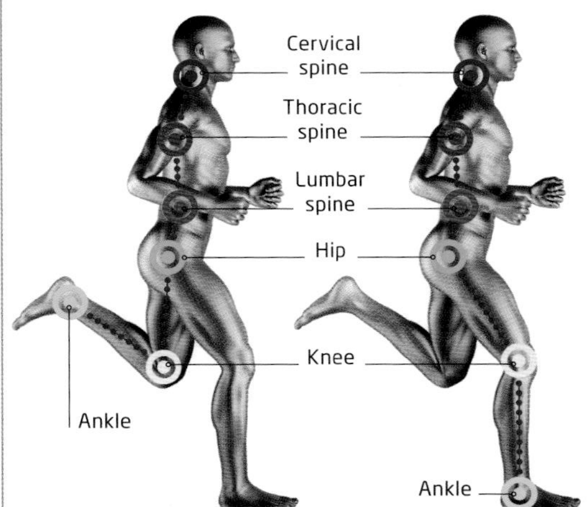

Open kinetic chain
This has reduced forces and increased motion as the runner's (left) foot is not in contact with the ground. This swing leg is "floating" in mid-air, ready for the next ground contact.

Closed kinetic chain
This features increased forces and reduced motion as the runner's (right) foot makes contact with the ground and in doing so absorbs many times the body weight of the runner.

THE MUSCLES

As a runner, your muscles are your best friends – they carry you along, tell you when you're doing well, as well as when you're overdoing it. If you look after them, they'll treat you well, but if you push them too far, you'll suffer for it. The main muscle type in human anatomy is skeletal muscle. This attaches to or covers bone, can be controlled by the brain via the central nervous system, and is the muscle type you use to create motion in any form of physical exercise, including running.

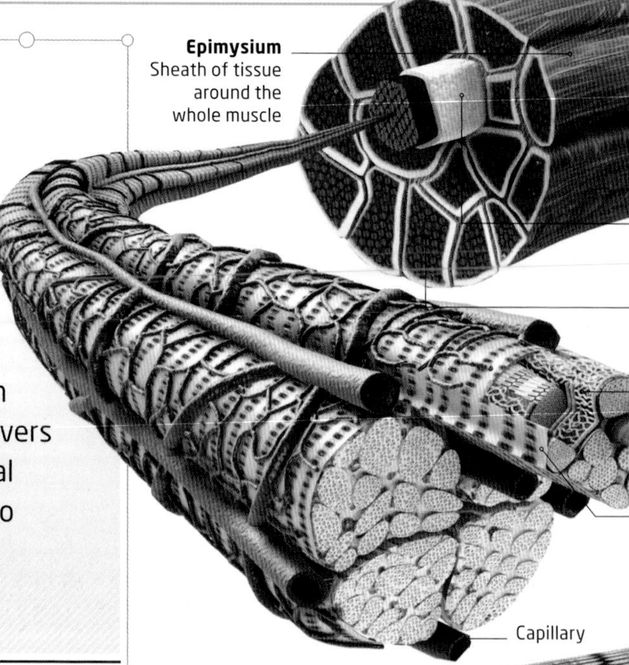

THE BODY'S PISTONS

Muscles have the unique ability to convert energy from fats and carbohydrates in food (see pp.50–53) into movement. In skeletal muscles, contractions are triggered by nerve impulses that arrive from the brain when we make a conscious decision to move. Muscle fibres shorten and thicken when they contract, causing them to pull (see box, below). Running uses either fast-twitch or slow-twitch muscles (see p.105).

MICROANATOMY OF MUSCLE CONTRACTION

Muscle is composed of fibres called sarcomeres, clustered in groups. Each group is controlled by a single motor neuron, which sends an impulse to the sarcomeres, telling them to enlarge and become thicker and shorter – to contract.

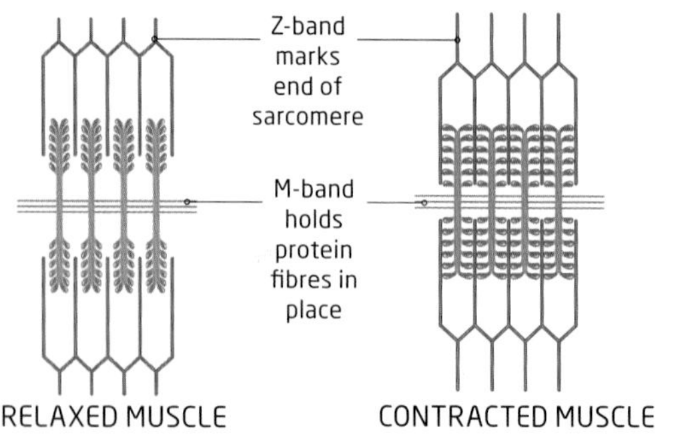

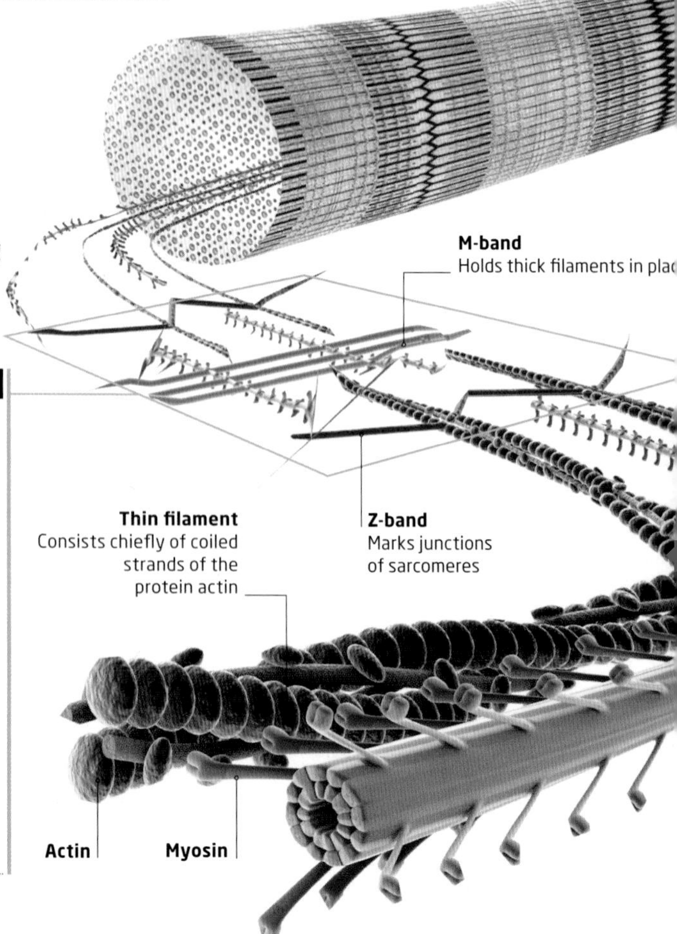

MUSCLES IN CLOSE-UP

Human muscle is made up mainly of water and protein, with small amounts of mineral salts, fat, and glycogen (see p.53). This artwork shows the components that make up a skeletal muscle.

INFO DASHBOARD

LEVERS IN THE BODY

Muscles, joints, and bones work together to create movement in the same way as levers pivoting around a fulcrum – the bones function as levers, the joints as fulcrums, and muscles provide the force. The force is magnified by the relative position of the bone and the joint.

FIRST-CLASS LEVER

The fulcrum is in the middle and the load and force at either end of the lever, like a see-saw. Here the elbow acts as the fulcrum to activate the tricep.

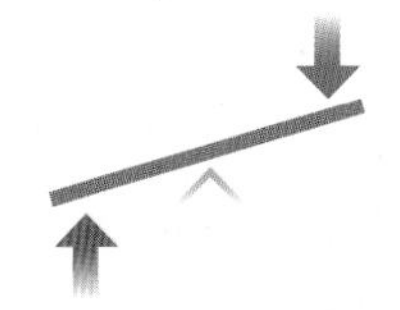

SECOND-CLASS LEVER

The fulcrum is at the end of the lever, with the force acting at the opposite end. The calf muscles provide the force to pull up the load of the foot, with the toe as the fulcrum.

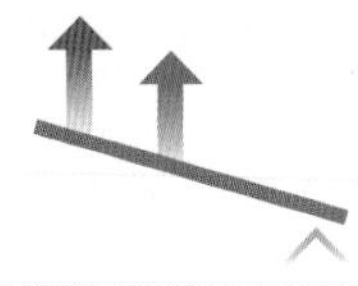

THIRD-CLASS LEVER

The most common kind of lever in the body, this uses a force in the middle to pull up a weight at the end, for example the leg muscles pulling up the lower leg and foot.

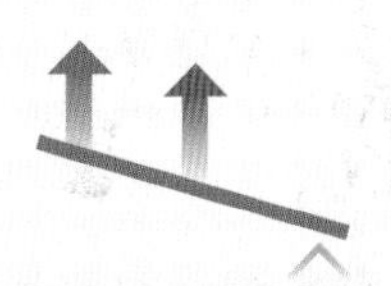

KEY »

AGONIST VERSUS ANTAGONIST

As they can only perform pulling and not pushing actions, muscles work in pairs. One muscle contracts and shortens, pulling on the bone to which it is attached and causing it to move. The bone cannot move back to its original state until the other muscle of the pair pulls it back.

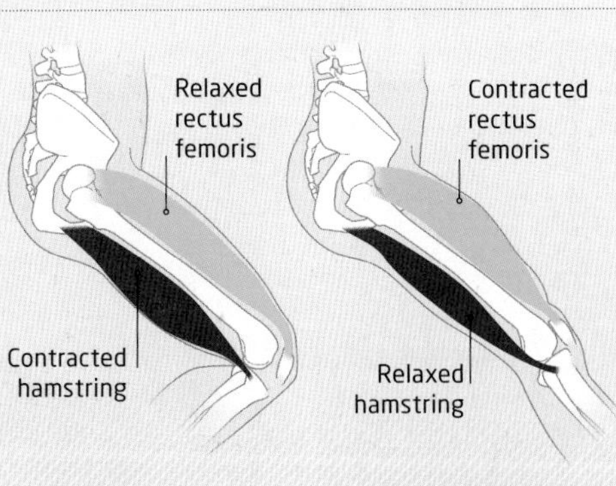

THE HEART AND LUNGS

Your cells need a continuous supply of oxygen that they combine with glucose to produce energy. When you exert yourself through running, this process is intensified. To enable you to carry out high-intensity exercise, the lungs must provide enough oxygen to the bloodstream, and the heart must pump it to the body's cells. This process will become more efficient as you get fitter, and can be improved by cardiovascular endurance training.

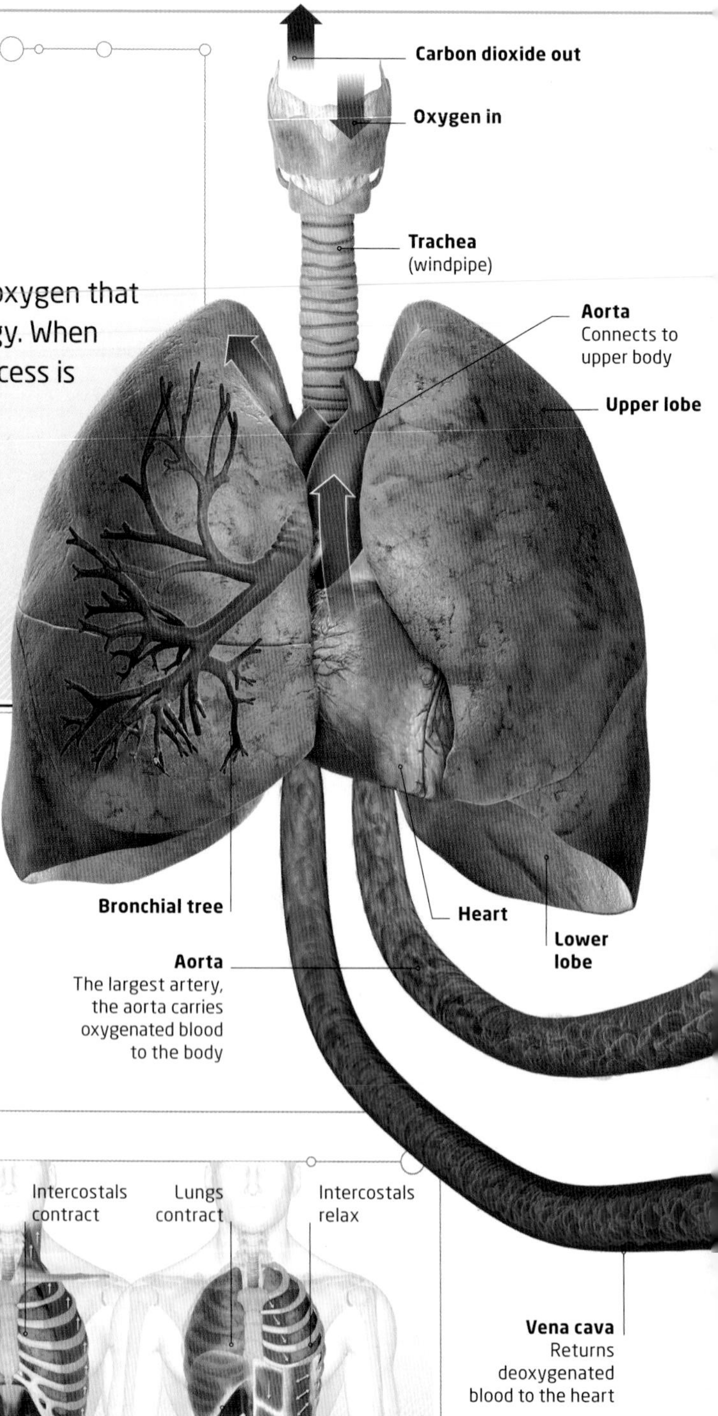

Carbon dioxide out

Oxygen in

Trachea (windpipe)

Aorta Connects to upper body

Upper lobe

Bronchial tree

Heart

Lower lobe

Aorta The largest artery, the aorta carries oxygenated blood to the body

Vena cava Returns deoxygenated blood to the heart

LUNG CAPACITY AND OXYGEN

As a runner, getting enough air into your lungs, and therefore oxygen into your bloodstream, is a high priority. However, this is not dependent on your lung capacity - the amount of air you can draw into your lungs - and many elite distance runners have comparatively small lungs. The real key factor in getting the most oxygen to your muscles is to increase your cardiovascular efficiency through training (see pp.95-103).

RESPIRATORY CYCLE

Air is drawn in and out of the lungs by the contraction and relaxation of the diaphragm and intercostal muscles, which move the chest walls. Once air reaches the lungs, oxygen is extracted via gas exchange (see box, right) and passes into the previously deoxygenated blood via the thin walls of the alveoli (microscopic air sacs). It is exchanged for the body's waste product, carbon dioxide, which is then exhaled.

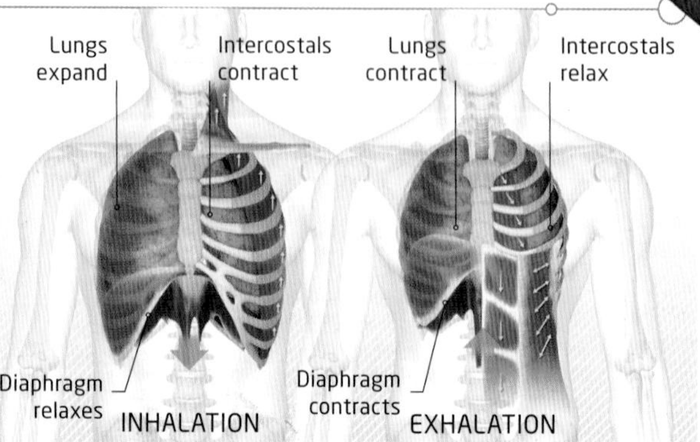

KEY >>

- OXYGENATED BLOOD
- DEOXYGENATED BLOOD

AEROBIC vs ANAEROBIC

This refers to the presence and absence of oxygen. Most body cells prefer to get energy by using oxygen to fuel metabolism. During mild exercise, with enough fuel and oxygen (aerobic exercise), muscle cells can work for long periods without fatigue. However, in harder exercise (anaerobic exercise), muscles must rely on other reactions that do not require oxygen to fuel muscle contraction. This metabolic process produces waste products such as lactic acid that can slow movement and cause fatigue.

Muscular wall of artery Pushes red blood cells through the body

Red blood cells Full of haemoglobin, which can bind oxygen

DELIVERY IN THE BLOOD

Oxygen absorbed in the lungs is taken in the blood to the left side of the heart, which pumps it through the body. When it reaches the capillaries (blood vessels with very thin walls), it is exchanged for carbon dioxide, which is transported in the blood to the right side of the heart, and then to the lungs to be exhaled.

Capillary bed

GAS EXCHANGE

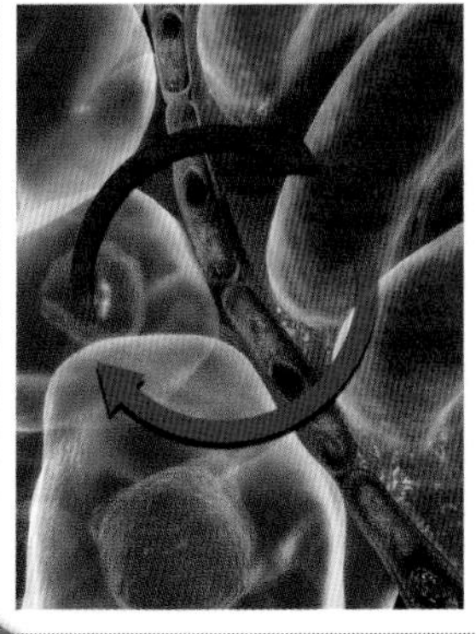

Blood flows through the capillaries, where haemoglobin releases oxygen, and carbon dioxide dissolves in plasma to be taken back to the lungs for exhalation. Molecules move easily across thin membranes from areas of high concentration to areas of low concentration (diffusion).

Deoxygenated blood cells

Body cells

THE CORE

THESE MUSCLES WORK TOGETHER TO PROVIDE CONTROL AND STABILITY TO THE LOWER TORSO AND PELVIS.

The key to efficient movement is keeping a stable pelvis and well-aligned spine - in running, where the arms and legs are moving cyclically, the core should fulfil this role and provide a stable anchor. The lower torso and pelvis, known as the lumbopelvic region, is important as an anatomical crossroads where forces from the upper and lower body meet when you run.

STRENGTH THROUGH STABILITY

When most of us think of the abdominal muscles, we picture the "six-pack" muscles, the rectus abdominis. In fact, there are many more muscle groups to consider. In combination, the abdominal muscles control the movement of the pelvis and spine in all three planes of direction (see opposite and p.19). However, specifically in running, much of their role is to resist unwanted motion in the torso, and maintain the lumbopelvic position as the arms and legs move.

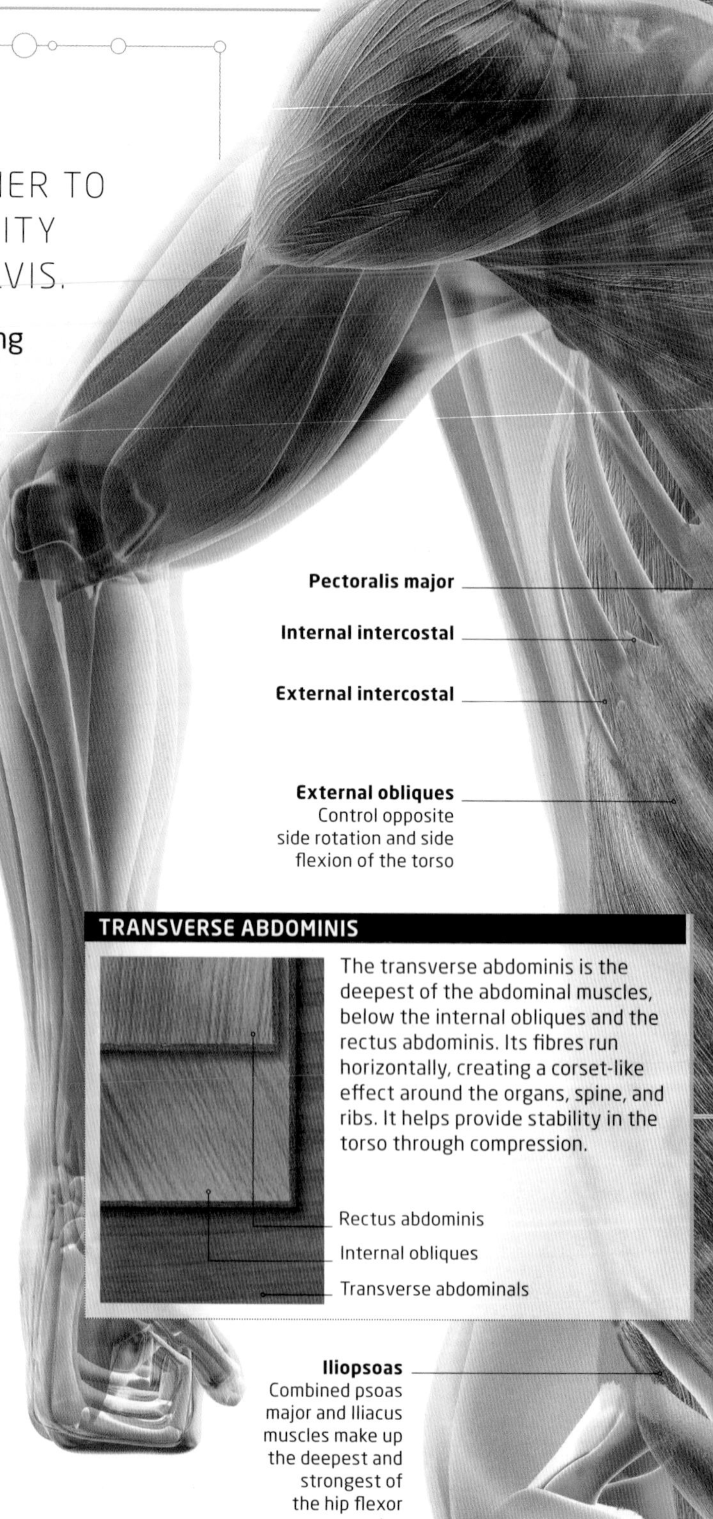

The transverse abdominis is the deepest of the abdominal muscles, below the internal obliques and the rectus abdominis. Its fibres run horizontally, creating a corset-like effect around the organs, spine, and ribs. It helps provide stability in the torso through compression.

THE ANTERIOR CORE

The abdominal muscles stabilize the core, with the chest muscles playing a minor role. The shoulders and arms, which are not part of the core, need a stable platform from which to cycle, providing balance to the leg action and helping set the pace during running.

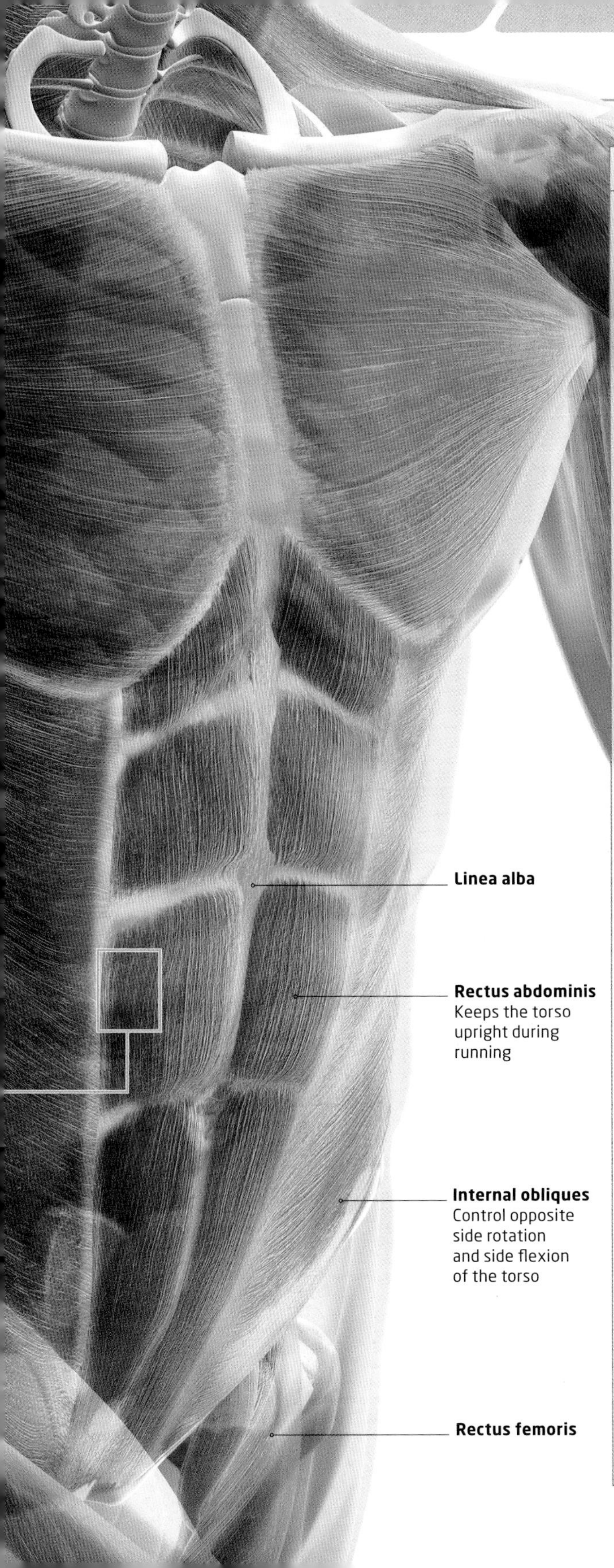

THE ABDOMINAL MUSCLES

The muscles of the abdomen control the movements of the core (see box, p.19) and help maintain its stability when you run. Strengthening them helps improve your overall stability and running form (see pp.112–27).

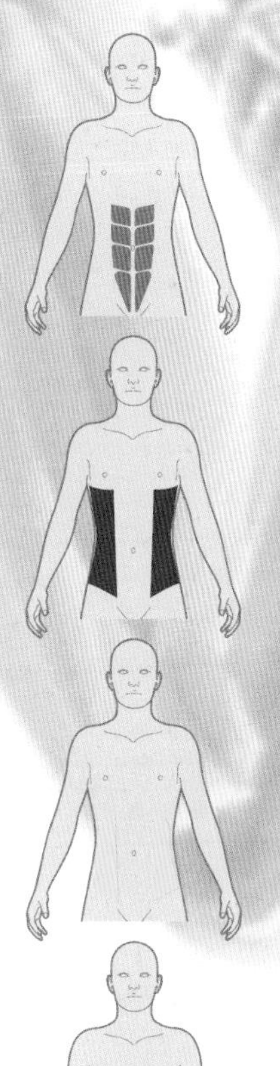

Rectus abdominis
This group of muscles runs from the pubis to the mid-lower ribs, and controls the movement of the front of the pelvis up to the rib cage and back again.

External oblique
This originates on the lower ribs, and attaches to the linea alba, hip bone, and upper pubis. It mainly controls the opposite-side rotation of the torso.

Internal oblique
This originates on the iliac crest (hip bone) and the inguinal ligament (see pp.22–23), and attaches to the linea alba and the lower ribs. It is primarily responsible for the same-side rotation of the torso.

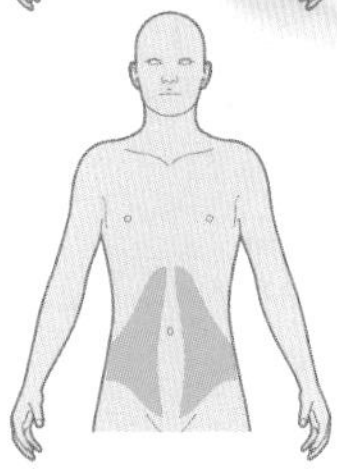

Transverse abdominis
Responsible for providing compressive stability to the lumbopelvic region, its many points of attachment pull together the pelvis, lower ribs and connective tissues of the abdomen.

KEY »

- RECTUS ADOMINIS
- EXTERNAL OBLIQUE
- INTERNAL OBLIQUE
- TRANSVERSE ABDOMINIS
- MUSCLES OF THE BACK (see p.18)

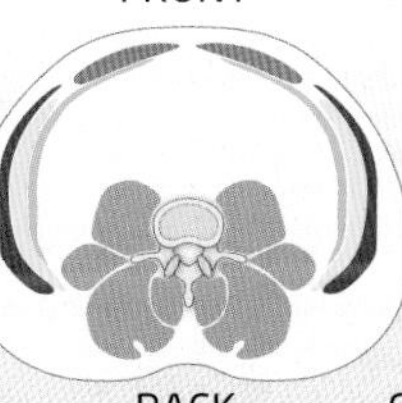

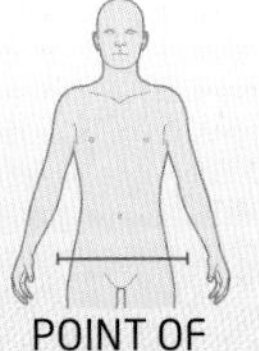

Linea alba

Rectus abdominis
Keeps the torso upright during running

Internal obliques
Control opposite side rotation and side flexion of the torso

Rectus femoris

THE LOWER BACK MUSCLES

The muscles of the lower back are extremely important and generally undertrained in runners. These are responsible for maintaining good postural alignment as you run, as well as for protecting your spine. The erector spinae are a deep muscle group, providing stability and control of the spine, while the large back muscle, the latissimus dorsi (see box, bottom right), lies near the surface, offering all-round stability from shoulder to lumbopelvic region.

THE THORACIC SPINE

A strong mid- and upper back are important for good running posture. Some people sit hunched over a desk all day with poor thoracic posture – running requires you to extend properly through the thoracic spine (upper torso) and adequately rotate (see pp.60–73). Due to poor posture, many runners are tense in the thoracic region, which can adversely affect breathing patterns.

Trapezius

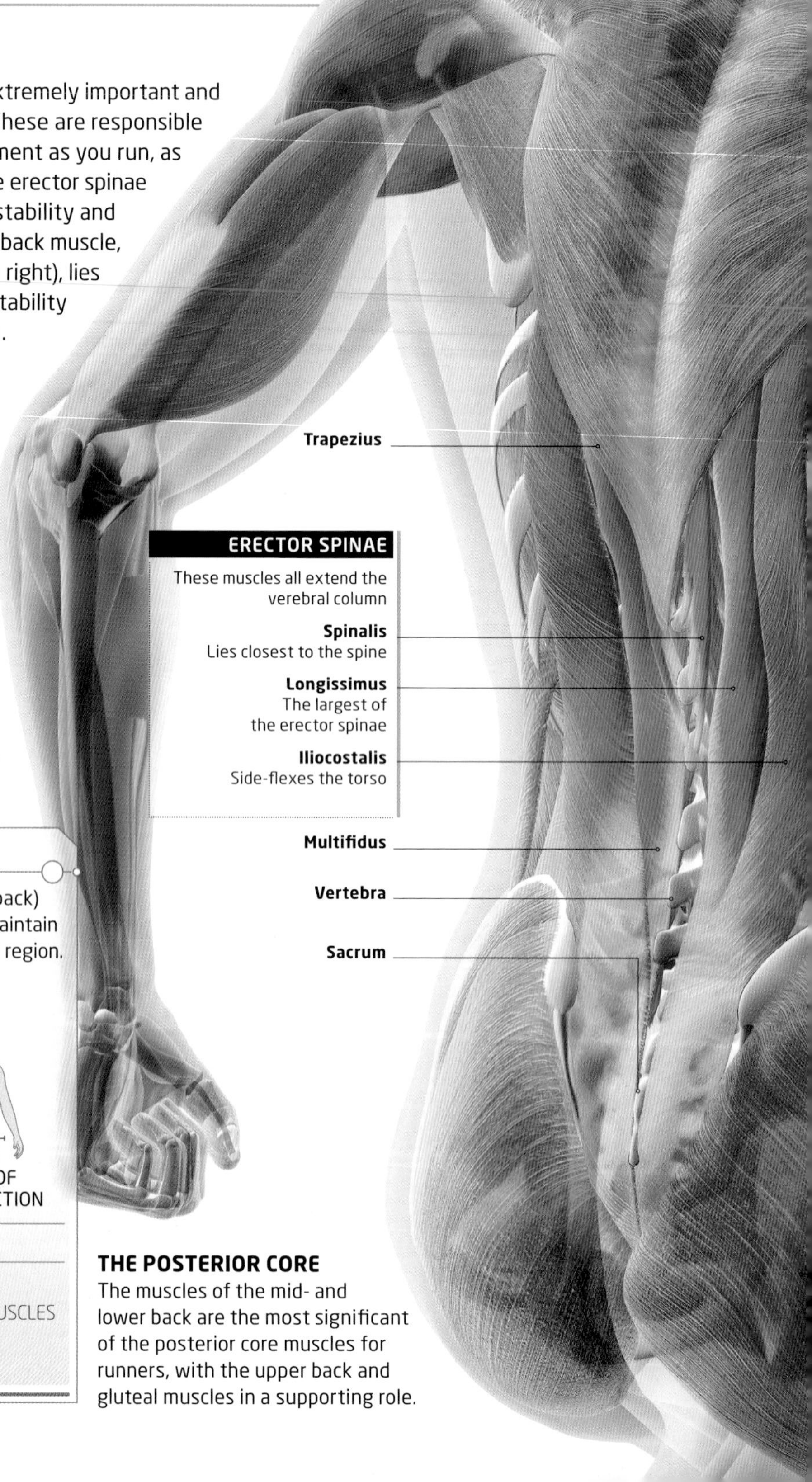

ERECTOR SPINAE

These muscles all extend the verebral column

Spinalis
Lies closest to the spine

Longissimus
The largest of the erector spinae

Iliocostalis
Side-flexes the torso

Multifidus

Vertebra

Sacrum

MUSCLES OF THE BACK

The anterior and posterior (front and back) muscles of the core work together to maintain a controlled position of the lumbopelvic region.

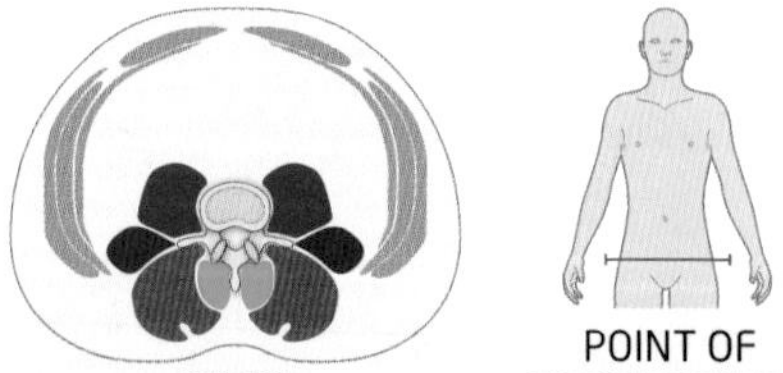

FRONT

BACK

POINT OF CROSS-SECTION

KEY »

- PSOAS
- QUADRATUS LUMBATORUM
- ERECTOR SPINEA
- MULTIFIDUS
- ABDOMINAL MUSCLES (see p.16)

THE POSTERIOR CORE

The muscles of the mid- and lower back are the most significant of the posterior core muscles for runners, with the upper back and gluteal muscles in a supporting role.

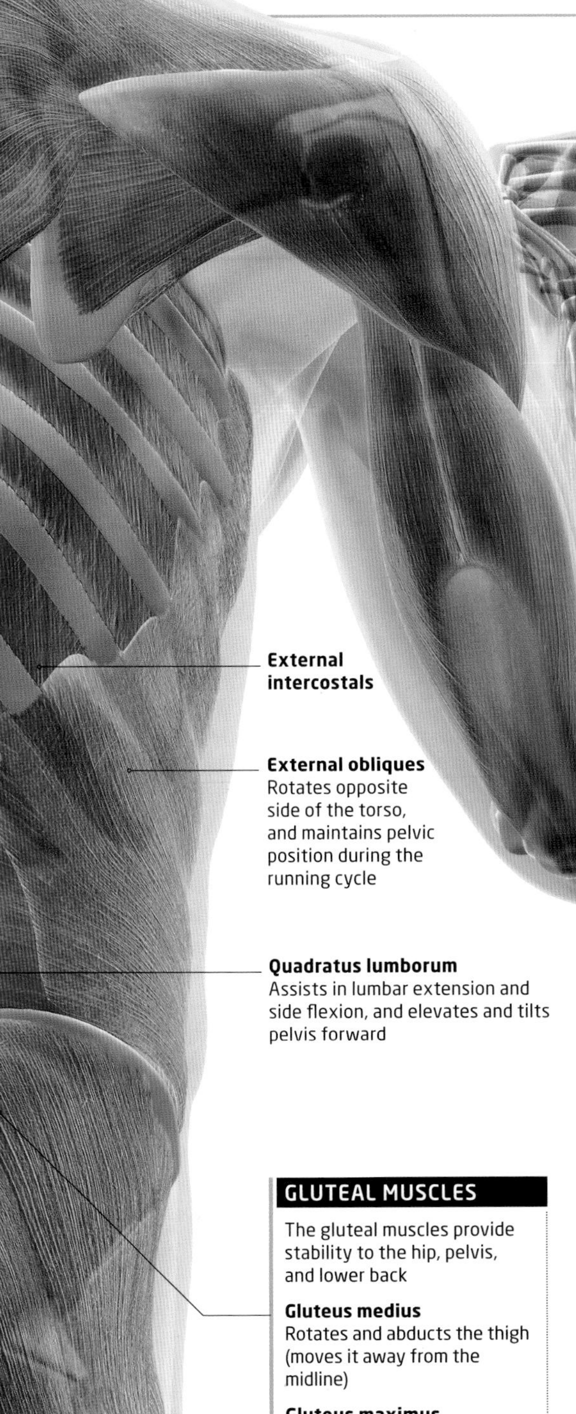

External obliques
Rotates opposite side of the torso, and maintains pelvic position during the running cycle

Quadratus lumborum
Assists in lumbar extension and side flexion, and elevates and tilts pelvis forward

GLUTEAL MUSCLES

The gluteal muscles provide stability to the hip, pelvis, and lower back

Gluteus medius
Rotates and abducts the thigh (moves it away from the midline)

Gluteus maximus
Powerful extensor and external rotator of the hip joint, key for propulsion in running

RANGE OF MOVEMENT

The core has three planes of movement – sagittal (vertically forwards and backwards), frontal (vertically side to side), and transverse (horizontally). It can also be activated when stationary, to act as a stabilizer.

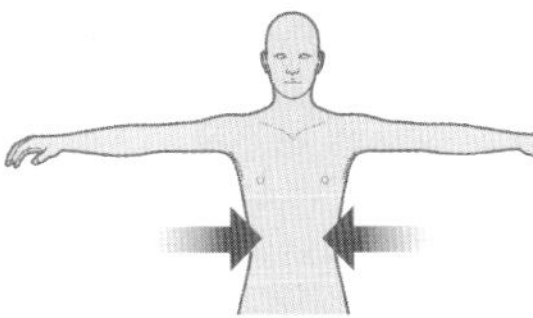

Isometric
An isometric movement involves holding the core in a fixed, stable position.

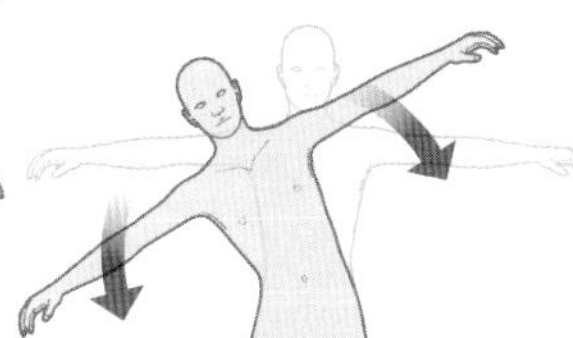

Side flexion
The core can also bend vertically from side to side, in a side flexion movement.

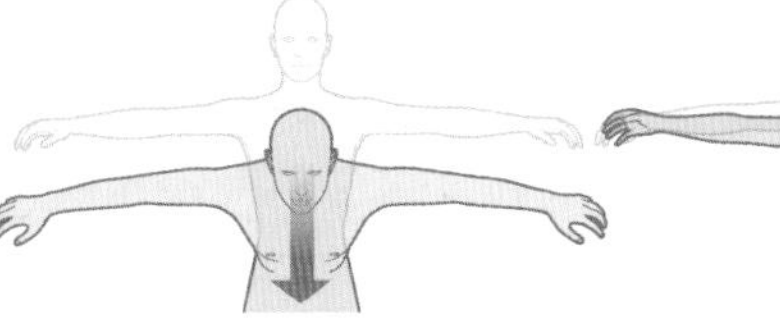

Flexion
When the core bends forwards vertically, it is known as flexion.

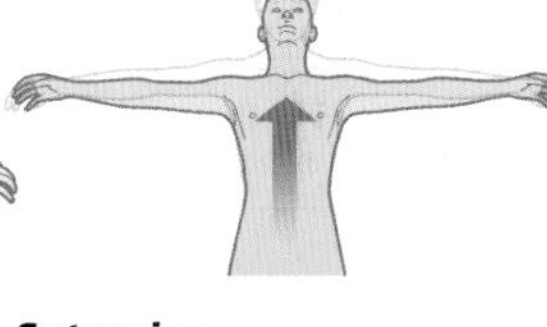

Extension
A backwards vertical bend from the core is known as an extension.

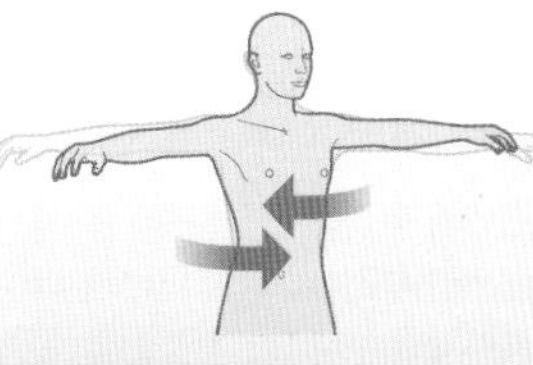

Rotation
This transverse movement involves turning or rotating from the waist.

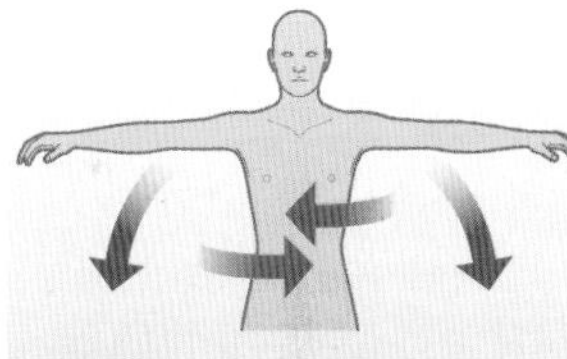

Complex
The core can also move on more than one plane, such as a flexion with rotation.

OTHER ELEMENTS OF THE CORE

The diaphragm, the pelvic floor, and the large superficial back muscle - the latissimus dorsi - are all important for providing stability and effective force transfer in the core region.

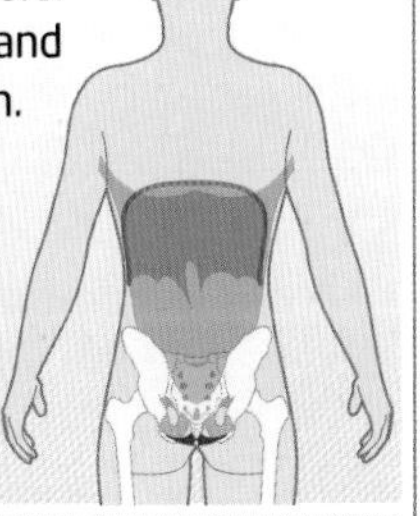

KEY »

- DIAPHRAGM
- PELVIC FLOOR
- LATISSIMUS DORSI

THE HIP

THIS IMPORTANT JOINT REQUIRES BOTH MOBILITY AND STABILITY.

While the hip joint itself can move through a large range of motion compared to many joints, as a runner you also need to be able to keep its movement under control, particularly when your weight is on one leg. The stability of the hip dictates both knee and lumbopelvic alignment, so poor hip control can often lead to knee and back injuries. Strong hips are the basis of a powerful, efficient running style.

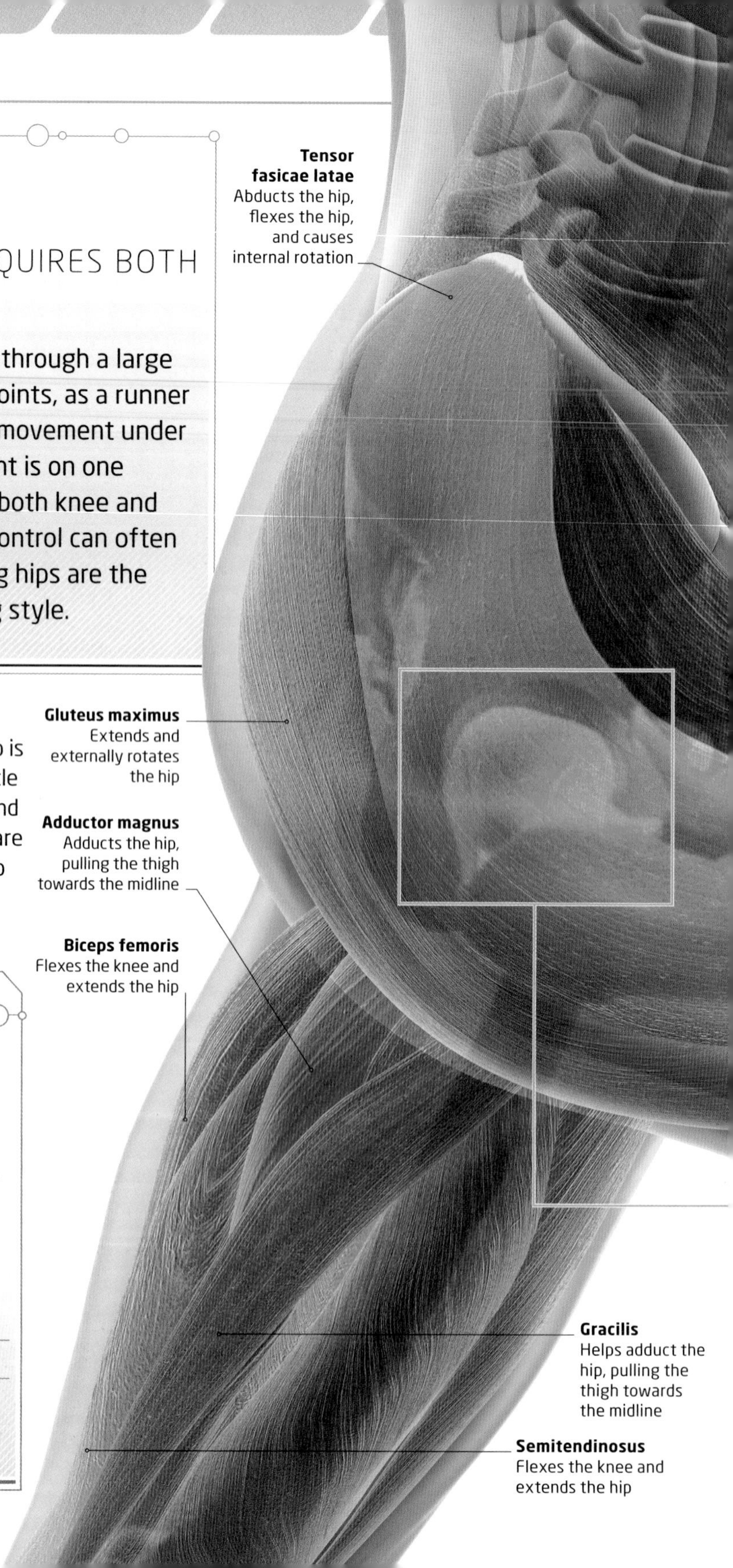

BALANCING THE HIPS

As with the majority of skeletal joints, the hip is acted upon by a number of antagonistic muscle groups (see p.13) working in pairs to create and control opposite actions. When these pairs are working in balance with one another, the hip generally functions well. However, when an imbalance occurs, injury often follows.

HIP FLEXORS

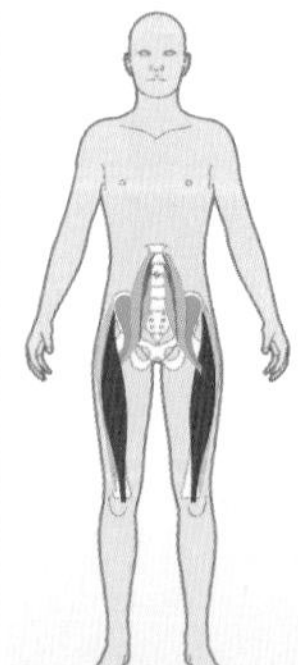

In the running cycle, the hip flexors swing the leg through from its fully extended position, to the highest point of the knee lift. In distance runners, the rectus femoris plays a major role in creating this hip flexion action. The rectis femoris is the only quadriceps muscle to cross both the hip and knee, and has the longest lever arm (see p.13) of all the hip flexors.

KEY >>

- PSOAS MAJOR
- PSOAS MINOR
- ILIACUS MUSCLE
- RECTUS FEMORIS
- TENSOR FASCIAE LATAE

Tensor fasicae latae
Abducts the hip, flexes the hip, and causes internal rotation

Gluteus maximus
Extends and externally rotates the hip

Adductor magnus
Adducts the hip, pulling the thigh towards the midline

Biceps femoris
Flexes the knee and extends the hip

Gracilis
Helps adduct the hip, pulling the thigh towards the midline

Semitendinosus
Flexes the knee and extends the hip

THE HIP AND ATTACHED MUSCLES

Several muscle groups are used to control the hip, and many of these muscles are responsible for more than one type of movement in the hip.

Tensor fascia lata
Raises the thigh away from the body and tilts the pelvis

Rectus femoris
Flexes the hip and extends the knee

HIP JOINT

This ball-and-socket joint between the femoral head and pelvic acetabulum (hip socket) is inherently very stable and allows for a lot of movement in all directions. Surrounding muscles and soft tissues need this to control joint movement during activities such as running.

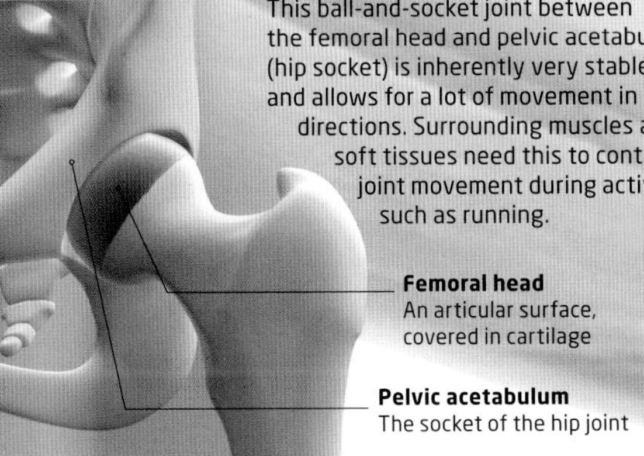

Femoral head
An articular surface, covered in cartilage

Pelvic acetabulum
The socket of the hip joint

RANGE OF MOVEMENT

The hip moves in three main directions: side-to-side, inwards and outwards, and up and down. It can also use a combination of these to make a circular movement – circumduction.

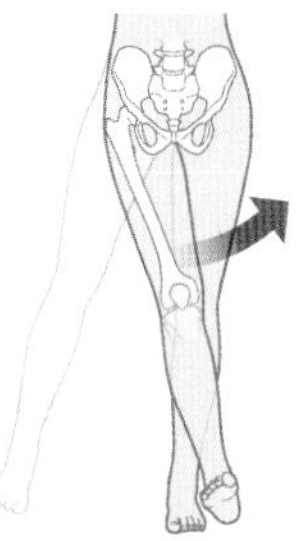

Adduction
A sideways movement of the leg towards the midline of the body is known as adduction.

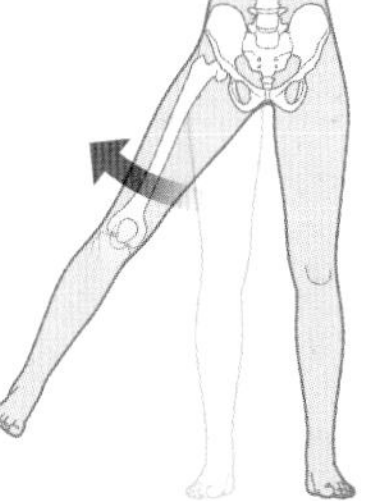

Abduction
Abduction is the sideways movement of the leg away from the midline of the body.

Internal rotation
The thigh can be turned internally, pointing the knee and foot inwards.

External rotation
The hip can also turn the thigh to point the knee and foot outwards.

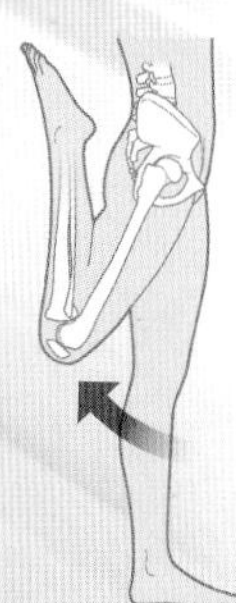

Extension
During extension, the thigh can be pushed backwards behind the body.

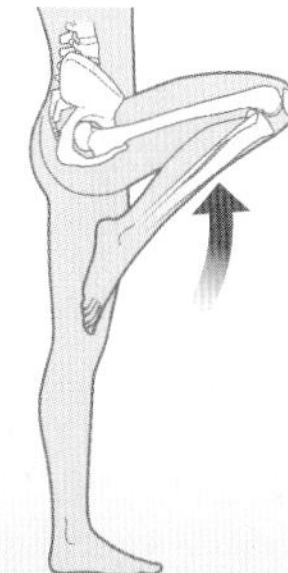

Flexion
The knee is lifted in front of the body, and the thigh is raised parallel to the ground.

PELVIC CONTROL IN RUNNERS

Many of the factors affecting running posture stem from pelvic position. If the pelvis is tilted or rotated away from the ideal neutral position due to muscular imbalances, this immediately alters the position and alignment of the lumbar spine above, and the standing leg below. Many of the most commonly reported running injuries can be traced back to poor function of the gluteal muscles and compromised pelvic position.

THE HIP AND PELVIS

The hip bones are connected to each other and, via the sacrum, to the pelvic skeleton. They connect the spine to the lower limbs at the hip joints.

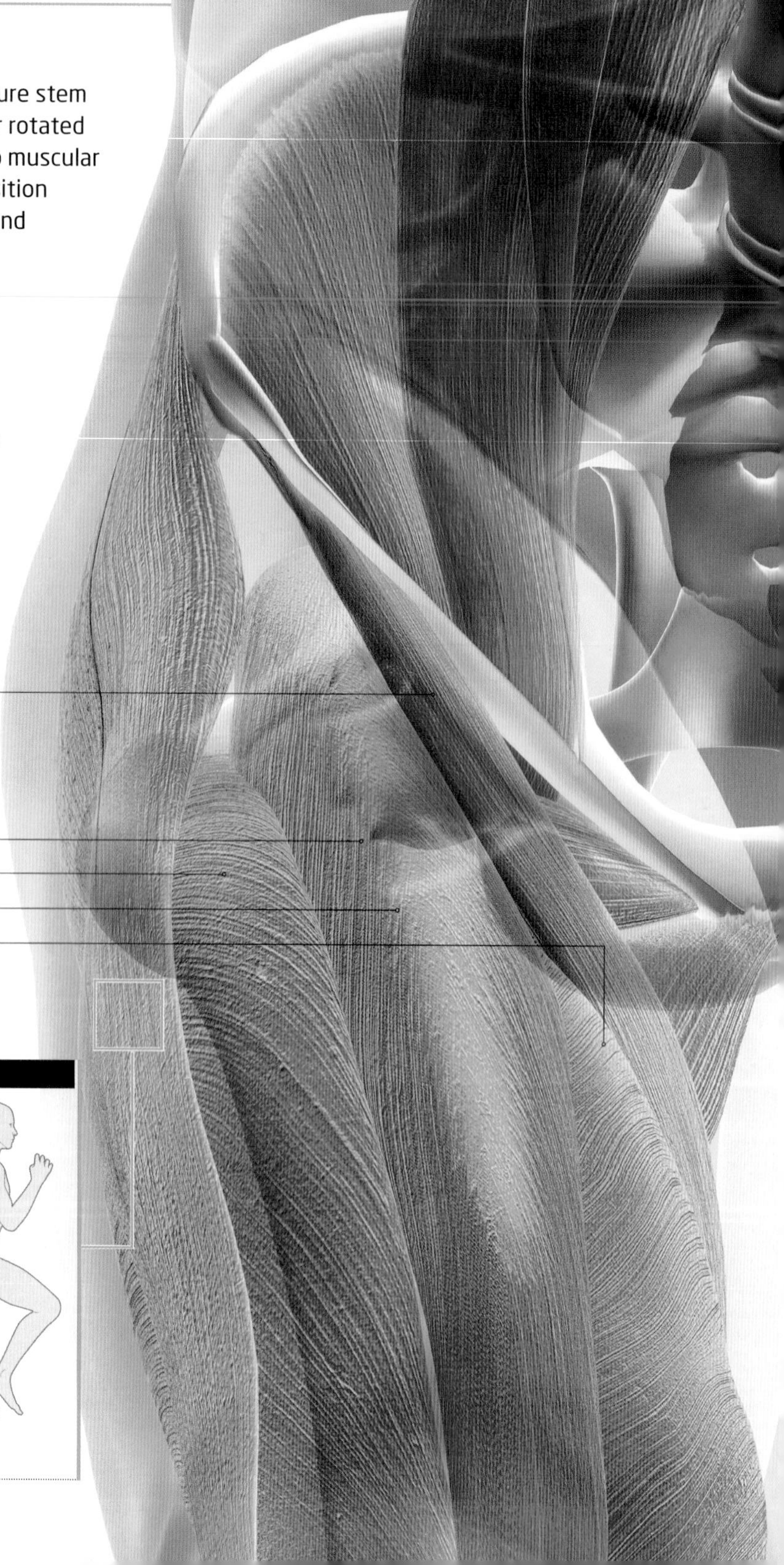

Sartorius muscle
Rotates the hip to the side, for example when sitting cross-legged

QUADRICEPS

Rectus femoris

Vastus lateralis

Vastus intermedius (behind)

Vastus medialis

ILIOTIBIAL BAND

Rather than being contractile tissue like a muscle, the iliotibial band (ITB) is a thickening in the fascial (connective tissue) system of the lateral thigh. The ITB doesn't have the capacity to get "tight" as a muscle would: tension in the ITB, which often results in knee pain, is usually caused by biomechanical flaws at the hip and foot that place this passive tissue under increased tension.

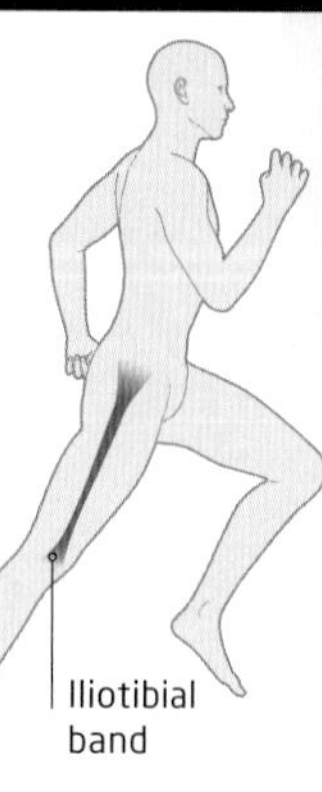

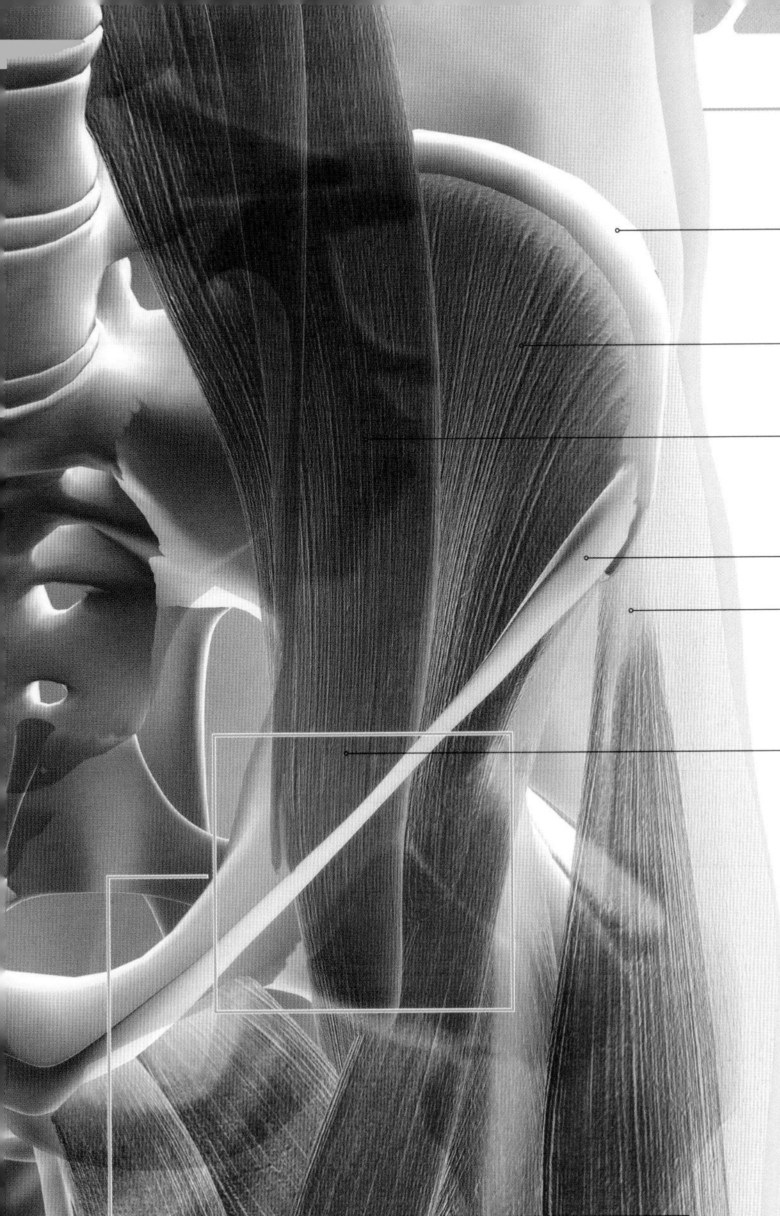

Pelvis
A ring of bones that protects the internal organs (see box, below)

Iliacus (hip flexor)
Originates from the inner ilium and creates hip flexion

Psoas
Originates from the lumbar spine and is the main muscle responsible for hip flexion

Inguinal band

Tensor fasciae lata
Assists in hip abduction, medial rotation, and flexion, and often gets tight in runners, causing ITB tension

Iliopsoas
The combined hip flexor unit of the iliacus and psoas muscles

PIRIFORMIS

The piriformis muscle lies beneath the gluteal muscles and is a deep lateral rotator of the hip. The piriformis is specifically important to runners as when it becomes tight, it can cause irritatation to the sciatic nerve.

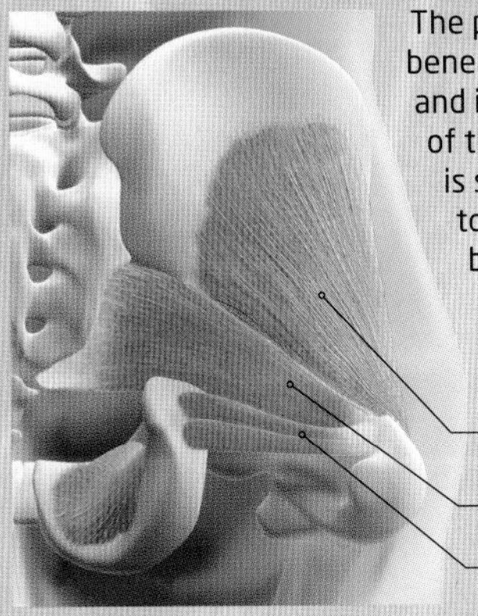

Gluteus minimus
Piriformis
Superior and inferior gemellus

THE PELVIC SKELETON

The ilium, ischium, and pubis form the pelvic girdle, not only providing a protective ring for the internal organs, but acting as an important structure for muscular attachments and the transfer of force between the lower body, the spine, and the upper body. The hip, pelvis, and lumbar spine are joined together by ligaments, providing stability to the structure.

Ilium
Femur
Ischium
Pubis
Sacrum

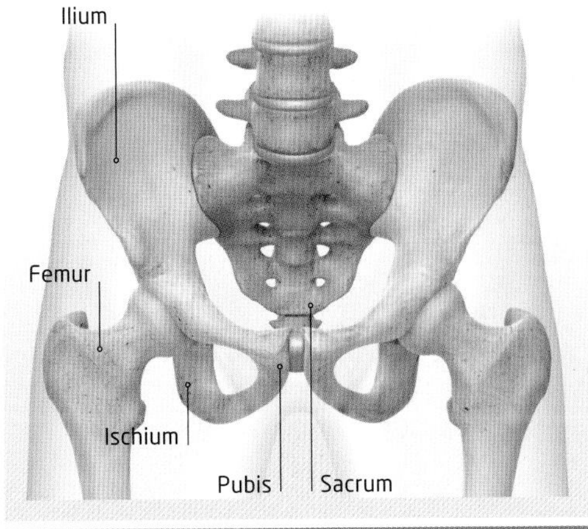

THE KNEE

One of the most commonly injured joints in runners, the knee joint forms the articulation between the femur (thigh bone) and tibia (shin bone). The patellofemoral joint, between the patella (knee cap) and the femur, is also part of the knee complex. A pivotal hinge joint, the knee joint moves mainly in flexion and extension (see box, below), with some rotational movement and little frontal plane motion. It is an extraordinarily strong joint: during running, the knee has to support up to eight times your body weight with each stride.

RANGE OF MOVEMENT

Like other joints, the knee's range of motion is dictated by its bone and ligament structure, with the muscles that cross the joint creating the force behind the movements.

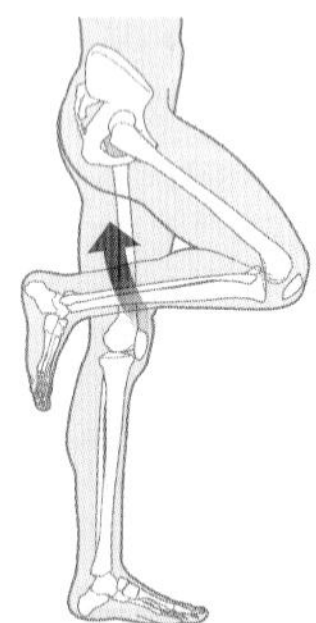

Flexion
This is the action of bending the knee. The motion is created mainly by contraction of the hamstring muscle group, or as a response to load-bearing.

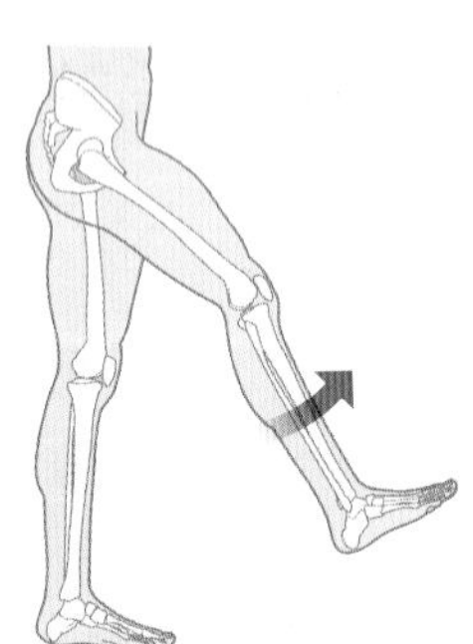

Extension
Knee extension is the action of straightening the knee. This movement is created predominantly by contraction of the quadriceps muscle group or by hip extension.

STABILITY AND KNEE CARE

The knee needs to be specifically aligned to carry load without injury – the freedom of motion in the hip and ankle above and below it can make it difficult to maintain good knee position. For a healthy knee, work on stability, strength, and control in muscles of the ankle and hip, and on maintaining muscle balance around the knee and hip – focusing on the knee alone is rarely sufficient. Exercises that strengthen the hamstrings and gluteal muscles (see pp.60–67) will help maintain knee alignment, as well as balancing out the action of the quadriceps.

Biceps femoris
Flexes the knee and helps to extend the hip

Semitendinosus
(behind) Extends the hip and flexes the knee

Semimembranosus
(behind) Straightens the hip and bends the knee

Fibula

Tibia

THE KNEE
The knee is situated between two highly mobile joints – the hip and ankle – which leaves it vulnerable to instability.

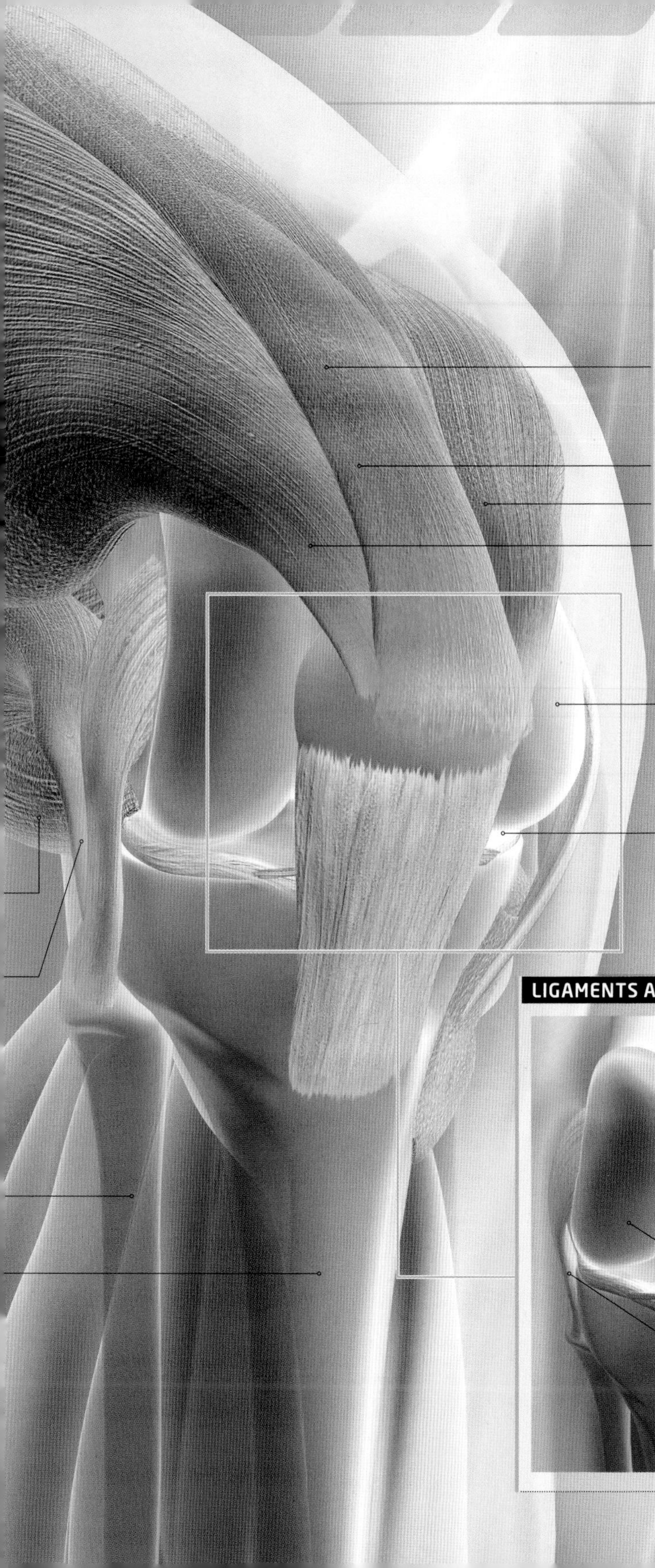

QUADRICEPS FEMORIS

The main muscles of the front thigh, used to extend the knee.

Rectus femoris
Extends the knee and flexes the hip; the only one of the group that crosses the hip

Vastus intermedius (behind)

Vastus medialis

Vastus lateralis

Patella
The knee cap. Acts as a focal point for the knee's extensor mechanism

Meniscus
Soft cartilage providing shock absorbency to the knee

LIGAMENTS AND CARTILAGE

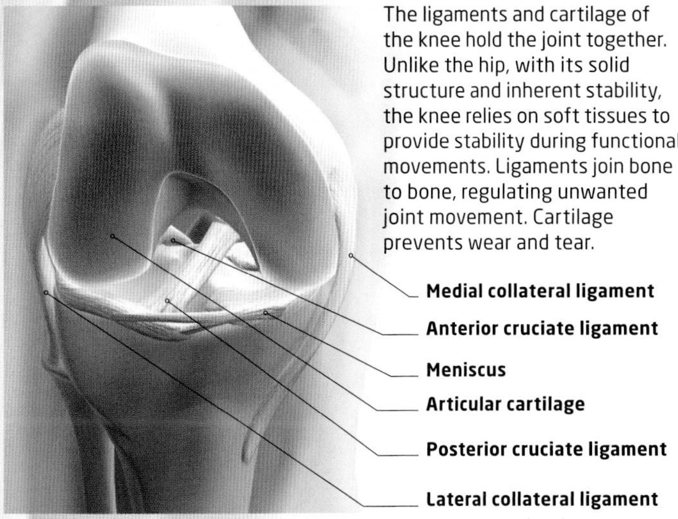

The ligaments and cartilage of the knee hold the joint together. Unlike the hip, with its solid structure and inherent stability, the knee relies on soft tissues to provide stability during functional movements. Ligaments join bone to bone, regulating unwanted joint movement. Cartilage prevents wear and tear.

Medial collateral ligament

Anterior cruciate ligament

Meniscus

Articular cartilage

Posterior cruciate ligament

Lateral collateral ligament

THE ANKLE AND FOOT

THESE STRUCTURES PROVIDE BOTH A STABLE BASE AND DYNAMIC MOBILITY.

The 26 bones and 33 joints of the ankle and foot form a complex mechanism capable of delivering both the mobility to absorb loads and the strength that enables you to push off, as well as being versatile enough to run on almost any type of terrain. The movements of the intricate joints of the foot and ankle are dictated by both the muscles of the foot and those in the lower leg.

THE FOOT DURING A RUN

Your foot is an intricate machine comprised of bone, muscle, and ligaments designed to provide stability, and to distribute load during foot strike and in response to weight-bearing when running. The shape of your feet can influence your running form, and can have an impact on your footstrike and technique (see p.36 and p.47). This is particularly true of the arches, the curves of the foot's underside, which provide much of its stability and shock absorbtion.

Soleus Along with the gastrocnemius, forms the muscle of the calf

Fibula

Achilles tendon

Calcaneus The heel bone

Plantar fascia Connective tissue supporting the arch of the foot

WHAT ARE LATERAL ANKLE LIGAMENTS?

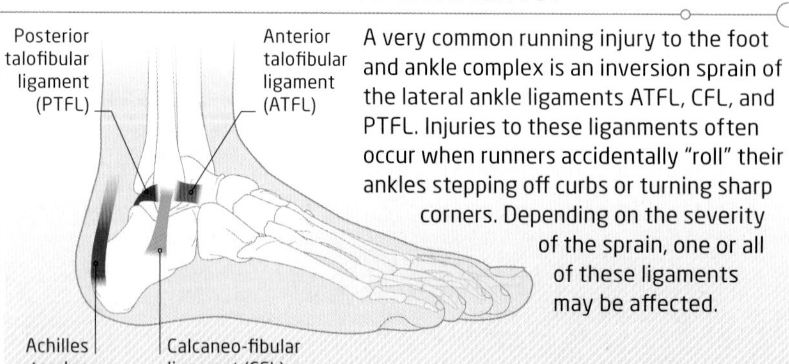

A very common running injury to the foot and ankle complex is an inversion sprain of the lateral ankle ligaments ATFL, CFL, and PTFL. Injuries to these liganments often occur when runners accidentally "roll" their ankles stepping off curbs or turning sharp corners. Depending on the severity of the sprain, one or all of these ligaments may be affected.

THE ANKLE AND FOOT

Highly active in the support and toe-off phases of the running cycle (see pp.30–31), the foot and ankle must exercise control over the strong forces involved during each phase.

Tibia
The largest bone in the leg, paired with the thinner fibula bone

Extensor digtorum longus
This muscle and tendon group works to flex the four smaller toes and dorsiflexes the ankle (see box, right)

Talus
Transmits the weight of the body to the foot

Cuneiform bones (behind)

Navicular bone

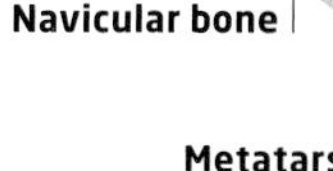

Metatarsals

Flexor hallucis tendon
Flexes the joints of the big toe; helps to flex the ankle

Proximal phalanges
The big toe has two phalanges, while the other toes have three

Distal phalanges
The tips of the toes

RANGE OF MOVEMENT

The foot and ankle can move through a number of key patterns to achieve the versatility to adapt to any terrain. These motions can either be active, as a result of muscle contraction, or passive, as a response to carrying weight.

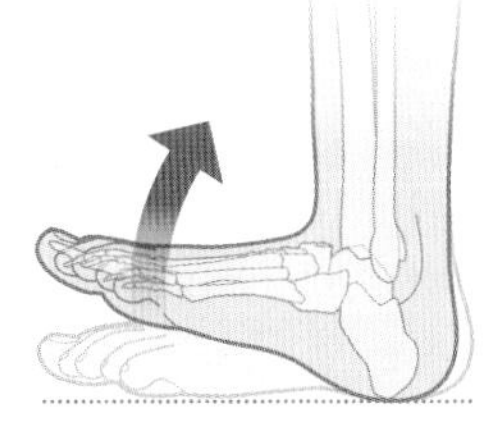

Dorsiflexion
The action of bringing the foot straight up towards the shin bone, this is performed either actively using the muscles, or passively as a reaction to weight and leg position during running.

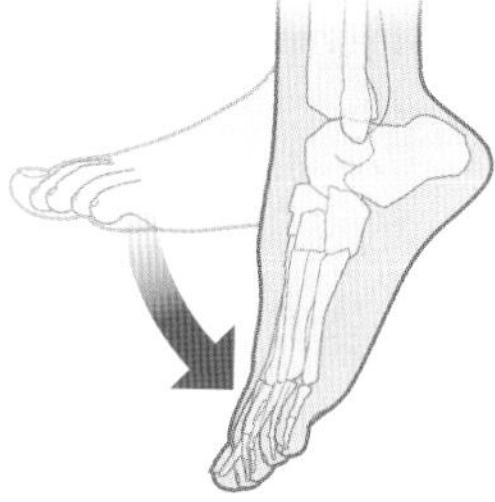

Plantar flexion
This action, pointing the foot down and away from the shin bone, is achieved through contraction of the muscles of the calf and posterior lower leg, such as gastrocnemius and soleus (see pp.28–29).

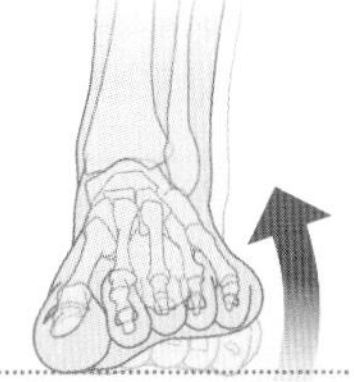

Eversion
This is one of the key motions that enables pronation of the foot (see p.36), deflecting the force of impact and allowing structural mobility through the foot and ankle. It mostly occurs when bearing weight.

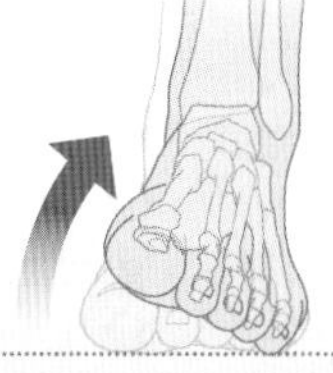

Inversion
This movement enables supination of the foot (see p.36), creating a stable base to push off in running gait. The tibialis anterior (see pp.28–29) and posterior are important in the inversion of the foot.

Gastrocnemius
Pulls up the heel and flexes the ankle

Soleus
Connected to the gastrocnemius to form the calf muscles; flexes the foot

Extensor digitorum longus
Extends the toes and bends the foot up

Fibularis longus
Flexes and turns the foot outwards

THE ANKLE AND LOWER LEG

The muscles, tendons, and ligaments of the lower leg are of vital importance to runners, and are all too commonly injured. This area includes the Achilles tendon, located at the back of the ankle and connecting the calcaneus (heel bone) to the gastrocnemius and soleus muscles. The Achilles tendon is structurally capable of transferring large loads during running (see box, below).

WORKING TOGETHER

While many of the movements of the foot and ankle are dictated by the muscles located within the lower leg, the intrinsic muscles of the foot control the toes and support the arches, which form the dynamic architecture of the foot.

THE ACHILLES TENDON

Upwards force via tendon

Body weight via skeleton

In running gait, the Achilles tendon is loaded with more than seven times the weight of the body. To push off the ground, the foot acts as a lever, and the downward pressure from the bone structure is countered with an upwards force through the tendon. The need to withstand this weight is reflected in the tendon's structure: it is the thickest and strongest tendon in the human body. Despite its strength, it is also a common site of injury through overuse or sudden tearing.

THE FRONT OF THE ANKLE

The tendons of the ankle and flexor muscles help provide the foot's range of movement, while the extensors allow control of the toes, which is vital to maintaining balance.

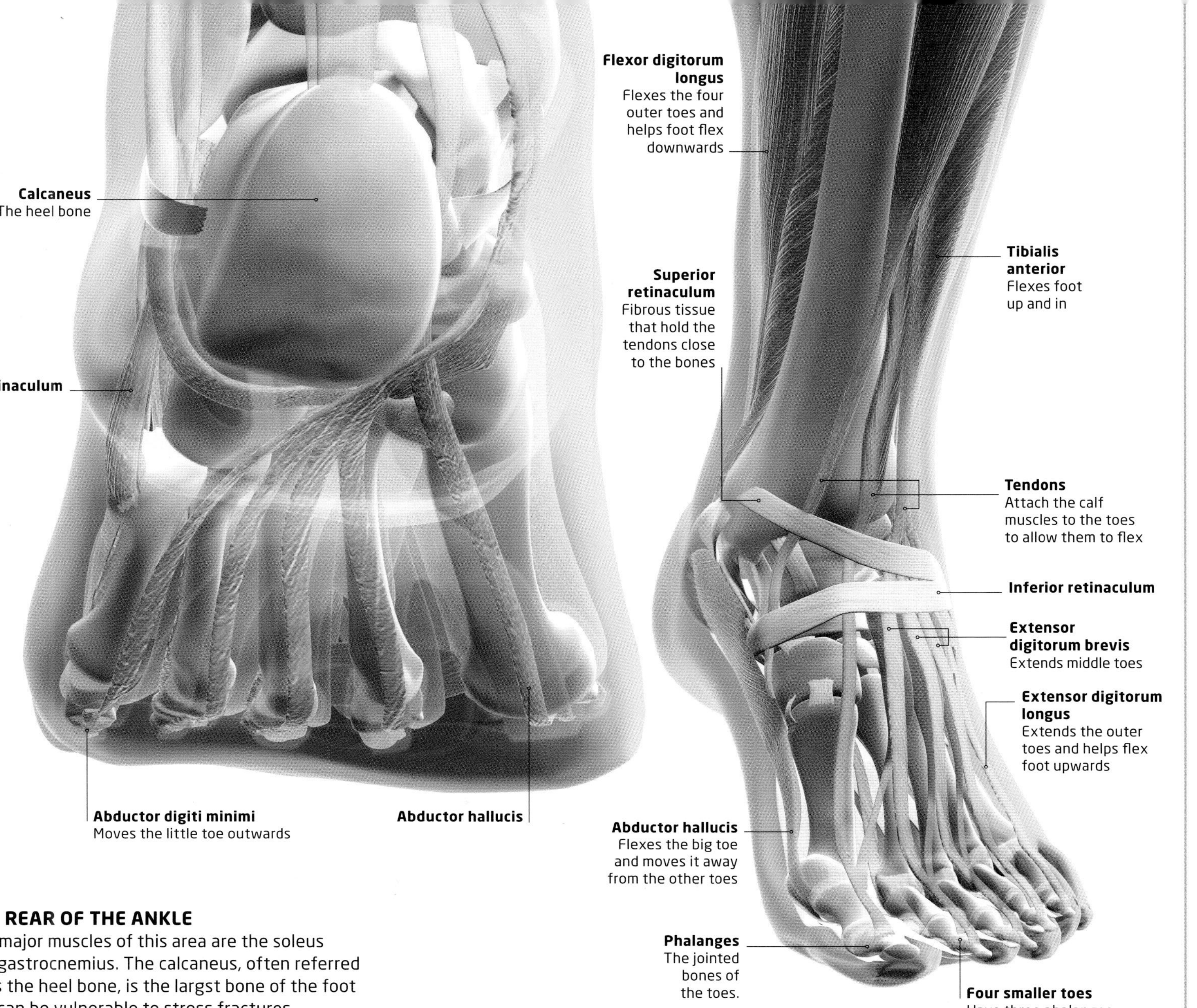

THE REAR OF THE ANKLE

The major muscles of this area are the soleus and gastrocnemius. The calcaneus, often referred to as the heel bone, is the largst bone of the foot and can be vulnerable to stress fractures.

THE RUNNING CYCLE

Running combines kinetic energy (motion) with the potential energy stored in tendons and muscles. The running cycle can be divided into two main phases: floating and stance. These can be further broken down into the toe off, swing, strike, and support phases. The floating phase, when both feet leave the ground, is the longest phase of the running cycle. During the stance phase, the body absorbs forces from the ground, storing energy in springy tendons and elastic muscle to propel the body forward.

THE RUNNING PHASES

Stance and floating (also called swing) are the two main phases. The stance phase is subdivided into strike, support, and toe off phases, which can be further qualified as early, mid-, or late.

KEY »

- STANCE PHASE
- FLOATING PHASE

- TOE OFF
- SWING
- STRIKE
- SUPPORT

TOE OFF

The knee of the leading leg drives forward, using the hip flexors, and the trailing (back) foot leaves the ground using energy stored in the Achilles tendon and calf muscle.

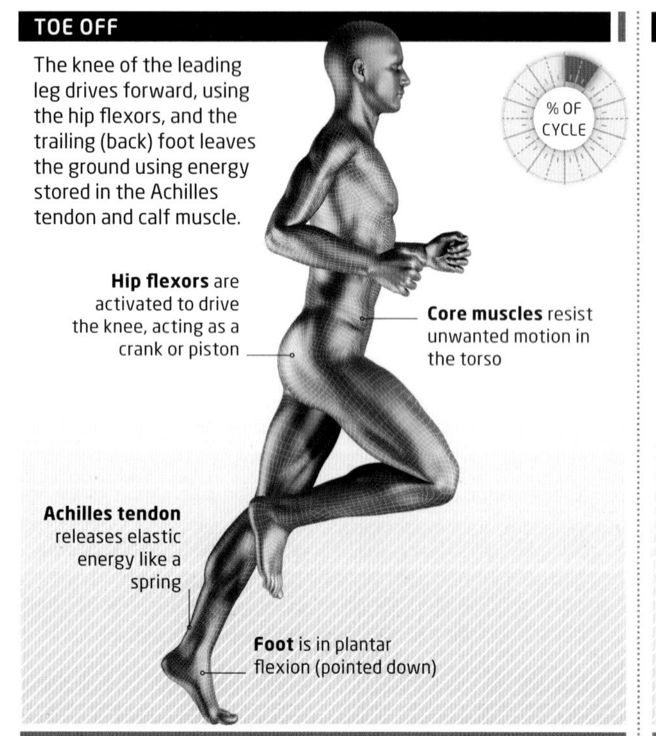

SWING

The longest phase of running is spent moving forward through the air, during which time you "swing" or cycle your legs through, ready for the next foot strike.

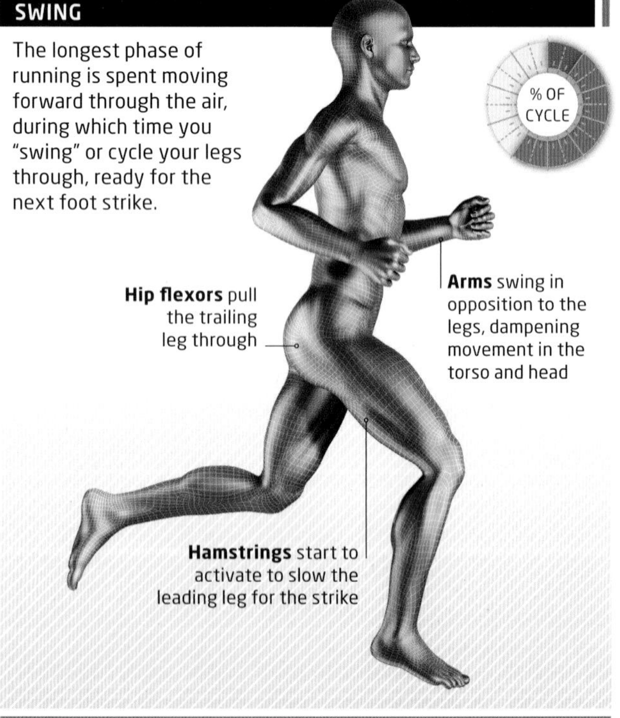

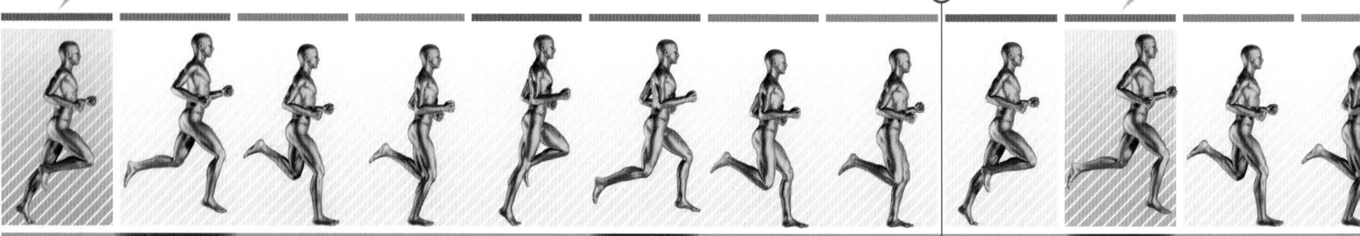

INFO DASHBOARD

MUSCLES USED DURING THE RUNNING CYCLE

This diagram shows the action of the muscles most used during each phase of running (although this is not necessarily representative of an ideal firing of muscles). Muscle activation varies through the cycle, with activation peaking during the strike and support phases, when increased kinetics (forces and torque) are at work on the body.

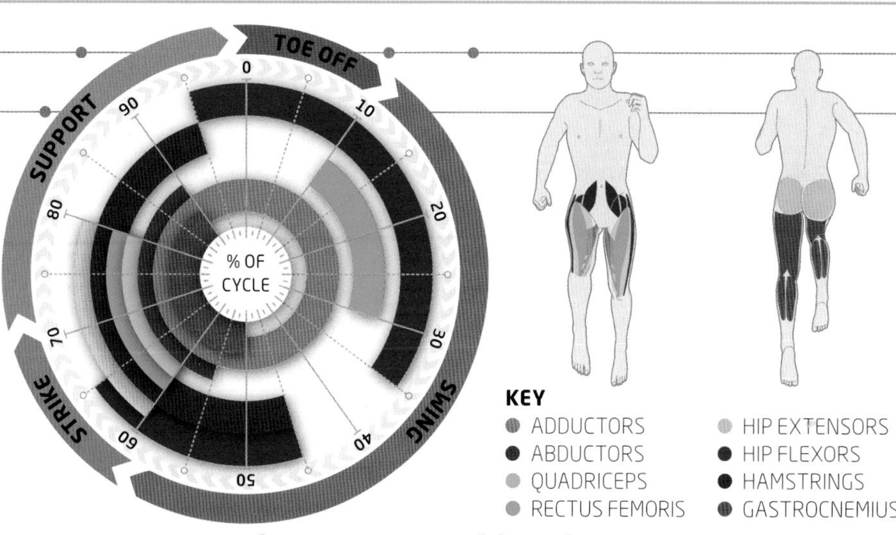

STRIKE

The body absorbs several times its own weight in terms of impact during the foot strike. Numerous muscles are active during this phase and in the support phase as the body absorbs the force of landing.

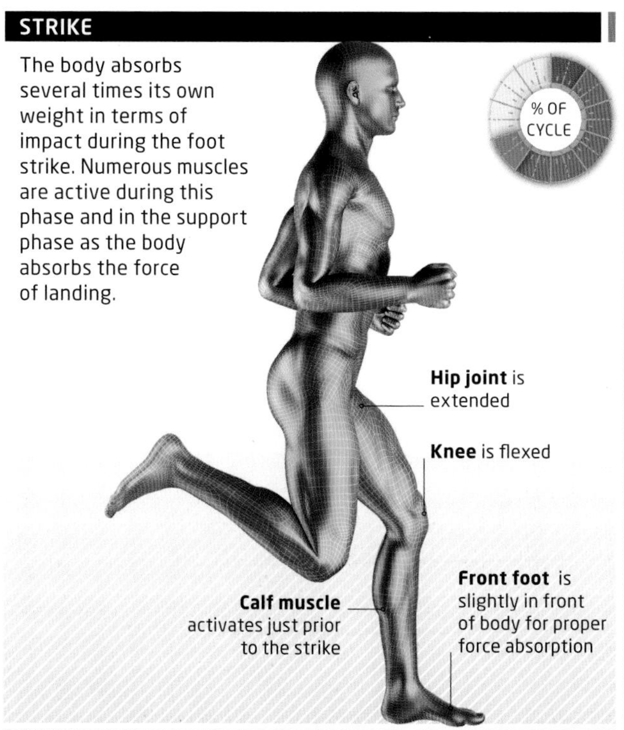

SUPPORT

During midstance, the leading leg is directly underneath the hips. The body then travels forward over the leg, extending the hip and knee, and enters the propulsion phase of toe off.

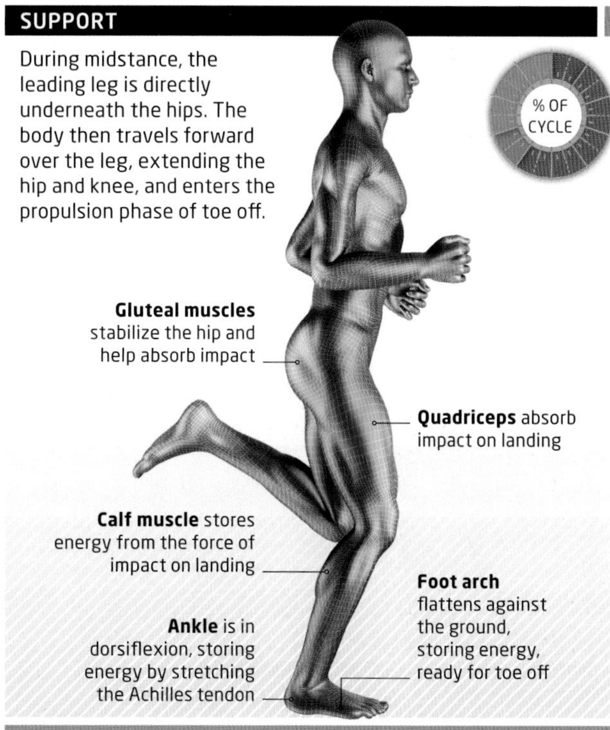

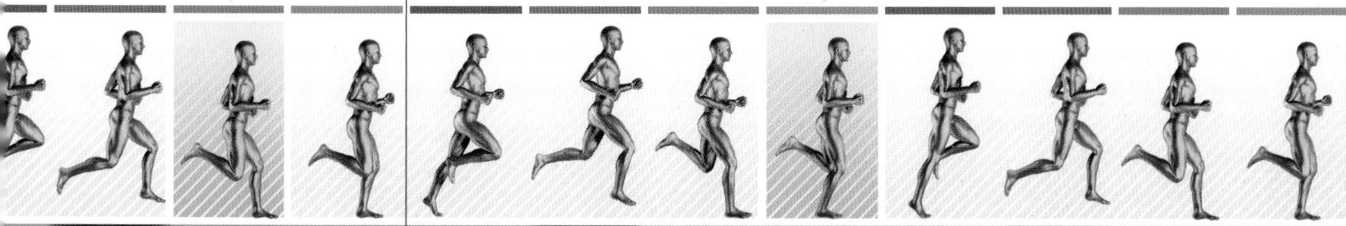

AN ECONOMIC CYCLE

Running is a skill, and learning good technique will ensure that you practise it with greater efficiency and sustain fewer injuries in the process. Runners should "run tall" with a slight forward lean and arms bent at about 90 degrees, and aim for a wide stride angle during toe off. During the footstrike, the foot should land in the area just in front of the body's centre of gravity, and as much as possible it should strike the ground relatively lightly. You should also consider the length of your stride and your cadence (stride rate).

THE NUMBER OF MILLISECONDS MIDFOOT-STRIKERS ALLEGEDLY SPEND ON THE GROUND PER STRIKE, AS OPPOSED TO 199 FOR HEEL-STRIKERS

TOE OFF: STAY TALL AND DRIVE THE KNEE

New runners tend to lean too far forward, inhibiting their stride angle. Stay tall, leaning from the ankle, and this will provide space for a wide stride angle when driving the knee at toe off. This will fully stretch your hip extensors, allowing the leg to slingshot through.

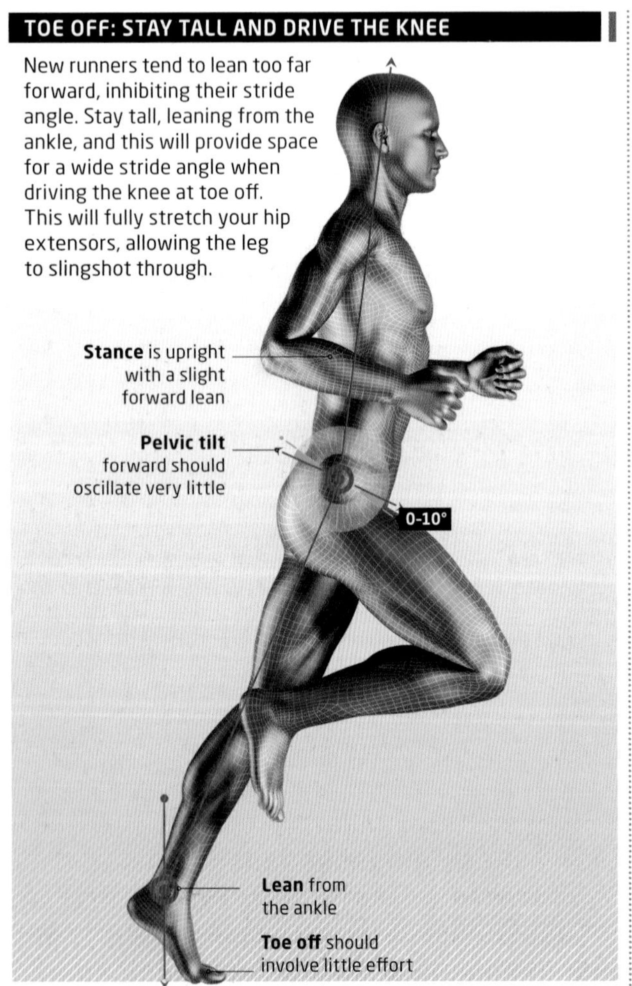

SWING: ALLOW NATURAL RECOVERY AND USE THE ARMS

Allow the trailing leg to cycle through naturally. Your arms should be engaged, rotating from the shoulder, and cycling parallel to the torso, bent at a right angle. This action balances the leg movement and also helps set your running pace or cadence.

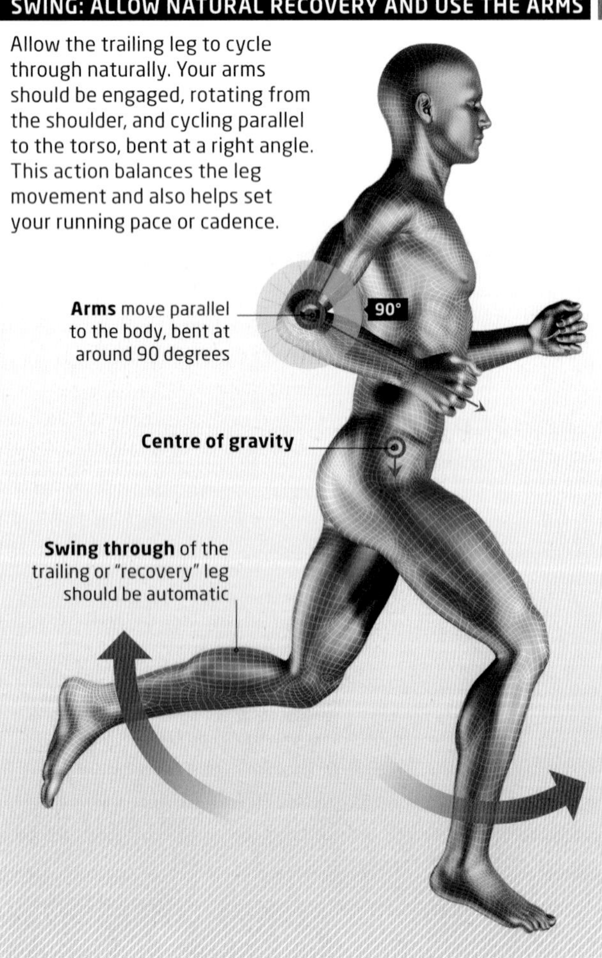

KEEP CENTRED

The body should remain as centred as possible during running, with the hips neutral. A small degree of rotation of the torso and of the hips is a natural consequence of lower limb action, but arms should be parallel to the body and should not cross over the midline of the body, and neither should the legs.

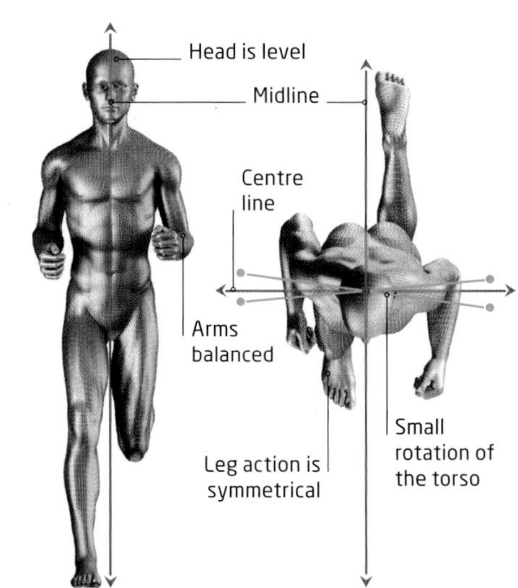

STRIKE: LAND BELOW THE CENTRE OF GRAVITY ON THE MIDFOOT

The foot strike should land just in front of the body's centre of gravity. This maintains momentum and avoids a braking action. It also protects the knee, and allows the muscles and tendons of the leg to absorb the force of impact, storing it as energy. The foot should also be relatively flat as it comes down.

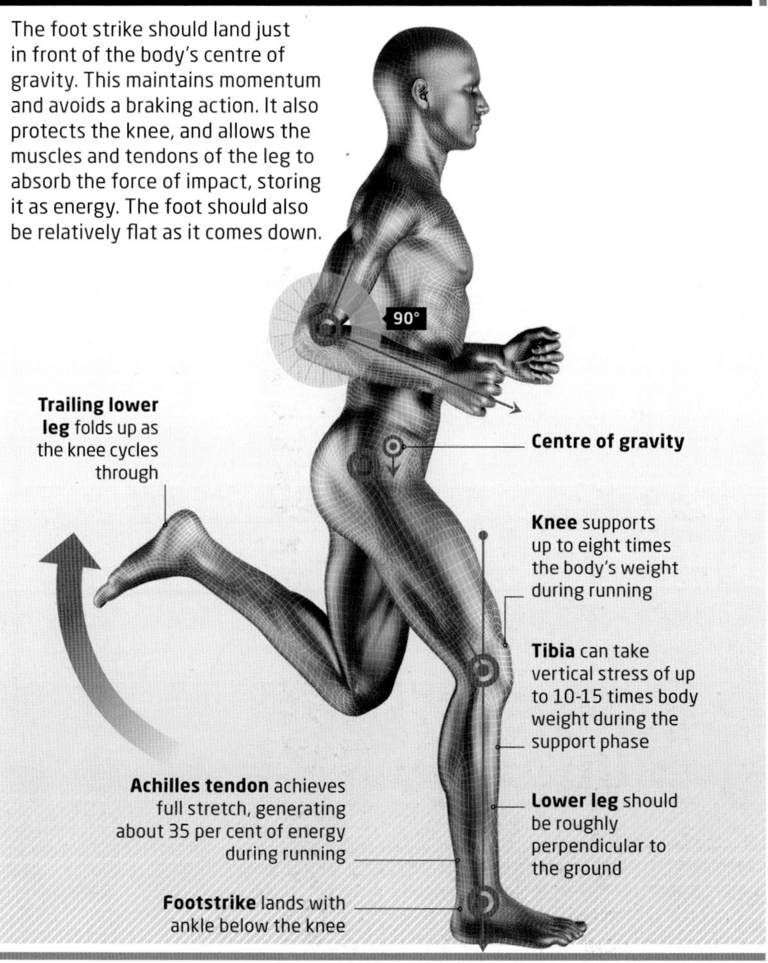

INFO DASHBOARD

FOOT STRIKE MECHANICS

What constitutes an ideal footstrike is still a subject of much debate and little data. Speed and distance both influence which type of foot strike is used. Whatever your strike, it is vital to avoid heavy landings and overstriding.

MIDFOOT STRIKE

This strike is on the ball of the foot and the heel more or less simultaneously, with the foot landing parallel to the ground. The arch is loaded on impact.

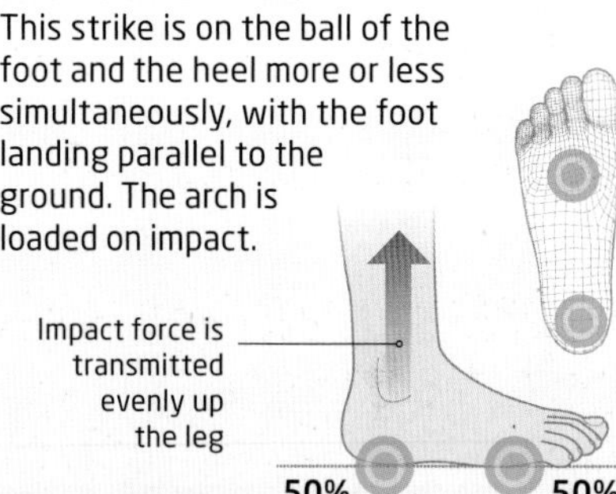

HEEL STRIKE

A good heel-striker lands first with the outside of the heel, then rolls inwards to load the arch, and then toes off. A heel strike has a double impact: the first of which is often seen as a braking motion. Despite this, most runners covering over a mile, running at slower speeds, are heel-strikers.

Braking force

Rotary motion

100%

FOREFOOT STRIKE

Often seen in faster short-distance runners, a good forefoot strike lands on the ball of the foot, on the outside edge, briefly touching down with the heel. The foot rolls slightly inwards, loads, and then toes off.

Force of impact can put additional stress on the ankle and calf

100%

THE EFFICIENT RUNNER

The different parts of the body are linked to one another via the joints in a connected system known as the kinetic chain. Each phase of running impacts on the next phase (see pp.30–31), and similarly the movement of one section of the running body will have a knock-on effect on other parts of the body. The posture or function of one part of the body can have a significant impact on running efficiency as a whole, and in some cases can determine whether or not the body sustains injury. Use these diagrams to help correct and finesse your running technique.

» THE HEAD

KEEP A LEVEL HEAD

It is important to keep your head up while you run. Looking down while running tires the neck muscles and affects the rest of the kinetic chain by introducing tension into the neck, shoulders, back, and even as far down as the hamstrings (see pp.20–21).

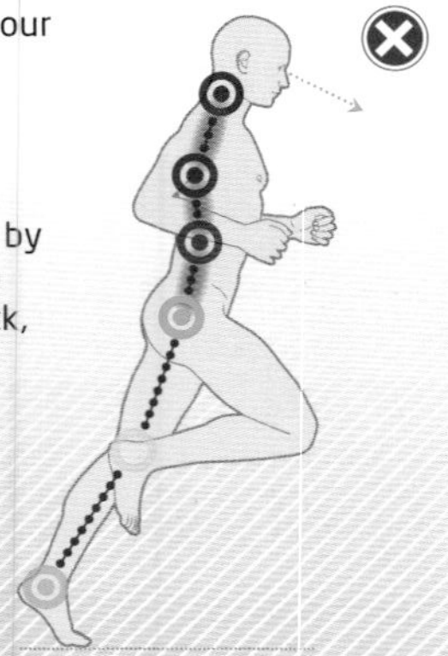

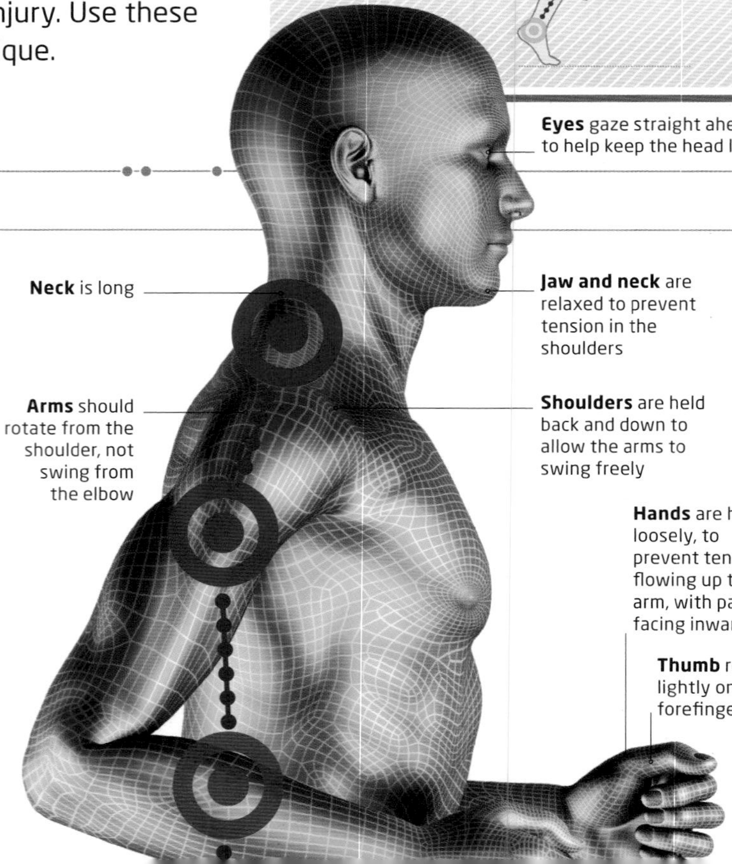

Eyes gaze straight ahead to help keep the head level

Jaw and neck are relaxed to prevent tension in the shoulders

Shoulders are held back and down to allow the arms to swing freely

Hands are held loosely, to prevent tension flowing up the arm, with palms facing inwards

Thumb rests lightly on the forefinger

Neck is long

Arms should rotate from the shoulder, not swing from the elbow

» THE ARMS

ARM POSITION CAN AFFECT STRIDE

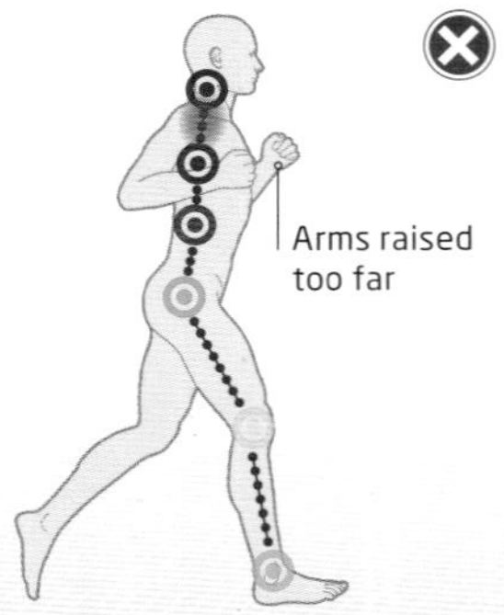

Arms raised too far

Arms held too high can cause shoulder tension and result in a shorter stride. Swinging them too low can cause excess forward lean and too much vertical movement.

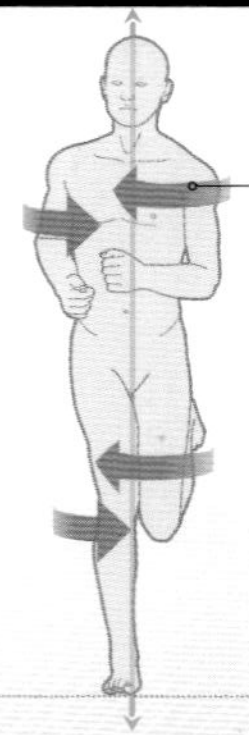

Lateral arm movement

Arms that swing across the midline of the body can exaggerate upper body torque, which then pulls the opposing leg in towards the midline and out of alignment.

» THE CORE AND HIPS

AN UNSTABLE PLATFORM CAUSES BAD FORM

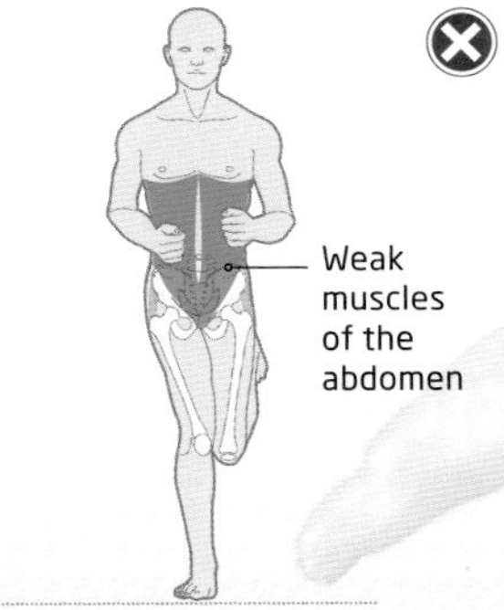

Weak muscles of the abdomen

Weak abdominal muscles and hip abductors (particularly gluteus medius and minimus) can make the pelvis unstable, causing the leg to turn in and the foot to overpronate.

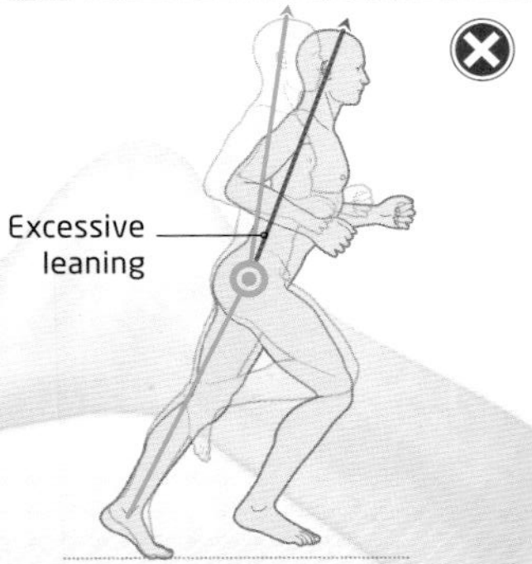

Excessive leaning

Weak abdominal muscles or poor technique can result in leaning forward from the waist, which in turn can cause a narrow stride at toe off.

» THE LEG AND FOOT

KEEP MUSCLES FLEXIBLE AND AVOID HIGH IMPACT

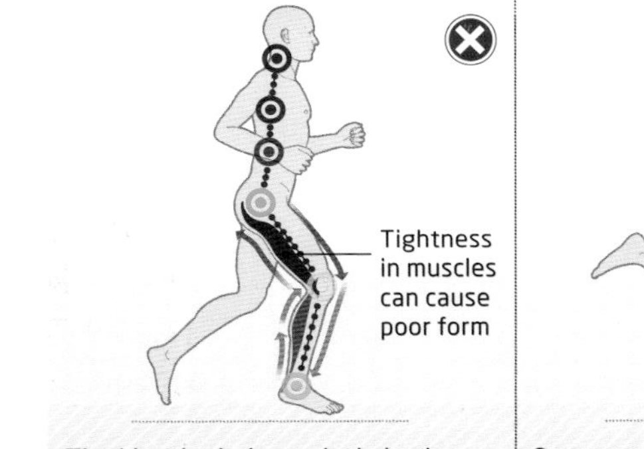

The kinetic chain works in both directions: tightness to a hamstring might cause limited hip extension and prevent good knee extension, tightening the calf muscle.

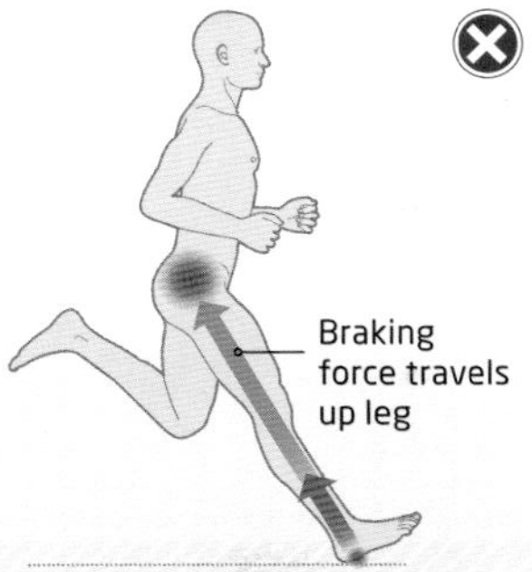

Braking force travels up leg

Overextending the knee during the foot strike sends force up the leg bone that can reach the hip and lower back. It also causes a braking action.

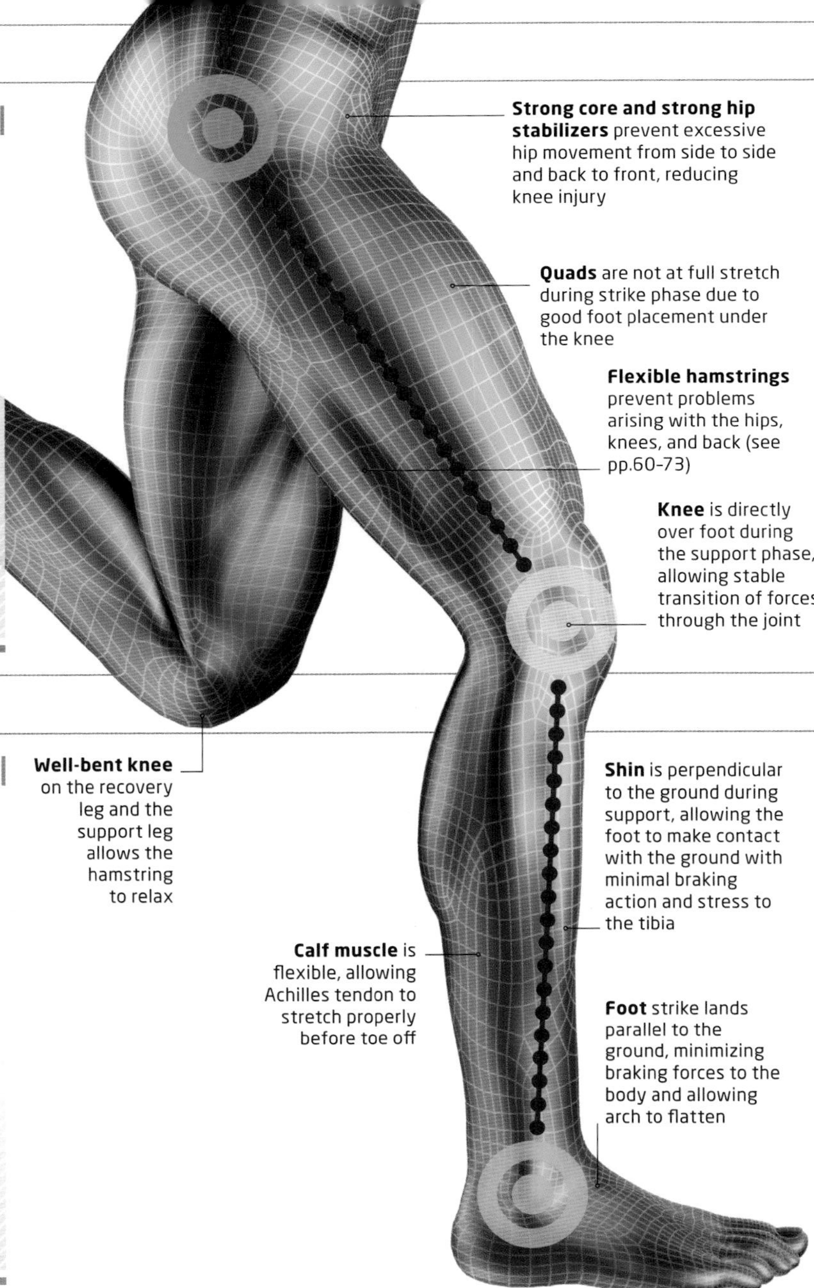

Strong core and strong hip stabilizers prevent excessive hip movement from side to side and back to front, reducing knee injury

Quads are not at full stretch during strike phase due to good foot placement under the knee

Flexible hamstrings prevent problems arising with the hips, knees, and back (see pp.60–73)

Knee is directly over foot during the support phase, allowing stable transition of forces through the joint

Well-bent knee on the recovery leg and the support leg allows the hamstring to relax

Shin is perpendicular to the ground during support, allowing the foot to make contact with the ground with minimal braking action and stress to the tibia

Calf muscle is flexible, allowing Achilles tendon to stretch properly before toe off

Foot strike lands parallel to the ground, minimizing braking forces to the body and allowing arch to flatten

ASSESSING YOUR RUNNING STYLE

Being able to assess your running form is a valuable tool. Every runner is different, and there is nothing wrong with having form that may not be "perfect". Rather, the aim of this section is to help you identify and address any elements that may be holding you back – making you more tired than you should be, or putting unnecessary strain on your body. Use the chart (right) to find small areas of improvement that can yield great benefits in terms of speed, efficiency, and enjoyment.

YOUR STRIKE AND POSTURE

A good footstrike lands slightly ahead of your centre of gravity, with your foot facing directly forwards. Your footstrike can affect your overall posture and alignment, as well as the transfer of energy via the kinetic chain (see p.11). A small level of pronation (rolling inwards) or supination (rolling outwards) is fine (see also p.47 and p.163).

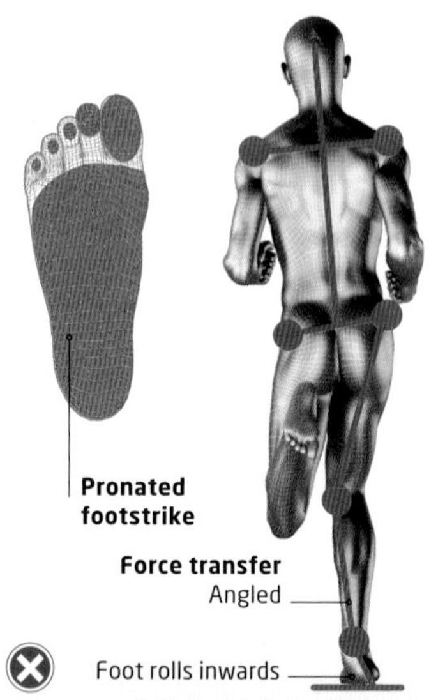

Overpronation The foot tilts inwards, transferring the force of the strike to the inside of the foot and ankle. This can put additional medial strain on the knee. The striking hip rotates, destabilizing the core.

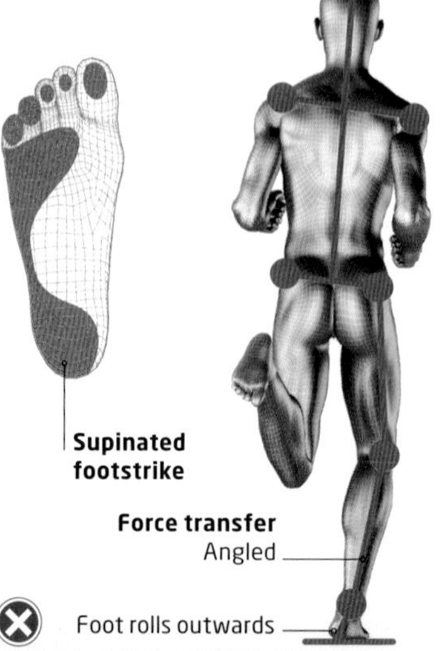

Oversupination (or underpronation) The foot tilts outwards, transferring the force via the outer side of the knee. Due to a lack of pronation, the runner's natural shock-absorbing mechanism is compromised.

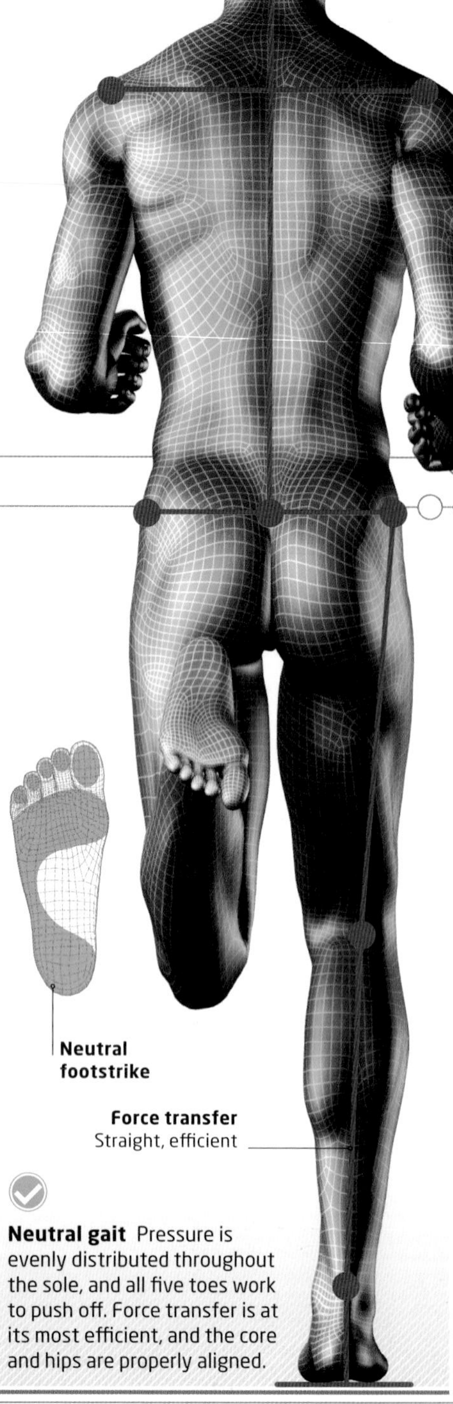

Neutral gait Pressure is evenly distributed throughout the sole, and all five toes work to push off. Force transfer is at its most efficient, and the core and hips are properly aligned.

HOW CAN YOU IMPROVE YOUR RUNNING?

WHAT TO LOOK OUT FOR		TELL-TALE SIGNS	WHAT IT MEANS	WHAT TO DO
POUNDING You may enjoy the comfort provided by a good pair of running shoes. However, some runners develop an overly heavy footstrike in response to their shoes' cushioning, hitting the ground with too much force.	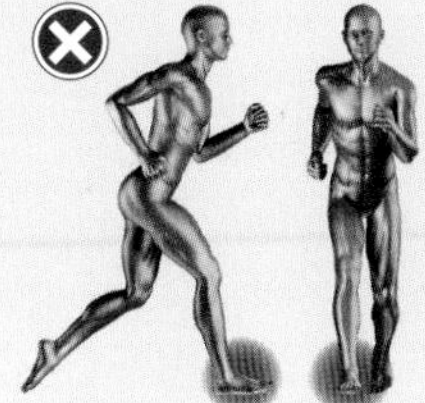	• You slam your feet heavily into the ground • You drag your toes • You quickly run out of energy • You suffer from injuries such as shin splints (see pp.170–71 and p.180)	• You are expending too much energy on the force of your footstrike • You are placing excessive force on the kinetic chain (see p.11) • You may be reducing your performance	• Use the Ankling drill on p.68 to help improve your strike • Focus on developing a light, even footstrike with a minimum of force (see pp.30–31) • Practise hill runs
OVERSTRIDING A long stride is not necessarily the best. When taking each step, your feet are striking too far in front of your centre of gravity, creating a braking force (see p.33) and reducing your running efficiency.		• Your feet are striking heel-first • Your strides are landing in front of your knees • Your lower leg stretches out at an angle	• You are taking overly long strides to the detriment of your cadence • Your footstrike is occurring too far forward, causing braking forces to be applied to your knee	• Use the Stride Outs drill on p.73 to work on your lower leg position • Keep your knee at the front of your stride, with your foot striking below the body
UNUSED ARMS New runners may be tempted to try to minimize arm movement in an effort to keep energy focused on the legs. In fact, proper arm movement is an important part of good running form.	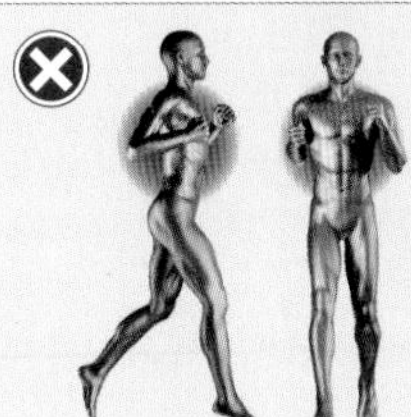	• Your arms are held tightly up around chest height • They feel tense and tired when you run • You suffer from shoulder or neck ache after running	• Your arm muscles are unnecessarily tense • Your are restricting your arms instead of using them to help your gait • Your energy transfer via the kinetic chain (see p.11) is restricted	• Hold your arms at a 90-degree angle to your body around waist height • Run with a long neck • Relax your shoulders • Use the B-walk drill on p.71 to mobilize your arms
TWISTING In contrast to unused arms (see above), twisting can occur when arm movement is both excessive and poorly directed. Your arms are swinging from side to side and causing lateral movement of the core.	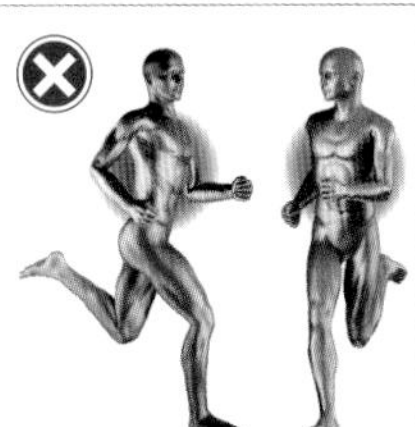	• Your shoulders and torso twist from side to side • Your arms and hands move laterally in front of your body	• You are expending energy on unnecessary sideways motion in your upper body • Your core is not staying in a stable position when you run	• Swing your arms in the direction of travel • Use the A-walk drill on p.70 to help improve your core's alignment • Practise core training (see pp.112–125) • Relax your hands
BOUNCING If you are an energetic runner, it can seem normal to run with a natural bounce to your gait. However, this is a waste of valuable energy and momentum – instead, aim for a smooth, level motion.	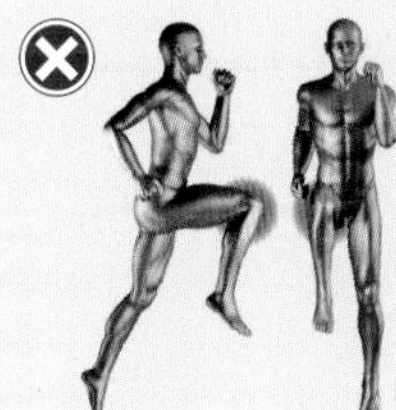	• Your knees are lifting towards your waistline with every stride • Your gait follows a bouncing movement rather than a smooth line	• You are wasting energy travelling up rather than forwards • You may be risking pulled muscles from the additional strain on your muscles	• Use the Stride Outs drill on p.73 to improve your form • Use your hip muscles to moderate the action of your legs and smooth your gait • Skim the ground rather than leaping in the air
SLOW PACE Some runners may adopt an overly slow pace in the search for efficiency or to save their energy – in fact, this has the opposite effect, using more energy for lesser results.	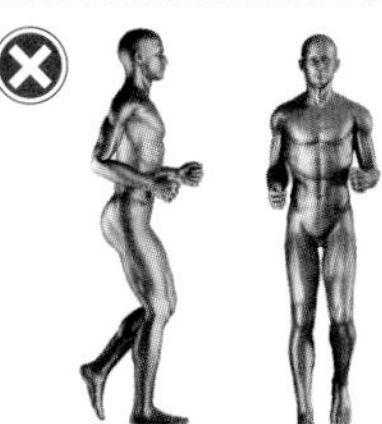	• You run at an extremely slow pace to try and avoid getting out of breath • Your running pace is similar to or less than your walking pace	• You are running too slowly • Your running technique is inefficient	• Use the Bounding drill on p.72 to improve your pace • Work on slowly increasing your speed • See pp.106–107 for more information on running faster

ASSESSING YOUR RUNNING FITNESS

UNDERSTAND YOUR GENERAL HEALTH AND HOW TO FIND THE RIGHT LEVEL OF INTENSITY IN YOUR TRAINING.

Your health and fitness should be your main priority as a runner, and being able to measure your exertion is a great way to ensure you don't over- or undertrain. Check your health before you start, and use the following methods to ensure you are training at the right intensity; establish your running fitness through time-trials or running-specific tests.

BMI: PROS AND CONS

Body mass index, or BMI, is a widely used system of determining human body shape. Devised in the mid-1800s, it is based on a person's height and mass and is used to measure whether an individual's body shape falls within a healthy range. To calculate your BMI, divide your mass by the square of your height. Some modern studies have found that BMI has its limitations, as it does not take into account tissue density. As a result some larger athletes who are extremely fit may have a BMI that is classified as unhealthy, or even obese, while people with a small frame but high body fat may have a "good" BMI.

Q WHAT'S THE FIRST STEP?

A As keen as you may be to get your shoes on and hit the road, before you start running, it is highly advisable to visit your doctor and have a general health check. You may feel fine, but there are certain risks that you cannot change, and that may be related to your genes or your age.

Q WHAT ARE THE MAIN RISK FACTORS?

A High blood pressure can cause damage to your heart and blood vessels (see pp.14–15), while an excess of the "bad" form of cholesterol – a fatty substance that is used to build cell membranes – can impede blood flow to your heart. Check for iron deficiency: iron is important in the production of haemoglobin, which carries oxygen to the muscles (see pp.12–15). Finally, get checked for diabetes, the condition that affects the regulation of blood sugar (see pp.50–53).

Q HOW CAN I MEASURE HOW FIT I AM?

A Once you have had a general health check, you can start assessing your fitness levels and planning your training accordingly (see pp.86–87). A good basic indicator is to take your resting heart rate (see box, right, and p.93). Once you have done this, you can progress to the tests on pp.40–41 used to find your maximal oxygen uptake (VO_2 max) – this is a more sophisticated way of analyzing your body's optimum capacity for exercise.

Q HOW HARD SHOULD I TRAIN?

A Your level of training will be dictated by your running goal – see pp.94–103 for training programmes for races of various distances. Use the RPE scales and heart rate zones (see boxes, opposite) to measure the intensity of the different types of running sessions (see pp.78–81).

Q CAN I RUN DURING PREGNANCY?

A If you want to continue running during your pregnancy, the first step is to talk to your doctor and/or midwife. It is certainly possible to run while pregnant, but you may have to limit your training, and be more aware of factors such as nutrition and body temperature.

FIND YOUR RESTING HEART RATE

Resting heart rate is used by athletes and coaches as a measure of fitness. It is best recorded in the morning after a night's rest. The lower your heart rate, the more efficient it is, suggesting higher fitness levels - your heart is a muscle, which becomes more efficient with training (see p.184). A reduction in heart rate during training can indicate increased fitness. However, dehydration can raise heart rate by 7.5 per cent, heat adds up to 10 beats per minute, and altitude causes a 10-20 per cent increase even when acclimatized.

HOW TO CARRY OUT THE TEST

- Lie down with a watch or clock within easy view
- Find a pulse at your neck or wrist
- Remaining motionless, count the number of beats in one minute

MEASURE YOUR TRAINING: THE RPE SCALE

The Rate of Perceived Exertion (RPE) scale measures the intensity of exercise. In this book, it is correlated to heart rate zones (see below). For example, an easy base run should be RPE 3-4, or 60-70 per cent of your maximum heart rate. The RPE scale is rated in a range of 1-10, and the numbers relate to descriptive phrases that are used to rate how difficult you find an activity - an RPE of 10 leaves you completely out of breath.

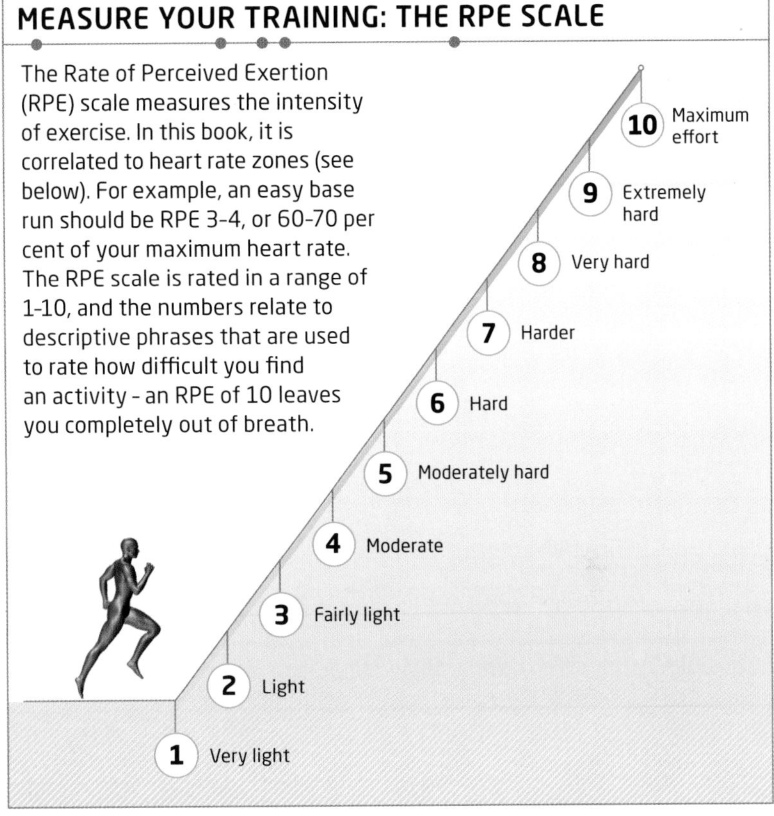

MEASURE YOUR TRAINING: HEART RATE ZONES

A good way of judging your running intensity is to measure your heart rate during exercise using a monitor (see p.49). In general, the faster you run, the more oxygen your muscles need, so your heart rate increases to pump oxygen to the muscles. Depending on the training session you need to work within different heart rate zones (see right), or percentages of your working heart rate. To find your working heart rate, subtract your age from 220 to get your maximum heart rate, then subtract your resting heart rate from this number. From this, you can calculate your ideal training heart rate zones. Use the information to ensure you do not over- or undertrain during your running sessions (see pp.78-81). Some monitors can be set to your heart rate training zones.

220 - YOUR AGE = MAXIMUM HEART RATE

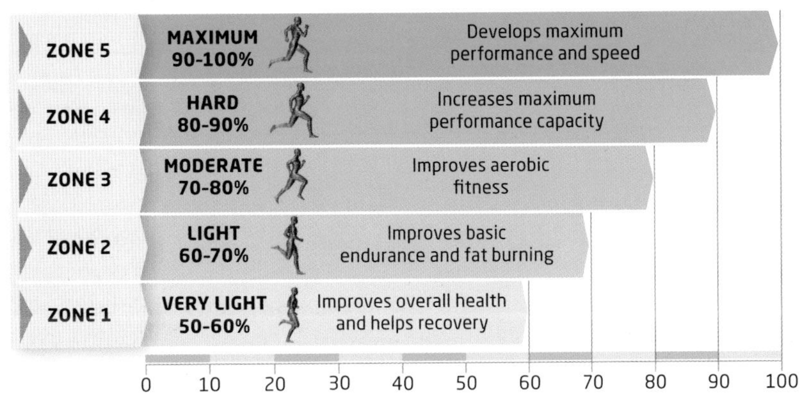

MAXIMAL OXYGEN UPTAKE (VO_2 MAX) TESTING

VO_2 max is an individual's maximal oxygen uptake - the maximum capacity of a person's body to take in and use oxygen while exercising. It is a useful way of measuring your optimum capacity for exertion, and elite distance runners typically have a very high VO_2 max score.

There are many ways to assess your VO_2 max, from simple gym-based equipment tests to more scientifically accurate methods. As a rule of thumb, if you are testing your VO_2 max for your performance in a certain sport, you would generally use the test most closely correlated to the sport.

Use the tests on these pages, their corresponding formulas, and the tables on pp.184–85 to assess your current VO_2 max score and your running economy (there are also a number of online converters for the different types of test - simply enter your test results into one of these for a quick answer).

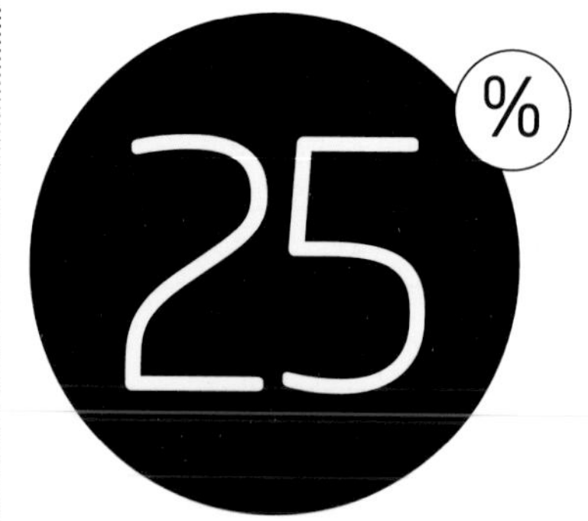

THE AMOUNT A MODERATELY FIT RUNNER CAN INCREASE VO_2 MAX THROUGH TRAINING

THE MULTI-STAGE FITNESS (BLEEP) TEST (P.184)

This test estimates an athlete's VO_2 max by pitting the athlete against a pre-recorded timer. To carry out the test, the athlete runs a 20-m (65-foot) distance between two cones, keeping time time to a recorded bleep. The speed starts at 8.5km/hour (5mph) and increases in 23 "levels" of 0.5km/h (0.3mph) until the athlete cannot keep up with the bleeps. From this, you achieve a score based on the number of repeats you manage, and can find your VO_2 max using an online converter. See p.185 for chart.

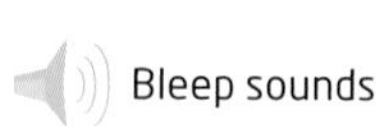

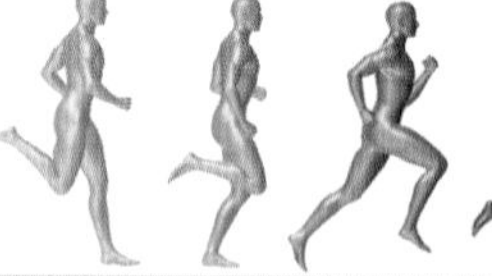

HOW TO CARRY OUT THE TEST

- The athlete warms up
- An assistant marks the 20-m (65-foot) course
- The test starts and the assistant plays the recording
- The assistant notes the number of bleeps successfully completed
- The test finishes when the athlete cannot keep pace with the bleeps

THE TREADMILL TEST

This test is very simple and requires the athlete to run on a treadmill. Each minute, the slope of the treadmill is increased as per the chart below until the athlete cannot maintain the pace. You will need an assistant to adjust the treadmill during this test as you will be working your body to its physical limits.

$$VO_2 \text{ MAX} = \mathbf{42} + (\text{time} \times 2)$$

TIME (MINUTES)	0	1	2	3	4	5	6	7	8	9	10	11	12	13	14	15
SLOPE	0°	2°	4°	6°	8°	10°	11°	12°	13°	14°	15°	16°	17°	18°	19°	20°

NB here, "time" is the total time of the test expressed in minutes and fractions of a minute

HOW TO CARRY OUT THE TEST

- The assistant sets the treadmill to 11.3km/hour (7.02mph) and a slope of 0° and runner warms up
- The test begins; the timer starts
- The assistant increases the slope of the treadmill (see left)
- The assistant stops the timer when the runner is unable to continue

THE COOPER 12-MINUTE TEST (P.185)

Developed in 1968 by Dr Ken Cooper, the inventor of aerobics, this test is a simple yet popular way of measuring aerobic fitness. To carry out the test, simply run around an athletics track for 12 minutes and use the track (400m/437 yards per lap) to work out your overall distance. If you have a GPS tracking watch (see p.49), set it to count down for 12 minutes and start running, and use it to measure the distance. The formulas (below right) calculate your VO_2 max.

HOW TO CARRY OUT THE TEST

- The athlete warms up
- The assistant starts the timer; the athlete starts running
- At the end of each lap, the assistant tells the athlete how much time is remaining
- The test finishes after 12 minutes

$$VO_2\ MAX = (22.351 \times km) - 11.288$$

OR

$$VO_2\ MAX = (35.96 \times miles) - 11.29$$

GET READY TO RUN

THE QUICKEST WAY TO START RUNNING IS SIMPLY TO PUT ON YOUR SHOES AND DO IT - HOWEVER, FOR THE BEST RESULTS, YOU'LL BENEFIT FROM SPENDING SOME TIME PREPARING YOUR BODY, YOUR MIND, AND YOUR KIT. THIS CHAPTER SETS OUT THE PREPARATION ESSENTIALS, FROM SETTING YOUR GOALS TO WHAT TO EAT, WHAT TO WEAR, AND HOW TO WARM UP AND COOL DOWN.

YOUR RUNNING GOALS

Before you start running, think about what you want to achieve. Your training will benefit strongly from forward planning and clear objectives - set yourself goals that are challenging and inspiring, but also realistic.

Q WHY SHOULD I SET GOALS?

A Goals give you something to work towards, providing focus and structure for your running training. Meeting targets will not only aid your development as a runner, it will also give you enormous confidence and motivate you to keep going and set further challenges.

Q HOW SHOULD I CHOOSE MY GOALS?

A When you start running, you might think that a simple goal, such as "to get fit", would be suitable, but this is too vague. You need to specify what your level of fitness will be and how you will measure it - your target must be structured. You may also be tempted to set yourself several goals, such as running a marathon, finishing it in under four hours, and running faster than your friend. Multiple goals are fine, but they should be complementary and developmental. If you set yourself too many large goals at once, you may not achieve any of them. Use the SMART criteria opposite to set sensible, focused goals.

Q HOW LONG DOES IT TAKE TO ACHIEVE MY GOALS?

A The scale and timeframe of your goals should vary. Setting short-, medium-, and long-term goals will keep you motivated. A short-term goal should be achievable within one month and should relate directly to your training load. Allow up to three months for medium-term goals so that you can focus on bigger challenges, such as improving a specific aspect of your running skillset. Your long-term goal will usually be your overall target for the year, such as running in a particular race. Your short- and medium-term goals, meanwhile, serve as markers of your progress towards this.

Q SHOULD I RELATE MY GOALS TO OTHER RUNNERS?

A In both training and racing, it is always best to focus on the factors you can control, rather than allowing your goals to be driven by the performances of others. You cannot plan for what other people are doing, and attempting to match them may have a negative impact on your performance.

SMART GOALS

Before you set your running goals, check them against the SMART criteria outlined below. If your targets are not SMART, think again.

CRITERIA	DEFINITION	EXAMPLE
SPECIFIC	Clearly and precisely define your goals. Ask yourself questions: What am I hoping to achieve? Why do I want to achieve it? Where will I achieve it?	I want to run a marathon in my local area. I want to run three times a week before work.
MEASURABLE	All your goals should be measurable: you should define both how you are going to achieve them and how you will keep track of your progress.	I want to run 10km (6.2 miles) two minutes faster than my current time. I want to complete a total of 30km (19miles) per week.
ACHIEVABLE	Unrealistic goals can make you feel disheartened and demotivated. However, goals that are too easy will not help you to develop or improve. Your goals should be achievable, but challenging.	I want to increase my hip flexibility. I am going to improve my running efficiency by strengthening my core.
RELEVANT	Ensure that your goals are relevant to your overall training programme and your running ambitions. Short- and medium-term goals should all contribute to your long-term goal.	I will improve my running technique by adding resistance exercises. I want to increase my stamina and endurance.
TIMED	Without the pressure of a deadline, it can be hard to focus on your goal. Set yourself an end date or target run time and work towards it in training.	In six months time, I will run a half-marathon. I will complete a marathon in under four hours.

CHOOSING YOUR SHOES

Buy your shoes from a specialist running shop, and make sure they are appropriate for your running style and intensity as well as the shape of your foot. Try to shop at the end of the day, or after a run, as your feet expand during the day, and wear your normal running socks when you try shoes on. Some of the larger shops can check your gait analysis on a running machine.

TRY A SELECTION

The most important elements to consider are: fit, shock absorption, and stability. When you put the shoe on, slide your finger into the shoe behind your heel; if you can't wiggle your toes, the shoe is too small. Feel for shock absorption by bouncing gently, and for stability by leaning forward and flexing your ankles. Try out several pairs until you find shoes that feel comfortable. If they don't feel right, don't buy them; running shoes shouldn't need to be broken in.

THE IDEAL TRAINER

The right footwear can make all the difference to your running, but finding it can be daunting. Check the features described here and ask the experts for advice as well.

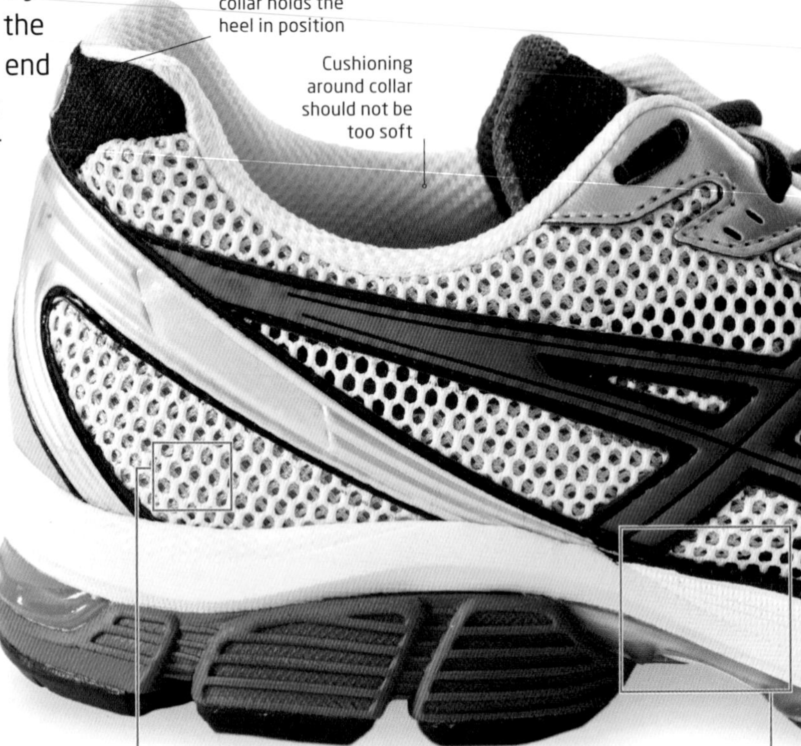

UPPER SHOE FABRIC

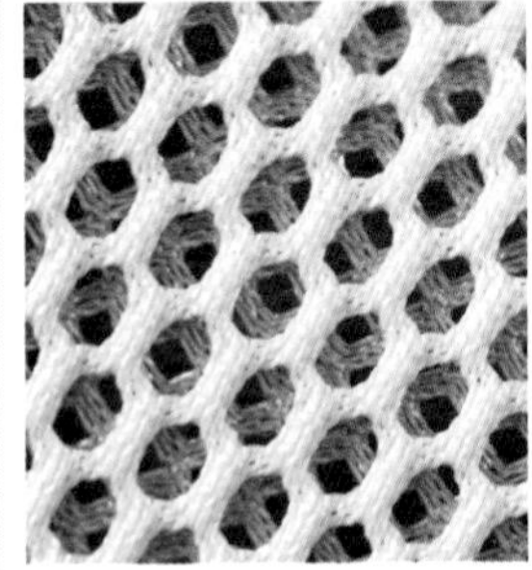

The upper shoe encases the foot. It is usually made of a light, breathable, synthetic fabric so that the heat from your foot can escape. Large, open-mesh fabric, left, is good for road running. Choose a tighter mesh for off-road running as it's more water-resistant and twigs and grit are less likely to become trapped in it.

MIDSOLE

The midsole layer sits between the inner liner and the outsole and protects against impact. Usually made of polyurethane foam, some midsoles feature gel sections for extra durability and cushioning. Some shoes have a firmer wedge of foam on the inner side that corrects excessive pronation (see opposite).

BAREFOOT RUNNING SHOES

Minimalist, or "barefoot" running, uses thin-soled shoes that provide little or no cushioning – its eventual aim is a "natural" style of running without artificial support. It requires correct technique and efficient stride, and runners who wish to try it should make the change gradually, using increasingly less padded shoes. The perfect shoe mimics running barefoot, by providing only a thin covering on the sole.

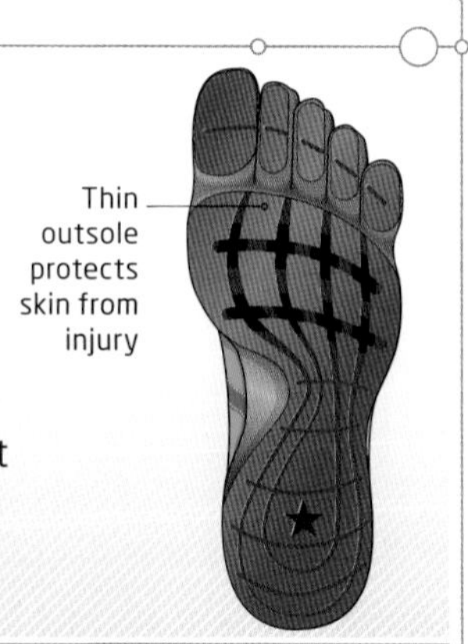

WHAT YOUR SHOES TELL YOU

The foot and ankle rotate naturally as you run, but the degree, or pronation, varies from one person to another. The wear pattern on your shoe indicates which part of your foot makes contact with the ground first. Uneven pronation (under or over) between the right and left shoe can affect your running mechanics and is a risk factor for injury. Consult a medical professional for advice as you may need orthotic insoles to correct any imbalance (see p.163). Wear your orthotics when trying new shoes.

NORMAL PRONATOR

If your foot rotates 15 per cent when you run, pronation is normal. The outer part of the heel makes initial contact with the ground, and your whole foot makes contact with the ground.

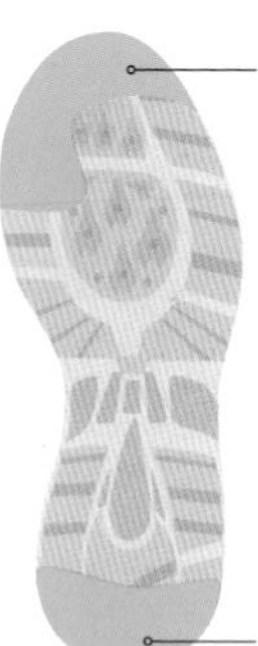

OVERPRONATOR

If your ankle rotates inwards by more than 15 per cent you overpronate. The foot arch tends to be lower. Overpronaters should choose motion control or stability shoes.

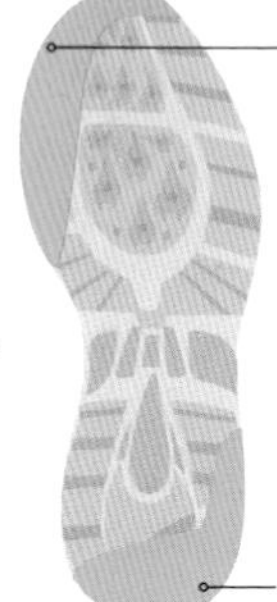

UNDER-PRONATOR

If wear is mainly on the outer side, you underpronate – your foot rotates less than 15 per cent. Choose a shoe with neutral cushioning.

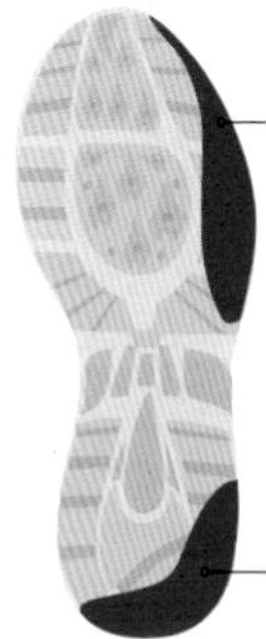

SHOE TREAD

Known as the outsole, the treaded bottom layer of the shoe is made of layers of carbon rubber. It should be flexible and able to grip a range of surfaces – wet or dry. If you are doing a lot of road running you will need a hard-wearing outsole; if you run on trails you will need a deeper tread.

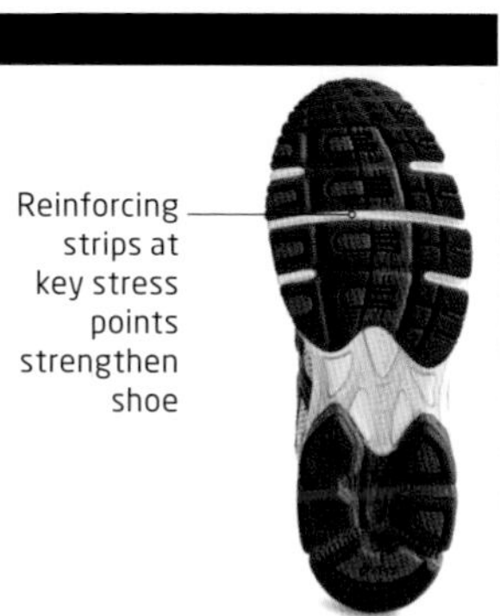

WHAT TO WEAR

Whatever you wear, it should be comfortable and functional. Sophisticated high-tech fabrics can be expensive but are worth it as they can help you stay cool, dry, and protected from the elements. Baggy cotton clothing should be avoided as it can chafe the skin. Tailor your wardrobe to the range of conditions you are likely to encounter on a regular basis.

AVERAGE NUMBER OF WASHES AFTER WHICH YOU SHOULD REPLACE YOUR SPORTS BRA

Q DO I NEED TO BUY SPECIAL CLOTHES?

A You could make do with the clothes that you might use for a workout. However, you'll find running gear made from high-tech synthetic "wicking" fabrics more comfortable (see opposite).

Assemble your running wardrobe in well-fitting, breathable layers. Be careful not to overdress as you will only have to carry it if you get too hot. Once you warm up, the extra body heat will make you feel 15–20 degrees warmer. Wear double-layered running socks to prevent blisters (never cotton).

For women, a good-quality sports bra is as important as the right footwear. Running is a high-impact activity, so you need a higher level of support than an ordinary bra can provide.

Q WHAT SHOULD I WEAR IN HOT WEATHER?

A If the temperature is above 12°C (55°F), you'll be fine wearing a T-shirt or vest and shorts made of breathable, wicking material. Avoid baggy, cotton clothing; sweat-logged cotton rubs the skin, causing runner's nipple (see p.170). Cool-max socks are best in summer. You'll also need a peaked cap and sports sunglasses to shield your face and eyes from the sun. Put sunscreen on any exposed skin.

Q WHAT SHOULD I WEAR IN COLD WEATHER?

A Wear long-sleeve tops and three-quarter or full-length leggings, depending on how cold it is. On your upper body you need a wicking base layer, then a warmer layer on top. If it's raining, wear a breathable, water-resistant outer jacket so that heat and moisture can escape. You generally need only one layer on your legs as your muscles create additional body heat.

Choose clothing with reflective stripes so that you can be seen when running on dark evenings. You can lose up to a third of your body heat through your head, so keep it covered. A thermal hat made of fleece material is ideal; if you get too hot, you can take it off and tuck it into your leggings. Wear a neck bandana, not a scarf, and pull it up over your face if it is very cold. Put petroleum jelly on exposed skin to protect it from the cold and wind, and wear sunscreen on your face on very bright days.

Q HOW DO I WASH RUNNING GEAR?

A Never dry-clean moisture-wicking fabrics. Wash them in cold water using a specially formulated detergent. Don't use bleach – even on your white clothes. Bacteria can become trapped in the fibres, which is hard to get out, so turn the clothes inside out for washing. Never put high-tech fabrics in a tumble dryer as it reduces the effectiveness of the sweat-wicking technology.

Q WHAT ELSE MIGHT BE USEFUL ?

A Carry water in a grip bottle, belt pack, or a marathon vest so that you can rehydrate on the go, and carry energy gels for longer runs. A fluorescent jacket or bib, or even clip-on lights, make you extra visible to cars on dark evenings.

COMFORT IS KEY
Clothing should be lightweight, allow your body to move freely, and not rub your skin. Function is more important than the look.

Headband
Keeps your ears warm

Base layer
Choose a top made of moisture-wicking material

Water-resistant, breathable jacket
Choose a zipped jacket so you can regulate your temperature

Gloves
Body heat is diverted from hands to core muscles so hands are susceptible to cold

Leggings
Make sure they are close-fitting and made of breathable fabric

GPS WATCH

This is a device with an integrated GPS receiver worn strapped to the wrist. Choose a multi-function watch that has features such as a heart rate monitor and running cadence and speed sensors. Information can be downloaded onto a computer and entered into your training log (see pp.92–93).

HIGH-TECH CLOTHING

These are clothes made of lightweight, stretchy, quick-drying fabrics that pull, or "wick" moisture away from the skin's surface. Clothing made of cotton, by contrast, holds sweat, which can actually make you feel cold and clammy. Worn close to the skin, high-tech fabrics absorb the sweat, which collects on the outer side of the fabric, then evaporates, so you stay dry and comfortable during your runs. As it's close-fitting, the clothing allows complete freedom of movement. On cold days, a couple of layers of thin (but insulating) pieces of high-tech clothing will keep you warm.

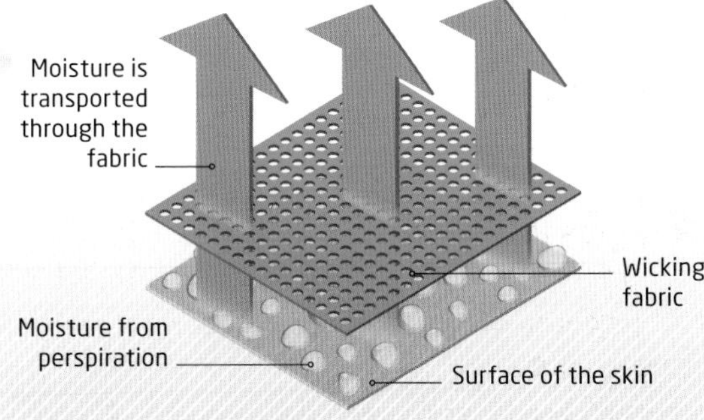

COMPRESSION CLOTHING

This is close-fitting clothing, from socks to base layers and T-shirts, with a relatively high proportion of elasticated material, which "squeezes" the muscles that are key to efficient running. In the upper body, the extra compression is designed to provide core support, help breathing, and improve posture. It is also intended to help blood circulation and increase the efficiency of your performance. The use of this clothing in sports is relatively new, and opinions vary as to its efficacy.

COMPRESSION SOCKS
The socks have a elasticated fabric woven into them, which applies pressure to the lower leg, ankle, and foot, designed to stimulate blood flow back to the heart.

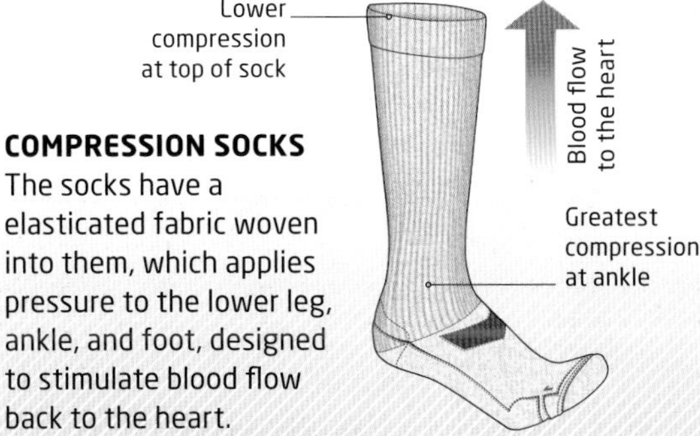

NUTRITION - THE ESSENTIALS

Variety, wholesomeness, and moderation are the three fundamental rules for a healthy diet - the key to running success. Following these rules will ensure that you eat a balanced diet that provides you with plenty of energy. In general, foods consumed in their natural state provide good nutritional value and contain few unhealthy ingredients. If you follow the first two rules, the third one usually follows - although allowing yourself a small treat now and then won't affect your performance, and can even be a good motivational tool.

HOW TO EAT

- Follow the recommended daily servings of the different food groups (see opposite)
- Try to avoid eating too many processed foods high in salt and fat
- Vary your diet to make sure you receive the full range of vitamins and minerals
- It is generally better to eat little and often - get used to having small meals every 3-4 hours
- While sports drinks are a vital tool for training and competing (see p.54), remember to factor in their high sugar content when planning your day-to-day diet

VITAMINS AND MINERALS

Vitamins and minerals are essential for healthy body function, and runners in particular need to consume sufficient quantities to ensure peak performance and avoid weakness, fatigue, and injury. A varied diet that encompasses the six key food groups opposite should provide most of the vitamins and minerals you need. The most important ones are listed in this table.

NUTRIENT	PURPOSE	GOOD SOURCES
CALCIUM	Helps build strong bones, regulate muscle contraction, and ensure that blood clots normally.	Milk, cheese, leafy green vegetables, soya beans, tofu, products containing fortified flour, fish bones (as in sardines).
IRON	Important in the production of red blood cells, which carry oxygen around the body.	Liver, lean red meat, beans, nuts, dried apricots, leafy green vegetables, brown rice.
VITAMIN D	Keeps bones and teeth healthy.	Sunshine is the best source. Food sources include oily fish, dairy produce, eggs, fortified breakfast cereals.
VITAMIN E	Maintains good cell structure by protecting cell membranes.	Nuts and seeds, wheatgerm, cereals, leafy green vegetables.
FOLIC ACID	Works together with vitamin B12 to form healthy red blood cells. Helps reduce the risk of central nervous system defects.	Broccoli, brussel sprouts, and other leafy green vegetables, asparagus, peas, liver, chickpeas, lentils, brown rice, citrus fruits.
POTASSIUM	Controls the balance of fluids in the body and helps to lower blood pressure.	Bananas, vegetables, pulses, nuts and seeds, fish, shellfish, beef, chicken, turkey, bread.
VITAMIN C	Maintains healthy cells. Necessary for the maintenance of healthy connective tissue.	Oranges and orange juice, strawberries, blackcurrants, broccoli, brussel sprouts, potatoes.
ZINC	Helps make new cells and enzymes. Processes carbohydrates, fat, and protein in food. Aids in the healing of wounds.	Meat, shellfish, milk and other dairy products, bread, wheatgerm.

INFO DASHBOARD

A HEALTHY DIET

The easiest path to healthy eating is to follow the guidance provided by this food pyramid, which illustrates the essential food groups and optimal servings. This will ensure that you consume the required intake of vitamins, minerals, amino acids, and other basic nutrients necessary for good health.

KEY »

RECOMMENDED DAILY SERVINGS

- FOOD AND DRINKS CONTAINING FAT AND SUGAR
- MEAT, FISH, EGGS, AND OTHER SOURCES OF PROTEIN
- MILK AND DAIRY PRODUCTS
- FRUIT AND VEGETABLES
- BREAD, PASTA, AND OTHER CEREALS

KEY FOOD GROUPS

The key to eating well is to ensure that your daily diet contains foods from these six different groups. Choosing healthy and minimally processed options from each food group is paramount for ensuring a wholesome and nutritious diet, and will go a long way to fuelling your training and enhancing your race performance.

FOOD GROUP	BENEFITS	GOOD CHOICES	PROPORTION NEEDED
WHOLEGRAINS AND STARCHES	Fuel your muscles, protecting against muscle fatigue. Also help to curb hunger and assist with weight management when wholesome choices (for example, wholegrain rather than processed) are made.	Wholegrain bread, bagels, cereals, and pasta, brown rice, rye crackers, stoneground wheat crackers, popcorn, oatmeal, bulgur.	55–65% of your daily food intake.
FRUIT	Rich in carbohydrate, fibre, and potassium, and also an excellent source of vitamins (in particular vitamin C), which help to promote healing after exercise and reduce high blood pressure.	Citrus fruits (such as oranges, grapefruits, and clementines), bananas, melon, kiwi, all berry varieties.	At least 2–4 pieces of fruit a day.
VEGETABLES	An important source of carbohydrate, and vitamins and minerals, especially vitamin C, beta-carotene, potassium, and magnesium.	Broccoli, all salad leaves, spinach, peppers (red, green, and yellow), cabbage, brussel sprouts, bok choy, kale.	At least 2–4 servings of different types a day.
PROTEIN	Provides amino acids, which are essential for repairing muscle. Darker meats provide increased amounts of iron and zinc.	Chicken, turkey, fish, lean beef, eggs, peanut butter, canned beans, tofu.	1 small portion (about the size of your fist) and 1 egg a day.
DAIRY PRODUCTS	A good source of protein, rich in calcium, vitamin D, potassium, phosphorus, and riboflavin. Help maintain strong bones and reduce the risk of osteoporosis and high blood pressure.	Low-fat milk, yoghurt, cheeses.	Several small portions a day: 1–2 glasses of milk, 1 yoghurt, 50–100g ($1^{3}/_{4}$–$3^{1}/_{2}$oz) cheese.
FATS AND OILS	So-called "good" fats and oils, omega-3, -6, and -9, help with immune system and brain function, vitamin absorption, and nerve activity, and also help reduce incidence of diabetes, stroke, and heart disease.	Omega-3: sardines, wild salmon, tuna, mussels; omega-6: olive oil, walnut oil, grapeseed oil, sunflower oil; omega-9: olives, avocados, pecan nuts, almonds, peanuts.	In moderation.

FUELLING YOUR TRAINING

Once you have built a healthy day-to-day diet, the next step is to tailor it according to the requirements of a training schedule (see pp.86–87). Running is an intensive physical process, and with the right knowledge you can fuel yourself to run further, feel better, and enjoy it more.

RUNNING SUPERFOODS

- ALMONDS
- BANANAS
- CHERRIES
- BROCCOLI
- SPINACH
- WHOLEWHEAT PASTA
- GREEN TEA
- OILY FISH
- PEANUT BUTTER
- SKIMMED MILK

YOUR ROUTE TO SUCCESS »

KNOW YOUR NEEDS

The average adult needs 2,000 (female) to 2,500 (male) calories per day just to function normally. Training for a race requires even more, and depending on the frequency, intensity, and duration of your training sessions your body will need different amounts each day. Calculating your energy requirements involves tracking your nutritional intake and exercise effort. A trained sports nutritionist can help devise a diet to optimize your training and recovery times.

TIME YOUR INTAKE

Leave 1–4 hours between eating and training, depending on the size and content of the meal (remember that protein takes longer to digest than carbohydrate). When it comes to carbohydrate, try to make your main meal before a run low GI (see box, top right), as this will help maintain higher blood-sugar levels. If you run in the mornings, have a small, carbohydrate-rich breakfast 20–30 minutes before you set out, as your energy stores will have depleted in the night.

At 15–20 minutes before a run, an isotonic sports drink (see p.54), half a banana, or 50g (1¾oz) of raisins with some water will provide good fuel, though bear in mind that liquids are digested more rapidly, meaning that energy is more readily available. Try to eat within 1 hour of finishing your run, as during this period more food will be converted to glycogen. If you can't face a full meal, have a small snack and/or a hypertonic sports drink.

SUPPLEMENT YOUR DIET?

Supplements are simply what the word implies. They are not magic potions or a replacement for a healthy wholefood diet, and taking the latest brand of protein powder or pre-workout drink will not help you break any world records. However, everyone has different nutritional needs and if used correctly, vitamin, mineral, and other supplements can provide nutritional back-up to a runner's diet to ensure all nutritional needs are met. The best advice is to seek the help of a qualified sports nutritionist and get a tailored programme made for you.

INFO DASHBOARD

THE GLYCAEMIC INDEX

High glycaemic index (GI) foods are quickly absorbed and will typically give you a "sugar rush" or spike in energy, followed by a trough when your energy levels drop below where they were before you ate. Low GI foods release their energy slowly. They are an excellent fuel for sport because they increase blood sugar levels slowly for ready use, and so provide a boost of energy without the "surge" triggered by high GI foods.

GI SCORES

The GI of foods is given on a scale of 0-100, with 100 being pure sugar. A GI of around 55 or less is considered low; 70 or more is considered high.

GI KEY »

HIGH
LOW

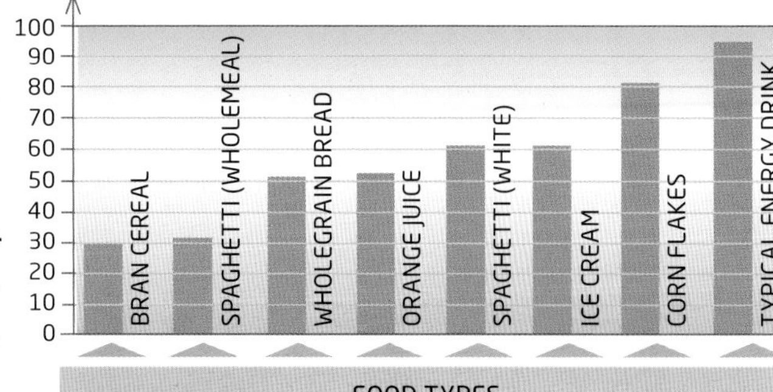

LOAD UP WITH CARBOHYDRATES

If you will be running competitively for more than 90 minutes – or even simply as part of your training programme – then "carb-loading" is a good way to saturate your muscles with glycogen (see box, right), which can then be released during the run. Just eating a large bowl of pasta the night before, however, is not the way to go about fuelling your muscles, and may cause stomach cramps. Instead, try to maintain a daily consumption of 9g (1/3oz) of carbohydrate per 1kg (2¼lb) of body weight in the days leading up to the race. Combine this with a taper in your training (see pp.146–47). The reduction in training will use less of your stored energy, meaning your glycogen stores are fully stocked up the night before the big race.

GLYCOGEN AND ENERGY

When you eat carbohydrate, any of the glucose it contains that is not immediately used by the body for energy is stored in your muscles and liver as a substance called glycogen. This substance then provides your body with easily accessible energy when you exercise. This is the main reason why carbohydrate intake is so important for runners, and why "carb-loading" (see left) can be a useful technique for providing the energy needed on longer runs.

The amount of glycogen you can store in your body varies according to your level of fitness and your inherited physiology – most people can store around 2,000kcal, which is approximately enough energy to run or walk around 32km (20 miles). You can, however, train your muscles to absorb more than this.

Once you have used up all the glycogen stored in your body, you may "hit the wall" – that is, suddenly experience extreme fatigue. To avoid this, make sure you are properly fuelled before your race, and top up with sports drinks or gels if necessary.

HYDRATION FOR RUNNERS

Water makes up 50-60 per cent of your body weight. It aids many of the body's processes, including sweating to stabilize body temperature, and forms 92 per cent of blood plasma, which helps transport nutrients to muscles and remove waste products, such as lactic acid and carbon dioxide, from them.

Q WHY IS HYDRATION IMPORTANT?

A Your running performance deteriorates when you are dehydrated, so it is crucial to drink enough water throughout the day and at regular intervals. Try keeping a full water bottle – tap water is fine – on your desk at work or in your car. This way you are constantly reminded to keep your levels topped up. If you like drinking caffeinated drinks such as tea and coffee during the day, remember to counteract their diuretic effect by drinking an extra glass of water.

SPORTS DRINKS

These drinks are designed to help replenish your levels of water and energy during and after exercise. There are three types, each containing different proportions of water, electrolyte, and carbohydrate. It is important to consume the right drink at the right time as this will strongly affect your performance. See below for a guide to which type of drink to consume and when.

TYPE OF DRINK	GLUCOSE CONCENTRATION	PURPOSE	WHEN BEST TO DRINK
HYPOTONIC	2%	Quickly replaces water lost during exercise and replenishes minerals e.g. sodium and potassium.	In hot weather and when you are sweating a lot. Can be drunk before, during, and after a workout.
ISOTONIC	4-6%	Replaces fluid and electrolytes lost during prolonged exercise sessions. Contains fructose or glucose, allowing the slow release of carbohydrates to maintain energy reserves.	During a workout or run. These drinks contain the same proportion of salt and water as your body's natural fluid balance, helping to maintain your carbohydrate-electrolyte balance during exercise.
HYPERTONIC	10%+	Supplements your daily carbohydrate intake. Provides the muscles with fuel, and can be used as a recovery drink after a hard session.	After exercise. Hypertonic drinks are very high in carbohydrates and can interfere with fluid and electrolyte absorption if drunk while exercising.

HOW HYDRATED ARE YOU?

The easiest way to check whether you are adequately hydrated is to check the colour of your urine. Use this simple colour chart to assess if you are drinking enough fluids. Ideally, your urine will be one of the first three colours shown in the chart. If it is any darker, you should rehydrate as soon as possible.

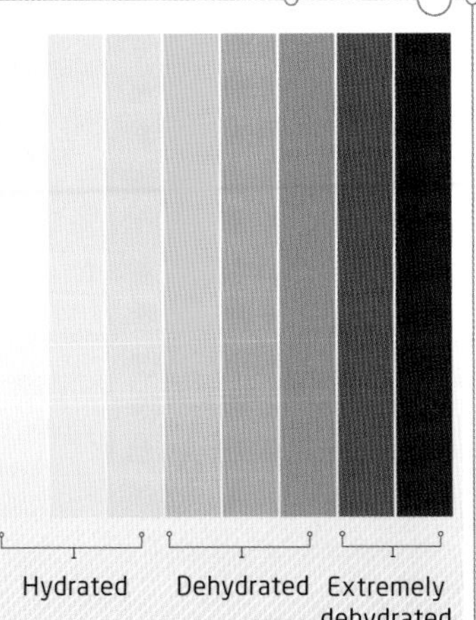

Q HOW MUCH SHOULD I DRINK?

A It is vital to ensure that you are fully hydrated before a run. In order to do this, drink 500ml-1 litre ($^3/_4$-1$^3/_4$ pints) of water between 60 and 90 minutes before you set off. This allows time for any excess fluid to be excreted from your body and avoids excess fluid sloshing about in your stomach while you are running. If you are fully hydrated and the weather is not too hot, you may be able to leave your water bottle at home for runs of less than 20-30 minutes. However, you should work out what you need during training sessions, and taking a water bottle allows you to monitor your own hydration strategy. Take three or four small sips (avoid big gulps) from your water bottle every 10 to 15 minutes, or more frequently in hotter weather.

Q SHOULD I DRINK CAFFEINE?

A A caffeinated sports drink or a small cup of coffee is a legal stimulant which has been shown to improve endurance, performance, and the ability to think faster during exercise. Consuming up to 200mg of caffeine one hour before training can also help improve your interval or speed-training performance. However, do experiment with the effects of caffeine before using it in a race - it doesn't suit everyone.

INFO DASHBOARD

FLUID GAIN AND LOSS

This chart shows the average loss and gain of fluid in humans. Drinking accounts for the largest proportion of fluid intake - use this to maintain your body's natural balance.

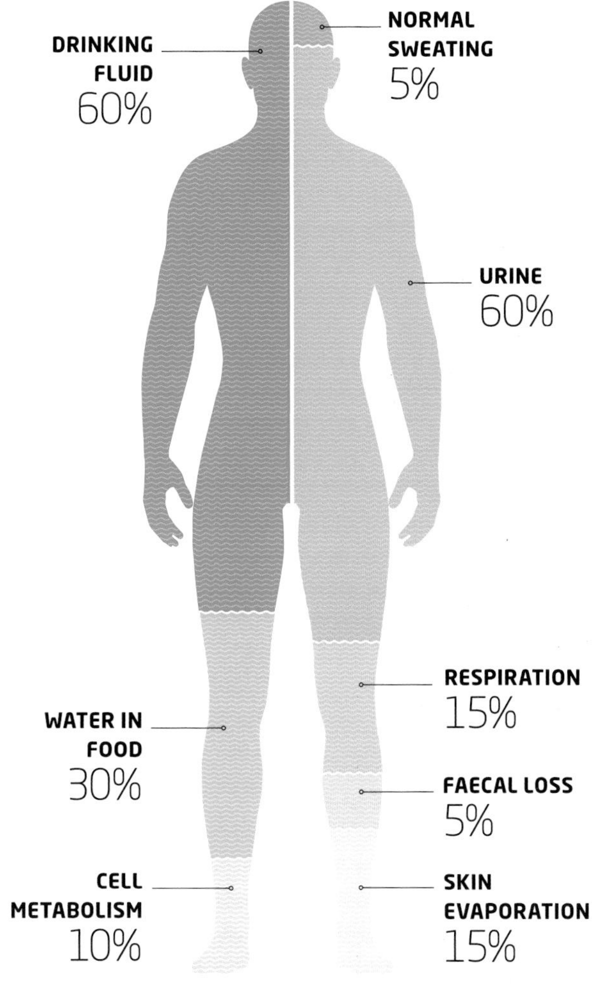

WATER INTAKE

Your body obtains hydration from three sources - drinking fluid, the water contained in food, and cell metabolism. This metabolic water is fluid that is liberated within the body when you burn carbohydrates and fats.

WATER LOSS

Your body loses water in five ways. Runners sweat at different rates according to environmental conditions such as altitude and weather, so your actual percentages will vary. They can also be affected by diet and exercise.

WARMING UP AND COOLING DOWN

Whether you are training or racing, a proper routine for warming up and cooling down is essential to maintaining fitness and peak performance. Always allow 10–15 minutes for a warm-up at the start of your session and approximately the same amount of time to cool down at the end.

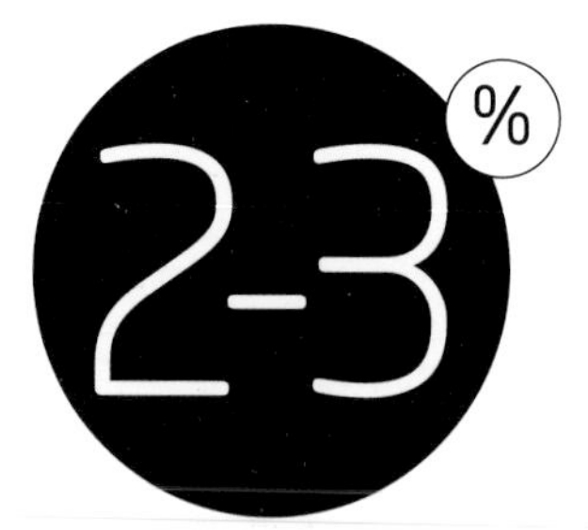

INCREASE IN BODY TEMPERATURE, LASTING FOR UP TO 45 MINUTES, PRODUCED BY A WARM-UP

YOUR ROUTE TO SUCCESS »

PHYSICAL PREPARATION

The main aim of a warm-up is to prepare your body for exercise by increasing your body temperature, breathing rate, and heart rate. This causes your blood vessels to widen – a process known as "vasodilatation" – allowing more oxygen to travel to your muscles. This helps to prevent the rapid build-up of lactic acid and other metabolic by-products such as ammonia and positive hydrogen ions, that can cause muscle burn when you start running without a warm-up. This elevated physical state will have a positive effect on your body's biomechanics: as your muscle temperature increases, so does the flexibility of your running joints – shoulders, hips, knees, and ankles – enabling you to run with a more fluid technique.

INJURY PREVENTION

Muscular injuries, such as pulled hamstrings or calf muscles, are common among runners. You will significantly reduce your risk of injury if you perform a thorough warm-up and cool-down. An inadequate warm-up will lead to an incorrect running technique and may cause injuries over time, not just to your muscles but to your ligaments and joints as well. Not cooling down properly can lead to stiffness and sore muscles.

IMPROVED PERFORMANCE

Warming up before a training run or a race will result in improved performance, because your body will be ready to run from the outset with good technique and at your desired speed. Cooling down is an essential part of running maintenance, enabling you to recover fully and quickly so you are in optimum shape for your next run.

WARM UP, COOL DOWN

BENEFITS OF A WARM-UP
INCREASES TRANSMISSION OF OXYGEN TO THE MUSCLES, PREVENTING BUILD UP OF LACTIC ACID AND OTHER METABOLIC
ELEVATES METABOLISM AND RAISES TEMPERATURE OF MUSCLES, INCREASING FLEXIBILITY
INCREASES MUSCLE CONTRACTION SPEED
INCREASES RUNNING EFFICIENCY AND REDUCES RISK OF INJURY
INCREASES HEART RATE TO AN APPROPRIATE LEVEL FOR RUNNING
INCREASES MENTAL ALERTNESS AND FOCUS

BENEFITS OF A COOL-DOWN
DISSIPATES LACTIC ACID AND OTHER METABOLIC BY-PRODUCTS, REDUCING NEGATIVE EFFECTS OF BUILD-UP IN MUSCLES
REDUCES THE POTENTIAL FOR DELAYED ONSET MUSCLE SORENESS (DOMS, SEE P.171)
REDUCES THE RISK OF DIZZINESS OR FAINTING CAUSED BY VENOUS BLOOD POOLING IN THE LEGS
REDUCES LEVELS OF ADRENALINE IN THE BLOOD
RETURNS HEART RATE TO RESTING LEVEL
INCREASES MENTAL ALERTNESS AND FOCUS

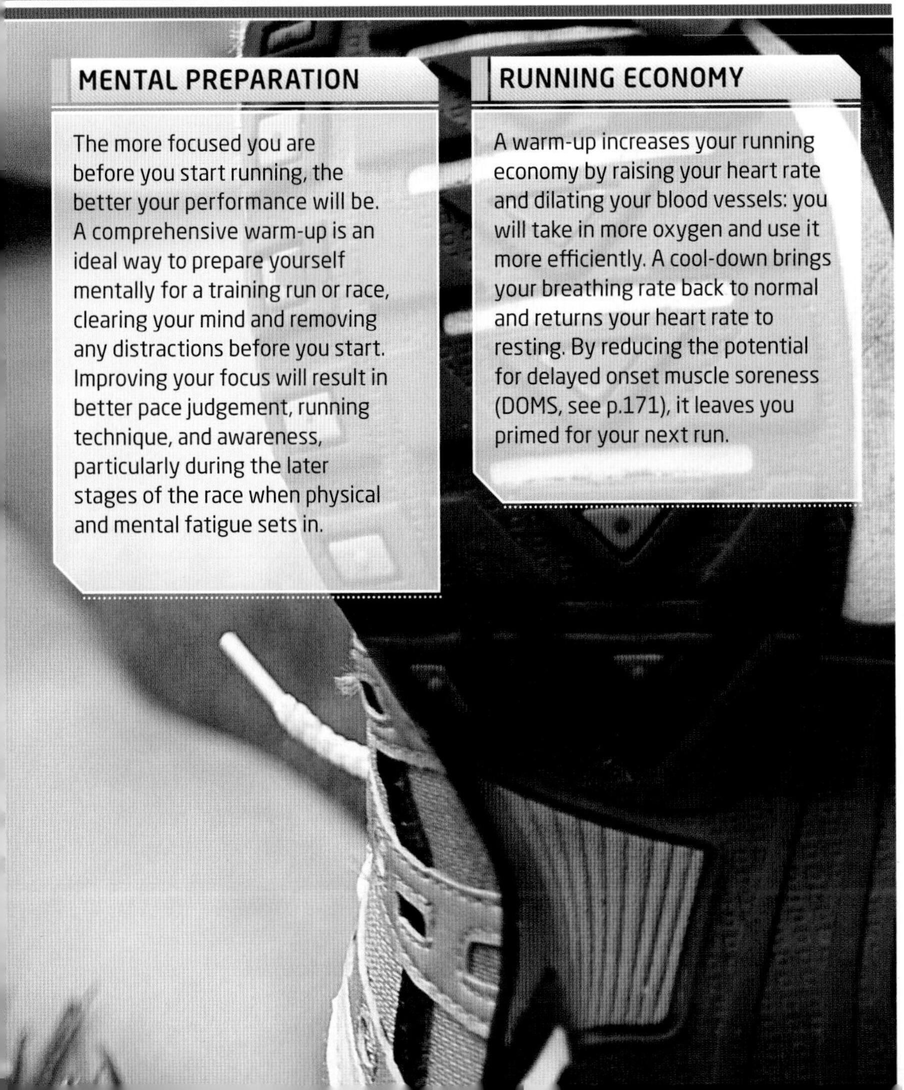

MENTAL PREPARATION

The more focused you are before you start running, the better your performance will be. A comprehensive warm-up is an ideal way to prepare yourself mentally for a training run or race, clearing your mind and removing any distractions before you start. Improving your focus will result in better pace judgement, running technique, and awareness, particularly during the later stages of the race when physical and mental fatigue sets in.

RUNNING ECONOMY

A warm-up increases your running economy by raising your heart rate and dilating your blood vessels: you will take in more oxygen and use it more efficiently. A cool-down brings your breathing rate back to normal and returns your heart rate to resting. By reducing the potential for delayed onset muscle soreness (DOMS, see p.171), it leaves you primed for your next run.

VASODILATATION

Active muscles rapidly consume oxygen during exercise. To replenish the oxygen, muscles produce by-products such as adenosine and carbon dioxide, which prompt blood vessels to dilate – a process known as vasodilatation. This allows a greater quantity of oxygenated blood to be delivered to the muscles. This takes place in the coronary blood vessels and those of the skin and muscles. At the same time, vasoconstriction – narrowing of the blood vessels – occurs in tissues that are inactive during exercise, enabling blood flow to be redistributed to the active muscles.

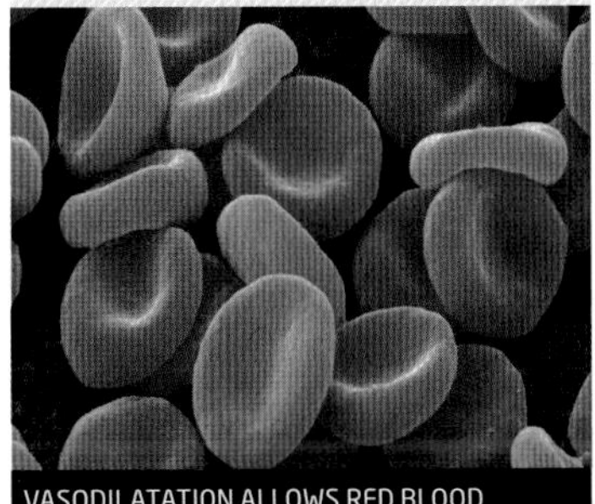

VASODILATATION ALLOWS RED BLOOD CELLS TO CARRY MORE OXYGEN TO ACTIVE MUSCLES

PRE- AND POST-RUN STRETCHING

EVERY RUNNER SHOULD HAVE A "TOOLKIT" OF WARM-UPS AND COOL-DOWNS – USE THESE EXERCISES TO PREPARE YOUR BODY FOR RUNNING, AND TO HELP IT RECOVER.

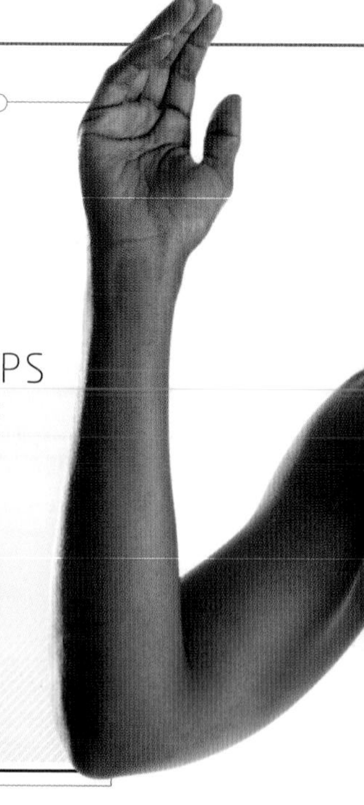

The concept of warming up before you run is well known, but it should mean more than simply spending a few minutes jogging gently. Preparing with dynamic stretches helps reduce muscle friction, while static stretches allow your muscles to transition back to their normal state after a run.

Q WHEN AND FOR HOW LONG SHOULD I WARM UP?

A You should warm up before every run, whether it is a training run or a race. A proper warm-up should start gently and increase in intensity over a 10- to 15-minute period.

Q WHAT WARM-UP EXERCISES SHOULD I DO?

A Before you begin stretching, spend a few minutes walking or jogging slowly, mimicking the types of arm and leg movements that you will perform during your run, but with a decreased range of motion. Gradually increase your pace during this exercise until you reach typical running speed.

It is good idea to perform dynamic stretches such as the Scorpion Stretch or the Hip Walk (see p.62) before you start your training session or race – they have been proven to increase muscle power output by up to 30 per cent more than static stretches. Once you have increased your heart rate and muscle temperature with the warm-up jog, perform some running-specific dynamic stretches, such as Straight Knee Walks (see pp.62–65). Additionally, you can incorporate some running drills such as Ankle Springs and Bounding (see pp.68–73) if you wish.

Q WHEN AND FOR HOW LONG SHOULD I COOL DOWN?

A You should cool down at the end of every training session and run – allow at least five minutes to return to your resting state. When you have finished your session or run, keep moving and gradually reduce the speed of your movements, ending up with a slow jog or walk, rather than suddenly coming to a stop.

Q WHAT COOL-DOWN STRETCHES SHOULD I DO?

A Incorporate some static stretches, such as the Hip Flexor Stretch (see p.65) and the Hamstring Stretch (see p.66) into your cool-down routine. During your run, your muscles may have tightened up due to the build-up of lactic acid caused by an increase in intensity and load – static stretches help muscles return to their pre-run state. Perform the Downward Dog, Hip Flexor Stretch, and Seated Spiral Twists (see pp.64–65) to stretch your leg muscles, and the Brettzel 1 and Brettzel 2 to stretch your whole body (see p.67).

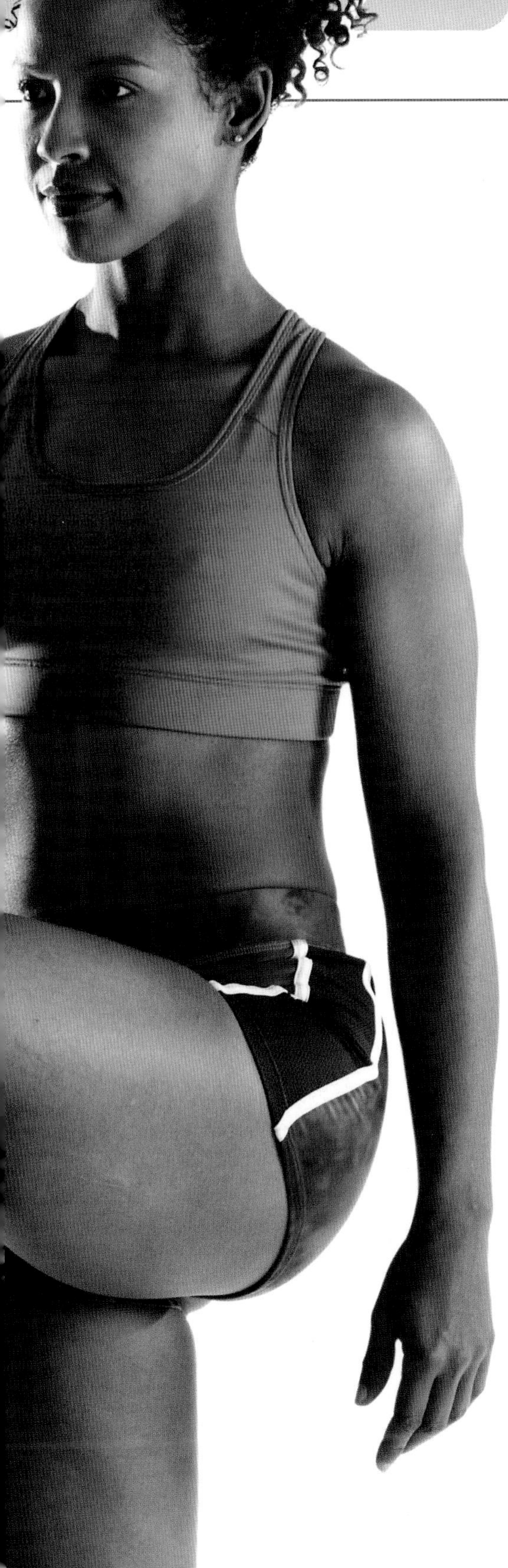

SAMPLE WARM-UP PROGRAMME

These sample warm-up stretching programmes are suitable for training sessions and short races – you can adapt them if you find that certain areas of your mobility or form benefit from particular exercises.

BASIC WARM-UP	
TOE WALK (P.60)	10-20M (11-22 YARDS)
HEEL WALK (P.60)	10-20M (11-22 YARDS)
INCH WORM WALK (P.61)	8-10M (8¾-11 YARDS)
SCORPION STRETCH (P.62)	10 REPS, ALTERNATING SIDES
SPIDERMAN (P.61)	8-10M (8¾-11 YARDS)
SUPERMAN (P.63)	10-20M (11-22 YARDS)
HIP WALK (P.62)	10-20M (11-22 YARDS)
STRAIGHT KNEE WALK (P.63)	10-20M (11-22 YARDS)

WARM-UP WITH EMPHASIS ON LEG MUSCLES	
TOE WALK (P.60)	10-20M (11-22 YARDS)
HEEL WALK (P.60)	10-20M (11-22 YARDS)
SUPERMAN (P.63)	10-20M (11-22 YARDS)
HIP WALK (P.62)	10-20M (11-22 YARDS)
STRAIGHT KNEE WALK (P.63)	10-20M (11-22 YARDS)

SAMPLE COOL-DOWN PROGRAMME

These cool-down programmes are based around moderate stretches designed to ease your muscles after their exertions. Use the advanced programme if you have had a particularly vigorous run.

BASIC COOL-DOWN	
SIDE LYING ROTATION (P.64)	20-30 SECONDS PER SIDE
DOWNWARD DOG (P.65)	20-30 SECONDS
HIP FLEXOR STRETCH (P.65)	20-30 SECONDS PER SIDE
SEATED SPIRAL TWIST (P.64)	20-30 SECONDS PER SIDE
HAMSTRING STRETCH (P.66)	20-30 SECONDS PER SIDE
ADDUCTOR STRETCH (P.66)	20-30 SECONDS PER SIDE

ADVANCED COOL-DOWN	
BRETTZEL 1 (P.67)	30-60 SECONDS PER SIDE
BRETTZEL 2 (P.67)	30-60 SECONDS PER SIDE
HAMSTRING STRETCH (WITH BAND) (P.66)	30-60 SECONDS PER SIDE

01/ **TOE** WALK

This exercise develops strength, stability, and functional range of motion around your ankle joints. It activates your shin and calf muscles, and the tiny muscles in your feet that are essential for runners.

TARGET MUSCLES

- Tibialis anterior
- Gastrocnemius
- Soleus
- Foot plantar flexors

Hold your shoulders back

Raise your heels up off the ground

1 Stand with your feet hip-width apart. Maintain a good posture, keeping your shoulders back. Raise your heels up off the ground and balance on the balls of your feet.

2 Step forwards with your left foot, trying to extend up onto your toes. Swing your right arm for balance. Repeat on the other side and continue, walking forwards.

Stay on your toes as you step from foot to foot

02/ **HEEL** WALK

Heel-walking activates the muscles in your lower leg, ankles, and feet, and mobilizes the Achilles tendon, combating tightness. It can also help to prevent shin splints (see p.180), a common complaint of distance runners.

TARGET MUSCLES

- Gastrocnemius
- Soleus
- Achilles tendon

Hold your shoulders back

Raise your toes up off the ground

1 Stand with your feet hip-width apart. Maintain a good posture, keeping your shoulders back. Raise your toes up off the ground and balance on your heels.

2 Step forwards with your left foot, trying to keep your toes pointing to the sky. Swing your right arm for balance. Repeat on the other side and continue, walking forwards.

Push your body weight into your heels

03/ INCH WORM WALK

This challenging, functional mobility exercise mobilizes your hamstrings, your calf muscles, the core muscles of your lower back, and your shoulders. Control of your shoulders, pelvis, and spinal position throughout the exercise is crucial.

TARGET MUSCLES

- Hamstrings
- Gluteals
- Gastrocnemius
- Soleus
- Achilles tendon

Maintain a straight line through your hips

1 Start from a Press-Up position (see p.138), with your hands under your shoulders and your arms straight. With your feet hip-width apart, balance on your toes. Keep your legs straight.

2 Walk your feet up as far as you can towards your hands, folding your body at the hips. Hold, then walk your hands forwards, back to the start position, and repeat.

04/ SPIDERMAN

This is a full-body exercise that will help to improve your mobility and core strength. Combining a crawling motion with a Press-Up (see p.138), it mobilizes your hip flexors and works your legs. At first, start from the Press-Up (Knees) position (see p.139).

TARGET MUSCLES

- Gluteals
- Quadriceps
- Hamstrings
- Iliopsoas
- Gastrocnemius
- Soleus

Keep your head up

Feel the stretch in your leg

1 Start from a Press-Up (Knees) position. Step forwards with your left foot to the outside of your left hand, bringing your left knee up, level with your left armpit.

2 Reach forwards with your right hand and step forwards with your right foot to the outside of the hand, stretching your left leg out behind you as you do so, and continue.

05/ SCORPION STRETCH

This is an excellent all-body stretch that improves your overall spinal flexibility, mobilizing your mid-section and opening up your hip flexors. Good technique is key, so focus on achieving the correct position rather than trying to stretch too far.

TARGET MUSCLES

- Transverse abdominis
- Rectus abdominis
- Obliques
- Iliopsoas
- Quadriceps

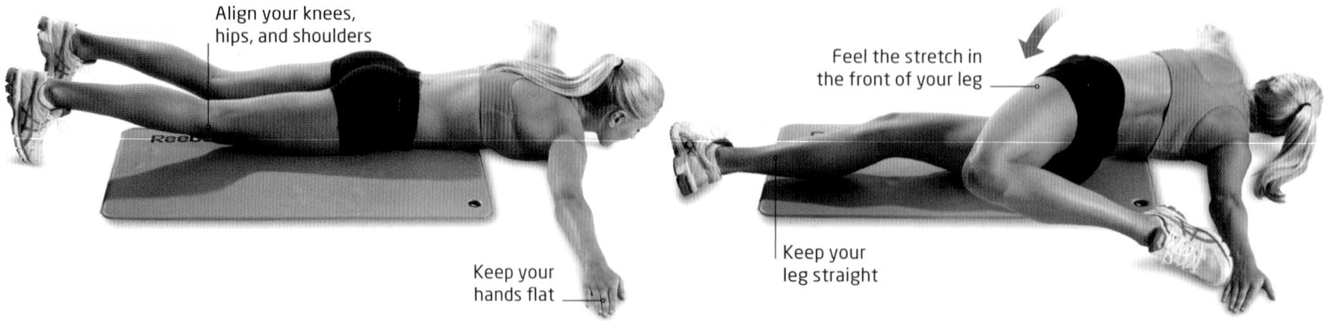

1 Lie face down on a mat. Stretch your arms out at 90 degrees to your sides, with your hands palms-down on the floor. Start to raise your left hip off the floor.

2 Bring your left foot up and over your back towards your right hand, twisting your lower back and bending your left knee. Hold briefly, then return to the start position. Repeat with your right leg.

06/ HIP WALK

Good hip mobility helps to keep your body steady, upright, and balanced. This simple but effective mobilizer opens up your hips and activates your glutes, increasing flexibility and range of motion.

TARGET MUSCLES

- Gluteals
- Iliopsoas
- Iliotibial band

1 Stand upright with your feet hip-width apart and maintain a good posture. Look straight ahead. Lift your left leg up and grasp the ankle with your right hand and the knee with your left hand.

2 Ease your left leg up, using your left hand to pull the knee gently up towards your chest. Hold the position briefly, then lower and repeat on the other side.

07/ SUPERMAN

This dynamic exercise opens up your hips, activates your glutes, and mobilizes your hamstrings before you run. It develops whole body balance, and stability around the hips, knees, and ankles.

TARGET MUSCLES

- Gluteals
- Hamstrings
- Gastrocnemius
- Soleus

1 Stand with your feet hip-width apart. Extend your left arm straight in front of you, with the hand palm down. Raise your left leg off the floor behind you and bend your upper body slowly forwards from your hips.

2 Push your left leg up until it is parallel with the floor. Stretch your left arm further forwards. Hold, then bring your left leg back down and step forwards with it to a new start position. Repeat on the other side.

08/ STRAIGHT KNEE WALK

This movement mobilizes your hips and hamstrings, and activates your calf muscles, improving flexibility before you run. It is good for preventing hamstring injuries.

TARGET MUSCLES

- Hamstrings
- Iliopsoas
- Gastrocnemius
- Soleus

1 Stand with your feet hip-width apart. Stretch your left arm out in front of you. Keeping your left foot flat on the floor, bring your right leg forwards in front of you.

2 Bring your right foot up to touch your left hand, or as high as you can. Hold briefly, then step forwards and repeat with your left leg and right arm and continue, walking forwards.

09/ SEATED SPIRAL TWIST

This stretch is useful for preventing inflammation of the iliotibial band (ITB) – the band of connective tissue that runs down the outside of your thigh – when you run. It is also a good glute stretch.

TARGET MUSCLES

- Gluteals
- Obliques
- Iliotibial band

Align your shoulders with your hips

Keep your upper body straight

1 Sit on the floor with both legs extended. Rest your hands by your sides. Bend your left leg and cross it over your right leg so that your left foot is flat on the floor by your right knee.

2 Reach across with your right hand and gently pull on the outside of your left knee until you feel the stretch. Return to the start position. Repeat on the other side.

10/ SIDE-LYING ROTATION

This exercise increases the mobility of the joints and muscles in your lower and upper back, working the thoracic spine and opening up your core from hips to chest. It is a good full-body stretch that works the front of your body.

TARGET MUSCLES

- Gluteals
- Obliques
- Rectus abdominis
- Pectorals

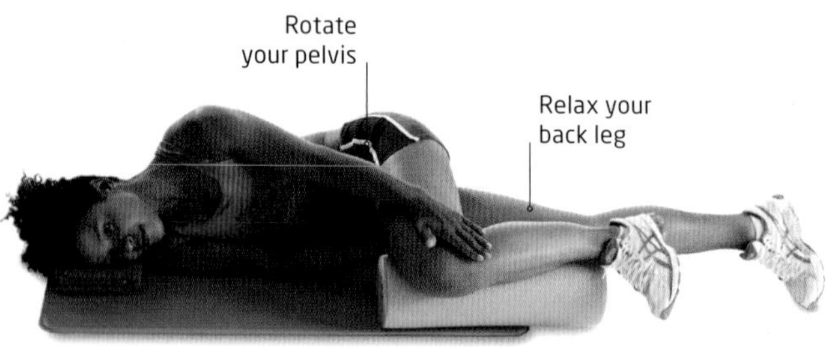

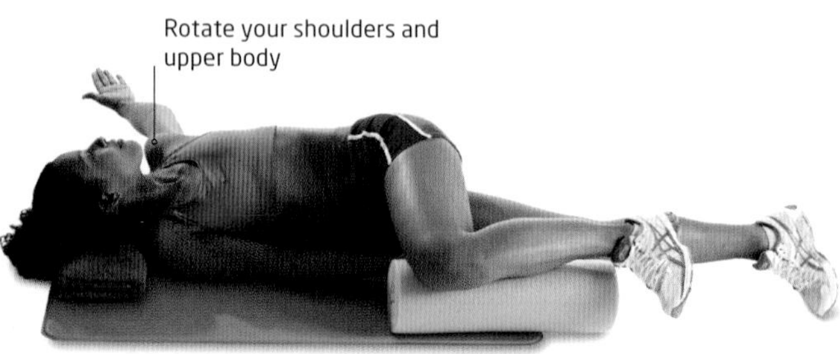

1 Lie flat on your back with your arms by your sides. Support your head on a folded towel. Bend your left leg at the knee and bring it across your body. Support it on a foam roller. Let your right leg bend and twist in the direction of the rotation.

2 To extend the stretch, reach your left arm behind you, in the opposite direction to the rotation. Return to the start position and repeat on the other side.

11/ HIP FLEXOR STRETCH

This exercise stretches your hip flexor muscles, helping to prevent imbalances around your pelvis and your lower back. Good hip stability and mobility are vital for balance and posture when running.

TARGET MUSCLES

- Iliopsoas
- Quadriceps
- Soleus

1 Kneel on your right knee and tuck your toes under. Position your left foot flat on the floor in front of you, with the knee bent at a 90-degree angle. Hold your upper body straight and place your hands on your hips.

2 Lean forwards, putting your weight on your left leg and bending your knee over your foot. Hold the position briefly, then reverse the movement to the start position, change legs, and repeat on the other side.

12/ DOWNWARD DOG

A classic yoga pose, this stretch strengthens your core and your calf muscles, elongates your back, and opens your hamstrings. It is a good stretch for avoiding Achilles tendon injuries.

TARGET MUSCLES

- Hamstrings
- Gastrocnemius
- Soleus

1 Start on your hands and knees, with your hands slightly forwards of your shoulders, your knees below your hips, and your back parallel to the floor. Without changing the position of your hands or feet, tuck your toes under.

2 Lift your knees off the floor and lower your heels. Straighten your legs and push your hips upwards into an inverted "V", extending your spine and legs. Hold briefly, then bend your knees and reverse to the start position.

13/ HAMSTRING STRETCH

The repeated knee flexion of running can cause tightness in your hamstrings: this stretch helps to loosen them. Hamstring flexibility is also important for your hips, knees, and back. You can use a resistance band around your foot to deepen the stretch.

TARGET MUSCLES

- Hamstrings
- Gastrocnemius
- Gluteals

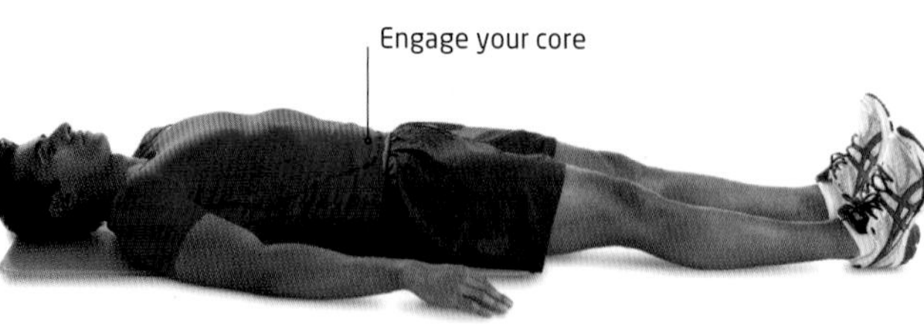

1 Lie flat on your back on the floor with both legs extended and your arms by your sides, hands palms-down. Align your knees, hips, and shoulders.

2 Lift your left leg, keeping your toes braced towards your body. Grasp your leg with both hands and gently pull back on it to extend the stretch. Lower your leg to the start position and repeat on the other side.

14/ ADDUCTOR STRETCH

This stretch works the short adductor muscles of your hips, down your inner thighs, and is good for keeping your hips mobile. Avoid pushing your stretch down too far in case of strain.

TARGET MUSCLES

- Adductor brevis
- Adductor longus
- Adductor magnus
- Gracilis

1 Stand with your feet wider than hip-width apart and your toes slightly turned out. Maintain a good posture. Place your hands on your hips.

2 Bend your right leg so that your right knee is over your right foot and your left leg is extended. Straighten your right leg to return to the start position and repeat on the other side.

15/ BRETTZEL 1

This is a total mobility stretch for your thigh muscles, hip flexors, piriformis, glutes, lower back, and thoracic spine. It is good for improving your overall thoracic mobility.

TARGET MUSCLES

- Quadriceps
- Gluteals
- Iliotibial band
- Thoracic spine

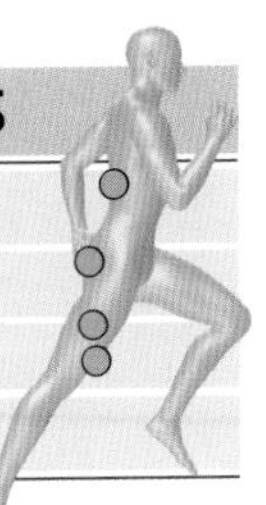

1 Lie on your left side with a folded towel under your neck for support. Draw your right knee up towards your chest and hold it with your left hand.

2 Reach your left leg back and grasp it with your right hand, rotating your shoulders to the right. Hold, then return to the start position and repeat on the other side.

16/ BRETTZEL 2

This is another full-body stretch. It works on the same muscle groups as the Brettzel 1 (see above), but with more emphasis on the ITB band, which can be an issue for runners suffering from runner's knee and ITB friction (see pp.170–71).

TARGET MUSCLES

- Quadriceps
- Gluteals
- Iliotibial band
- Thoracic spine

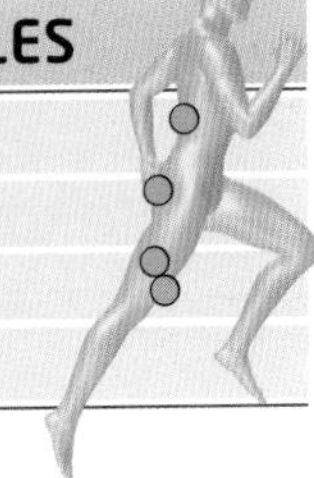

1 Sit on the floor with your legs extended. Bend your left knee at 90 degrees and tuck your left foot in towards your right thigh. Bend your right knee behind you at 90 degrees, so that your thighs are at right angles to each other.

2 Rotate your upper body in the opposite direction to your legs. Place your right hand on the floor with your left hand on top of it to hold the position. Return to the start position and repeat on the other side.

01/ ANKLING

This drill teaches correct foot-landing mechanics for running, helping increase your stride and making you a faster, more accomplished runner. It improves your running coordination, while developing your ankle strength and mobility. The movement is a bit like running over hot coals, with small, rolling steps in quick succession.

DRILL GUIDE

- 10–20m (10–20yd)
- Walk back recovery
- 3–6 reps

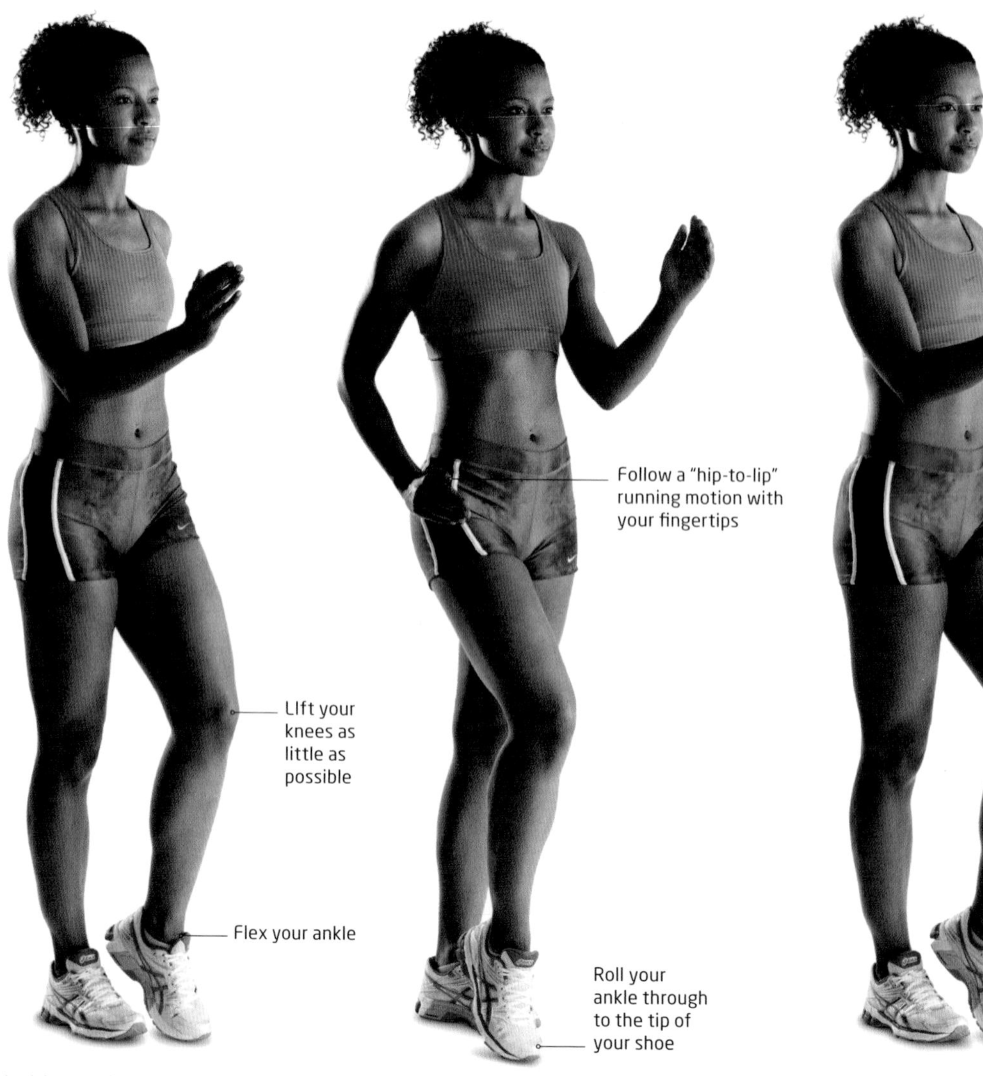

1 Stand with your feet hip-width apart. Take a half shoe-length step forwards with your left foot, landing on your heel. Roll your left foot forwards from heel to toe so that every part of your sole comes into contact with the floor.

2 Step forwards in the same way with your right foot. Land with your right heel first and roll your sole forwards until your right foot is in a tiptoe position. Lift your knees just enough to allow your ankle to move through the full range of motion.

3 As soon as your right foot reaches the tiptoe position, take a step forwards with your left foot. Roll through your ankle's full range of motion until your foot is in a tiptoe position. Continue, alternating feet.

02/ ANKLE SPRINGS

Ankle Springs work to create a bouncier stride for runners by teaching better foot-loading mechanics. Running requires forwards motion combined with the ability to spring off your feet. This drill maximizes the release of energy from your Achilles tendon and plantar fascia, adding spring.

DRILL GUIDE

- 10-20m (10-20yd)
- Walk back recovery
- 3-6 reps

Follow a "hip-to-lip" running motion with your fingertips

Keep your knees straight

Maintain a fixed 90-degree foot position

Maintain minimal foot contact with the floor

1 Stand with your feet hip-width apart. Keeping your feet rigid at a 90-degree angle and your legs straight, perform a forwards skip – a bit like performing a mini can-can.

2 Alternate foot contact about one shoe-length apart. Emphasize explosive foot contact on the balls of your feet, to develop both the toe-off and contact phase of the running cycle.

03/ ANKLE SPRINGS VARIATION

Hold your upper body, arms, and shoulders still

1 To work your legs harder, grasp a broomstick in both hands with an overhand grip, lift it over your head and hold it across your shoulders while doing the drill.

04/ A-WALK

This high-knee walking, or marching, drill emphasizes upright body posture, coordinated arm and leg movements, and a driving knee lift. Use exaggerated arm movements throughout the exercise.

DRILL GUIDE

- 20-30m (20-35yd)
- Walk back recovery
- 6-8 reps

1 Stand with your feet hip-width apart and your hands hanging loosely by your sides. Maintain a relaxed posture, while engaging your core muscles.

2 Step forwards with your right leg, lifting your knee until it is at a 90-degree angle. Bend your left arm, following an exaggerated "hip-to-lip" running motion with your fingertips.

3 Lift your right leg until the thigh is parallel to the ground, then step forwards with your right foot. Repeat with your left leg and right arm, and continue, alternating sides.

05/ B-WALK

Like the A-Walk (see opposite), this marching drill emphasizes upright body posture and coordination of the arms and legs. In addition, it works on hamstring flexibility and body control. Both drills increase the range of motion at the hips, knees, and ankles, and help to improve stability of movement.

DRILL GUIDE

- 20-30m (20-35yd)
- Walk back recovery
- 6-8 reps

1 Stand with your feet hip-width apart and your hands hanging loosely by your sides. Maintain a relaxed posture, while engaging your core muscles.

2 Step forwards with your left leg, raising your left knee until it is at a 90-degree angle. Keep your left foot flexed. Bend your right elbow, following an exaggerated "hip-to-lip" running motion with your fingertips.

3 Swing your left foot forwards and extend your knee until your leg is almost parallel to the ground. Let the momentum carry you forwards. Step forwards with your right foot and continue, alternating legs and arms.

06/ BOUNDING

A high-intensity plyometric exercise, Bounding requires your muscles to exert large forces over short explosive forwards steps. This will help to improve your speed, power, and running economy. You need to have a good lower-body strength training base before engaging in this highly explosive exercise.

DRILL GUIDE

- 20-50m (20-55yd)
- Walk back recovery
- 3-6 reps

1 Start running forwards at a slow jog. After a few strides, bound as far as you can up and forwards with your left leg. Use a high knee lift to propel yourself, driving with your left knee. Swing your arms in opposition to your legs and land on your left foot.

2 Bound as far as you can with your right leg, as if doing a triple jump, using a high knee lift to propel yourself upwards and forwards. Use your arms to sustain the bound in midair. Land on your right foot. Continue, bounding on alternate legs.

07/ STRIDE OUTS

Stride Outs or strides are comfortable sprints that exaggerate the running cycle and help you to practise your running technique by improving leg coordination, speed, and mobility. Perform stride outs on a firm, flat surface. They can be used as a part of your warm-up before a run or as a specific technique session.

DRILL GUIDE

- 50-200m (55-220yd)
- Walk back recovery
- 5-10 reps

1 Start runing fast and relaxed with an exaggerated running cycle. Maintain a good, upright posture without tensing your shoulders.

2 Drive forwards with your legs and arms at about 75-85 per cent of your top sprint speed, keeping your breathing relaxed and in time with your running.

3 Build up to your stride pace and hold it for 85 per cent of the distance before gently decelerating. Walk back to the beginning, shaking out your legs.

PLAN YOUR TRAINING

THE AIM OF ANY TRAINING IS TO FOCUS YOUR PERFORMANCE TOWARDS A CERTAIN POINT. THIS MIGHT BE A RACE OR A RUNNING EVENT, OR SIMPLY BUILDING YOUR DISTANCE OR SPEED UP TO A TARGET LEVEL. THIS CHAPTER SHOWS YOU HOW TO PLAN YOUR TRAINING USING DIFFERENT TYPES OF SESSIONS, AND PROVIDES SAMPLE PROGRAMMES FOR A SELECTION OF RACE DISTANCES.

GOOD TRAINING PRINCIPLES

Once you have set your goals and prepared yourself, it's time to plan your training. This book contains the tools and technical information to set up a training regime, and sample programmes, but you will also benefit from adhering to some basic principles, whether you are a beginner or a seasoned marathon runner.

THE PERCENTAGE BY WHICH YOU SHOULD TYPICALLY INCREASE THE DISTANCE YOU RUN, WEEK BY WEEK

YOUR ROUTE TO SUCCESS »

RUN AS MUCH AS YOU CAN

When you run, you use muscles that only work specifically when you are running. So, although muscle- and core strengthening exercise programmes will help to improve your fitness and strength, and swimming and cycling can help with your aerobic fitness, the most effective form of training is running itself. Quite simply, the more you run, the better you will become at it.

BUILD UP GRADUALLY

If you are new to the sport, you should spend your first four to six weeks building your aerobic endurance. Concentrate on gradually increasing the distance you run week by week (but no more than 5-10 per cent a week), while also using cross-training (see pp.82-83) to develop aerobic fitness, flexibility, mobility, and stability. Use the foundation programme (see pp.94-95) as a guide. The more solid the base of your training, the easier it becomes to progress onto tougher challenges.

AVOID OVERTRAINING

Do not allow an overambitious personal best time or distance to tempt you to increase your mileage or speed significantly, as this can lead to overexertion and injury. Although your body will adapt to the stress of training, it's critical to ensure that you don't apply too much. Each time you overload your body, it needs to time to recover, adapt, and rebuild. If you overtrain - and do not allow sufficient recovery time - the body does not have time to adapt, so cannot cope with extra load or intensity, which increases your risk of injury. See pp.84-85 for more information on overtraining.

INFO DASHBOARD

COMPONENTS OF A TRAINING SESSION

A training session should always consist of a warm-up, a main activity (the focus of your session), and a cool-down. The main activity usually involves running, but you can vary it by changing the run type (see pp.78–81) or doing a cross-training session (swimming, rowing, or core and resistance exercises, see pp.112–43).

WARM-UP

This acclimatizes your body to exercise by increasing blood flow to the muscles and making them more supple. For more on warming up, see pp.58–59.

RUNNING

Use the training programmes (see pp.94–103) as a starting point to plan your runs. Gradually increase the distance, difficulty, and speed as you improve.

CORE AND RESISTANCE TRAINING

These exercises help improve running technique, resulting in better performance and reduced risk of injury (see pp.86–119).

LOW-IMPACT TRAINING

Try other forms of low-impact training such as swimming, rowing, or cycling to increase aerobic fitness or recover after a run (see pp.82–83).

COOL-DOWN

This reduces the lactic acid in muscles, lowers heart rate, and lets your body return to a resting state. For more on cooling down, see pp.58–59.

BE CONSISTENT

Running requires dedication, and improvement only comes with regular practice. No matter how detailed and graded your training programme, there will be days when you simply don't feel like running. However, unless you are ill or injured, you should always complete your planned training session – a consistent and committed attitude to training will eventually cement running as a habitual part of your life. Conversely, taking an extra few days off can set your plans back weeks.

UNDERSTAND YOUR BODY

Although every runner uses the same parts of their body (muscles, tendons, bones, and ligaments, heart, and lungs) to run, no two people respond to the training in the same way. In addition, people enjoy different aspects of running; some find hill running easy, while others are more adept at running long distances. The programmes in this book are there to guide you. If you understand how your body copes with the different demands of running, then you can develop a rewarding and effective training routine tailored to your own particular strengths and weaknesses.

KEEP A TRAINING LOG

Build up a portfolio of training experiences – a training log (see pp.92–93). After each session, make a note of the distance and type of run (see pp.78–81) or cross-training activity you undertake. Describe how you felt during the session, how you felt afterwards (physically and mentally), and what you think you could improve. Make a note of which sessions you enjoyed, and any that you found difficult. Reading through the log gives you an accurate view of your progress, which can give you a sense of achievement. The log also helps you to identify your strengths and weaknesses, enabling you to build up an effective training programme that helps both. You can add other useful information to your log, for example, your average pace, running and resting heart rate, calories burned, and your general state of health.

VARY YOUR RUNNING

GOING FOR A RUN SEEMS SIMPLE: PUT ON YOUR KIT, LACE UP THE TRAINERS, SET THE STOP WATCH, AND OFF YOU GO.

If you run regularly a few times a week, every week, you will improve your fitness, but you may plateau or become bored with following the same old routes, in the same way, or just increasing the distance you run week-by-week. If you vary your sessions, you will feel better prepared and more motivated. These runs are ideal for foundation and base-phase training (see pp.94-103).

BASE RUNS

This type of running is key to any running programme. Base runs are performed frequently and at your natural pace, so help to improve aerobic capacity and running economy. This type of run also forms the basis for later, harder training programmes.

- Base runs should be comfortable and enjoyable
- You should be able to hold a conversation while running (recite the alphabet if you are on your own) – slow down if you can't

TARGET
RPE 3–4
HEART RATE 60–70%

PROGRESSION RUNS

Start out at your normal running pace and gradually increase it during the session. They should be harder than base runs, but not as strenuous as tempo, hill, or interval runs (see pp.80–81). There are two ways to plan the run (see right).

- Increase your pace slightly every 1km (0.6 mile) or 1.6km (1 mile) throughout the run
- Increase your pace over blocks of 3km (1.8 miles)
- Start at a 9 mins per 1.6km (1 mile) pace and increase your pace by 30 seconds per 3-km (1.8-mile) block

TARGET
RPE 3–6
HEART RATE 60–80%

ALTERNATE RUNNING SESSIONS WITH DAYS OF CROSS-TRAINING (SEE PAGES 82–83)

INFO DASHBOARD

TARGET HEART RATE AND RPE

Before you set out on a session you need to set your target working heart rate. In addition, set your target rate of perceived effort (RPE) - a scale of 1 to 10, where 1 is a very light activity and 10 is the maximum and renders a person completely out of breath (see p.40).

WORKING HEART RATE

Your working heart rate is the difference between resting and maximum heart rate (see p.39). Set your target and use a heart rate monitor or GPS watch with a built-in monitor to check your heart during a run (see p.49). Record the results in your training log (see p.92-93).

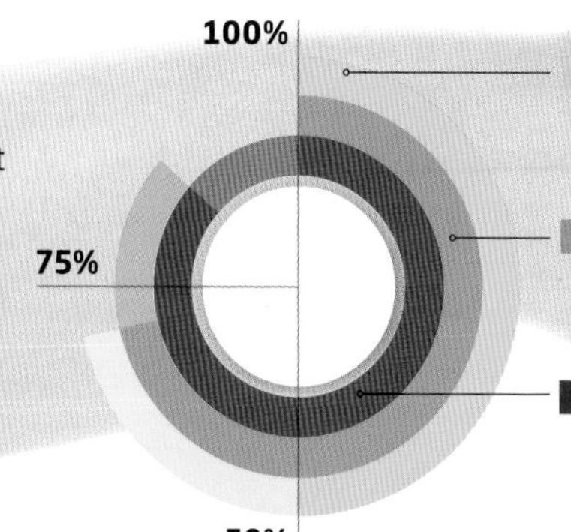

HEART RATE 50-70%
EASY RUNS
Includes base and recovery runs

HEART RATE 70-85%
MODERATE RUNS
Includes fartlek and long runs

HEART RATE 85-100%
HARD RUNS
Includes tempos, hill repeats, and intervals; only attempt the higher limits if you are very fit

TARGET
RPE 4-7
HEART RATE 70–85%

LONG RUNS

A long run tests endurance levels - it should leave you feeling exhausted, but not as if you have been racing. This type of run is mainly used for half-marathon and marathon training.

- If training for a half-marathon, aim to run 14.5-19km (9-12 miles)
- If training for a full marathon, aim to run 25-37km (16-23 miles)
- Perform a run by time to prepare for a race. Calculate your anticipated race time, then run for that length of time, but at a lower intensity and speed, so covering a shorter distance

TARGET
RPE 4-6
HEART RATE 70–80%

FARTLEK

These are medium-intensity training sessions that combine base running with short bursts of faster-paced running. Fartlek is similar to interval training (see p.81), but not as structured. It's good for the early stages of your training as it improves running economy. Developed by a Swedish coach Gösta Holmér in 1937, fartlek means "speed play".

- Alternate between slow jogs and fast segments; fartlek should be unstructured
- Experiment with increasing pace and endurance over short distances (200m/218 yards) or time intervals (30 seconds)
- Helps aerobic capacity and speed
- Prepares runners physiologically and psychologically for more demanding runs (see pp.80-81)

ADVANCING YOUR TRAINING

To improve your performance, train smart and run fast by working more challenging running sessions into your training programmes. Hill repeats, tempo runs, and interval training can be used to work on speed and/or strength endurance (see pp.104–107). By including these alongside your base-phase runs and recovery running, your performance will improve dramatically, and you will feel full of energy every time you run.

HILL REPEATS

Hill repeat runs combine strength and speed training. They are beneficial even if you only ever run on flat courses, but they're essential if you are going to be racing on a hilly course.

- Perform hill repeats towards the end of the base-phase training to introduce your body to higher-intensity running
- Choose a hill with a gradient of four to six per cent
- Run up hill fast for 45 seconds, then do a two-minute recovery run back down; repeat 10 times

RPE 6–9
HEART RATE 80–95%
TARGET

TEMPO RUNS

Tempos, or lactate threshold (LT) runs, are running sessions performed at a sustained effort over a predetermined distance or time. They teach the body how to use oxygen more efficiently, so you can run faster (see opposite).

- Run tempos over a distance of 3.2-8km (2-5 miles) or for 15-40 minutes; beginners should start with no more than 20 minutes
- Run 30-45 seconds per 1.6km (1 mile) slower than your 5-km (3.1-mile) time trial pace; don't run at this pace for more than an hour, even if you are very fit

RPE 8–9
HEART RATE 85–95%
TARGET

INFO DASHBOARD

RAISING LACTATE THRESHOLD
When you run at a higher intensity than normal more lactate and hydrogen ions are released into the muscles (see pp.12–13). This leads to a build-up of waste products, which causes an increase in the acidity in the muscles, preventing muscles from taking up oxygen - they have reached their lactate threshold. To run faster, you need to raise your lactate threshold.

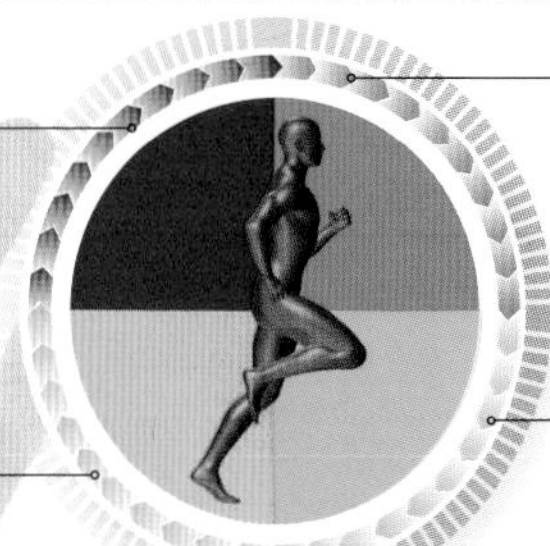

TARGET
RPE up to 2
HEART RATE 50–60%

RECOVERY RUN

This is a very low-intensity run, typically performed the day after a hard training session of hill repeats, tempos, or interval runs.

- The ideal distance is 3.2-8km (2-5 miles), but it can vary depending on your race goal
- Recovery runs are not necessary during base-phase training, but are an essential part of race-specific training
- Recovery runs help you recover mentally from the hard training, while also improving fitness levels and running economy

TARGET
RPE 9–10
HEART RATE 85–100%

INTERVALS

These are high-intensity, fast-paced short runs, performed at race pace or higher to push your running performance to the next level. The aim of the run is to strengthen the heart muscle so that it can pump oxygen around the body more efficiently.

- Interval runs are best performed on a track or a flat course
- Short interval runs (100–400m/ 109–437 yards) help speed training (see pp.104–105)
- Long interval runs (600–1,200m/ 656–1,312 yards) help strength endurance (see pp.106–107)

THE BENEFITS OF CROSS-TRAINING

In this book, cross-training includes any form of training that improves your fitness, performance, or recovery that isn't running – swimming, cycling, yoga, and core and resistance training. It forms an important part of the training programmes on pp.94–103, particularly the base and recovery phases.

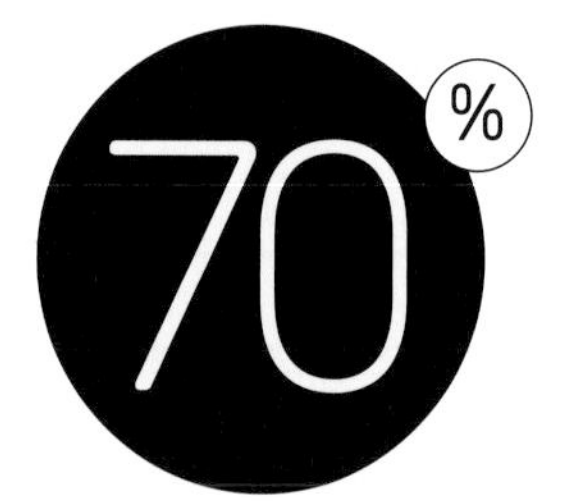

PERCENTAGE OF YOUR MAXIMUM HEART RATE THAT SHOULD BE MAINTAINED OR EXCEEDED DURING CROSS-TRAINING

YOUR ROUTE TO SUCCESS »

REDUCE YOUR INJURY RISK

Running is a high-impact, weight-bearing sport, which places stress on your musculoskeletal system, particularly around your back, hips, knees, and ankles. As a result, it is not advisable to run every day – if you do, you can place too much strain on these areas and risk injury. Adding low-impact or non-weightbearing cross-training sessions to your programme is a great way of giving your body a break from running, while still working on your fitness and keeping active.

IMPROVE YOUR FITNESS

Cross-training also helps to improve your general fitness levels. Alternative endurance activities such as cycling or swimming will increase your aerobic capacity. In addition, undertaking core and resistance training will help you become a stronger and more mobile runner.

VARY YOUR TRAINING

Doing the same thing time and time again can become tedious after a while. However, it is possible to substitute 25–30 per cent of your running mileage with cross-training options such as cycling, swimming, running in the pool, steppers, and ski ergos. Cross-training makes your training programme more varied and interesting, and will keep your motivation at a healthy level. It also enables you to take an active interest in other sporting disciplines.

INFO DASHBOARD

CROSS-TRAINING TARGET AREAS

Different areas of running and fitness benefit from different types of cross-training. This chart shows the benefits of a variety of cross-training activities.

KEY »

- HIGH BENEFIT
- MEDIUM BENEFIT
- LOW BENEFIT

TYPES OF CROSS-TRAINING	FLEXIBILITY	MOBILITY	STRENGTH	STABILITY	ENDURANCE	RECOVERY
SWIMMING	High	High	Medium	Medium	High	High
CYCLING	Low	Medium	Medium	Low	High	High
ROWING	Low	Low	High	Low	High	Medium
SKI ERGOS	Low	Medium	High	Medium	High	Medium
YOGA	High	High	High	High	Low	High
CORE	Low	Medium	High	High	Low	Low
RESISTANCE	Low	Medium	High	High	Low	Low

BOOST YOUR PERFORMANCE

Building strength using weight training can help increase your leg strength. This will give you a more powerful running stride and, as a result, you'll get faster, you'll find hills easier, and you'll take fewer steps to complete your runs.

Core strength is vitally important to running. Following a running-specific core programme (see pp.112–27) will increase your pelvic stability and the power transfer through your stride, while reducing your propensity to injury. It also strengthens the deeper muscles that form the foundation of your running strength.

AID YOUR RECOVERY

Incorporating cross-training into your main training programme (see pp.94–103) gives your body a chance to recuperate from the intensity of regular running. In addition, swimming is a good way to recover from a hard training day – it gives a wide range of muscles a vigorous yet low-impact workout. Completing a few lengths using all of the swim stroke variations is a great way to increase mobility and help your running muscles to recover. Doing some of your mobility exercises (see pp.58–59) in the pool is also great for recovery. If you become injured (see pp.172–83), swimming can form part of your rehabilitation programme.

ADVANTAGES OF CROSS-TRAINING

- Increases general fitness and improves running efficiency
- Maintains training motivation through a varied programme
- Decreases weight bearing and joint impact
- Helps recovery from running, especially after a race
- Reduces the chances of becoming injured
- Forms part of a balanced fitness programme for the whole body, not just the muscles required for running
- Helps increase overall strength and stability
- Provides low-intensity days in a training programme
- Helps avoid overtraining
- Allows you to be flexible in your day-to-day training
- Produces a higher level of all-round mobility
- Can be used as part of a rehabilitation programme

HOW TO AVOID OVERTRAINING

Your training schedule should be balanced, structured, and not excessive. It must include plenty of rest and also fit in with your other commitments, such as work and family. If you train too much, in the wrong way, or don't allow time for recovery, you are likely to damage your body and set back both your progress and your motivation.

SIGNS OF OVERTRAINING

- Chronic fatigue, lack of energy
- Persistent leg soreness
- Persistent muscular and joint pain
- Insomnia
- Lack of appetite and decreasing body weight
- Frequent injuries
- Decreased performance
- Frequent colds or respiratory infections

Q WHAT DOES OVERTRAINING MEAN?

A There is a big difference between feeling tired after a training session and overtraining. The former is a natural part of training, which will lessen as you become fitter, while the latter is a serious problem. Overtraining occurs when you place too much stress on your body. It is caused by training too hard or too often, lack of recovery time, insufficient sleep, or poor nutrition. You might feel that excessive training will make you stronger, but the opposite is true. It weakens the body and leads to an accumulation of fatigue. You will eventually burn out or suffer an injury, which means you will be unable to train. Overtraining can affect anyone, not just elite athletes.

AVERAGE NUMBER OF HOURS' SLEEP PER NIGHT NEEDED TO PREVENT EXCESSIVE FATIGUE

Q HOW DO I AVOID OVERTRAINING?

A If you follow a structured training programme (see pp.94–103), you are unlikely to overtrain. This will build your fitness and running distance gradually, and include plenty of rest days to give your body time to repair and recover. Rest, recovery, and a good night's sleep are as important to your training as actually running. You should try to be aware of your body and be alert for signs of excessive fatigue or injury. Use your training logs (see pp.92–93) to monitor performance and general well-being, and don't be afraid to miss a training session if your body is telling you that it has not recovered sufficiently. It is also vital that you fuel your training efficiently (pp.50–53), ensuring that what you eat and drink is working with your body, rather than against it. Always refer back to your SMART training goals (see pp.44–45): if you overtrain and get injured, you are unlikely to achieve them.

Q HOW DO I RECOVER FROM OVERTRAINING?

A The only way to recover from the effects of overtraining is to stop training immediately. You must simply rest and give your body time to recover. To help this process, you should eat an increased amount of carbohydrate (see p.53) to help replenish muscle glycogen and get your energy levels back up. Dehydration may also be a factor, so be sure to keep your fluid levels high (see pp.54–55). Although you won't be training, you should still complete your training log so you can monitor your recovery. In particular, you should take your morning resting heart rate and note your general well-being. In some cases you may also need to consult your doctor to deal with any injuries. Usually, a complete break from training for as long as you need to recover will be sufficient.

INFO DASHBOARD

THE OVERTRAINING CURVE
This graph shows in very simple terms the trajectory of overtraining. If you are maximizing your effort, but your performance is decreasing and/or your health is getting worse, you may well be on the downwards part of the curve - overtraining. If you feel this is the case, you should stop training immediately and allow your body to rest and recover. Persisting will only make things worse.

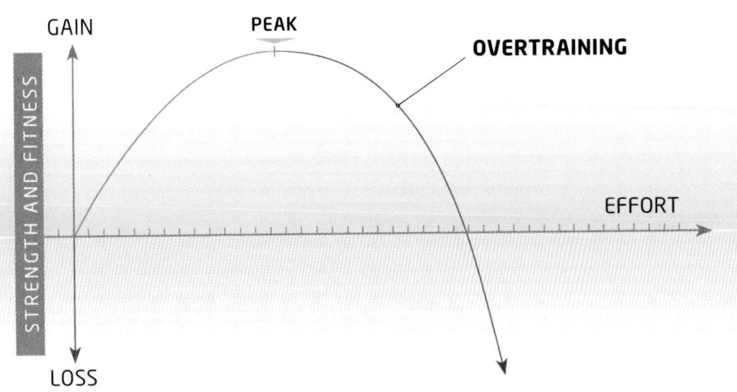

PLANNING YOUR TRAINING

The main objective of any training programme, for beginners and elite athletes alike, is to reach peak performance at a specific time. To achieve a target you need to plan a structured training programme that consists of several phases: a base phase, a specific phase, then an optional performance phase.

NUMBER OF MUSCLES THAT YOUR BODY USES EVERY TIME YOU TAKE A STEP

YOUR ROUTE TO SUCCESS »

SET YOUR TARGET

Before you start you need to know where you are currently and from that, what you want to achieve. First, complete a fitness test or time trial (see pp.38–41). Now use the results to set yourself a realistic, achievable SMART goal (see pp.44–45): this might be a single race or event, a personal target to cover a certain distance within a certain time, or a whole year's events.

Use your SMART goals, together with the sample programmes given on the following pages (see pp.94-103) to plan your training. Pick the programme that best suits your objectives, and tailor it to your own needs. Aim to build up your strength and endurance gradually. This is often best achieved by beginning with shorter distances such as 5km (3.1miles), and working through the different distances in progression (see pp.94-103).

BUILD YOUR BASE

Without a solid foundation to your training not only can you not progress on to greater challenges, but you are likely to injure yourself, which can set you back physically and psychologically. The purpose of a base phase is to build running fitness, increase your running economy, and generally get your body used to the sport. All of the race programmes in this book include a base phase. However, if you are aiming to cover distances of 10km (6.2 miles) or more, you need to complete the foundation programme (see pp.94-95) before starting a race-specific programme.

Your base training should feature a variety of running sessions (base, progression, Fartlek, and long runs, see pp.78-79). In addition, build in cross-training days (see pp.82-83) with yoga, swimming, and/or core strength exercises, which increase aerobic fitness and your muscular strength. An effective base phase not only helps your long-term running performance, but also reduces your risk of injury.

GET SPECIFIC

The second training phase focuses on developing the strength and endurance needed for a specific event. This can be done through continued use of cross-training days (see pp.82-83), but more important is your choice of running sessions. Long runs, tempo runs, and intervals (see pp.80-81) are all great ways of building your running strength. But you should always consider the type of terrain you will be running on when you compete in a race and tailor the training accordingly so that you achieve the best results. For example, if a course is particularly hilly, include extra hill repeats in your specific training phase to build hill-running strength.

INFO DASHBOARD

SINGLE OR MULTIPLE RACES

If you are training for one race, following this simple training principle will help you to achieve your running goals. If you are planning several races throughout the year, you should apply the same formula for each event, ensuring that you build in sufficient recovery time. Your training logs (see pp.92-93) will help you to develop your goals and manipulate your training programme throughout the year (see also the sample training programmes on pp.94-103).

MAXIMIZING YOUR RUNNING PERFORMANCE

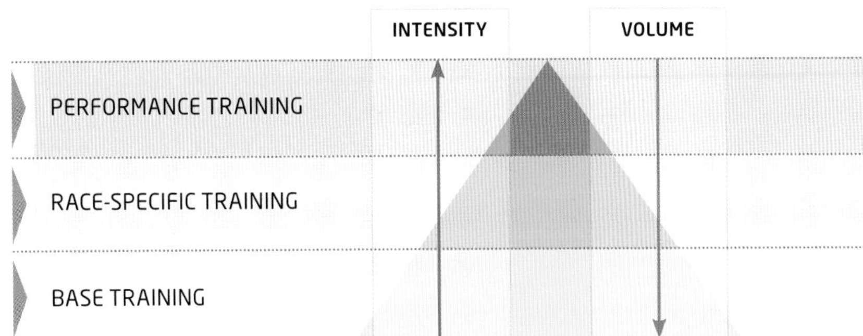

PERFORMANCE TRAINING

All training is about performance, but the performance phase of your race programme is about improving your strength and endurance, and maximizing your running speed. This is best achieved through tailored tempo runs as well as short or long runs, or intervals (see pp.104-107). These training sessions can be built into the last weeks of your race-specific training, and the tapering weeks. Remember, however, if you have not completed effective base and specific phases, you will not get the full benefits of this last stage of training.

LET YOUR BODY RECOVER

Once you have completed a race, have a rest. The further you have run, the more rest your body will need. As a general rule it's a good idea to take one day off for every mile you ran during the event. Although everyone is different - some people need more and others less - it's best to listen to your body. This is also a time when cross-training - for example, swimming, cycling, rowing, and yoga - can be used to maintain cardiovascular fitness while also giving your running muscles time to recover from the rigours of the race (see pp.82-83).

TIPS FOR PLANNING YOUR TRAINING

- Make sure daily training sessions include warm-ups (see pp.60-63), a main activity (running, cross-training, or strength and core training) and a cool-down (see pp. 64-67)
- Vary the type of running sessions you perform (see pp.80-81) to help improve fitness as well as prevent boredom and maintain your motivation
- Don't run every day: running is a high-impact sport and your body needs time to recover between sessions
- Use foam roller exercises (see pp.164-69) to help mobilize tight muscles before or after training
- Alternate running with non-weightbearing exercise such as swimming, cycling, or rowing to aid recovery between running sessions as well as after a race
- Incorporate sessions of core and resistance exercises to help with balance and stability when running

IF YOU ARE A BEGINNER

Making the decision to start running is great, but if you've never run before, or not for a long time, you need to approach the sport in the right way. Start by exploring the biomechanics of running (see pp.30-35) to help you understand and assess your body and prepare it for the challenge ahead.

TIPS FOR BEGINNERS

- Assess your fitness level (see pp.38-41), then set your targets, for example, a 5k (3.1-mile) race
- Increase training volume, load, and frequency slowly
- Utilize non-running activities as well as core and resistance exercises to build fitness and develop strength and stability
- Warm up at the beginning of each session and cool down at the end

YOUR ROUTE TO SUCCESS »

START AT THE BEGINNING

Before you begin training, it is important to understand why you want to take up running. Assess your current fitness level and running style (see pp.38-41); set clear, realistic goals (see pp.44-45) based on the results. Finally, plan a structured training programme that will enable you to achieve them.

FOUNDATION TRAINING

As a beginner you should take time to develop your running ability and general strength and fitness by undertaking a foundation programme (see pp.94-95). Taking time at the beginning to build up your all-over body strength and core stability will make you a better runner in the long term. A good foundation programme includes running sessions as well as cross-training (see pp.82-83). The non-running activities not only help your overall fitness, mobility, strength, and balance, but also allow the running muscles time to recover between runs.

TEST YOUR PROGRESS

Potentially, you could be ready to run a 5k (3.1-mile) race within eight weeks of beginning your training (a six-week training programme followed by two weeks' tapering, see pp.96-97). The 5k is the shortest race distance and the ideal length for a first event as it enables you to building your running endurance gently. For your first race, choose a local one (see Chapter 5 for tips on race preparation).

However, you don't have to race to test your progress. You can set goals that are based on your own personal development and achievement, for example, covering a route in a certain time, losing weight, or simply setting (and sticking to) a training schedule.

INFO DASHBOARD

THE BUILDING BLOCKS TO YOUR FIRST EVENT

A good training programme should be varied, whatever the level. Combine different running sessions (see pp.78-81), with some non-running actvities to aid recovery, as well as days when you focus on core strength and resistance exercises. All of the race-training programmes consist of a base phase and specific phase, which includes activities that will help with particular goals.

RAISE THE BAR

When you have achieved your initial goals, you deserve to feel a sense of accomplishment. You're a runner now! But don't bask in your achievements for too long: you need to set some new SMART goals. Think about where you want to go next. For example, do you want to increase your distance, or run faster - or possibly both? Don't forget that the more challenging the goal, the longer it takes to achieve.

BE REALISTIC

When planning your new goals, don't get carried away and set yourself unrealistic training targets. If, for example, you ran a personal best in your first 5k race, it does not mean you are nearly ready for a half-marathon. Longer runs such as a half-marathon and beyond require an extended period of careful preparation (see pp.100-101). You risk both injury and disappointment if you try and force yourself to do strenuous runs before your body is ready. Follow the natural trajectory of your development by gradually increasing your training until you are ready for your next challenge.

LISTEN TO YOUR BODY

Pay attention to your physical responses to the training programme. Stop or slow down if you feel any pain or discomfort - pain is your body's way of saying it needs more recovery time. See Chapter 6 for information on common runners' complaints and injuries and how best to treat them. By the same token, if you feel you can do more, don't be afraid to step up your training a little bit at a time - but by no more than 5 to 10 per cent a week, even if you feel you could do more. If in doubt, err on the side of caution (see pp.84-85).

ADVANCING YOUR TRAINING

Now that you have completed a foundation programme and have successfully competed in your first 5-k (3.1-mile) races, you will have built up your running fitness. Enjoy the sensation of achieving your first goals. So, what next? You have a choice - try running further or aim for the same distance again, but faster.

Q HOW DO I PLAN FOR RUNNING FURTHER?

A The natural progression would be to complete all the race distances in order - 5km (3.1 miles), 10km (6.2 miles), half-marathon (21km/13 miles), then a full marathon (42km/26 miles). But increasing your race distance also means spending more time training so that your body can adapt to the demands. Before you decide what you want to aim for, read through your training logs (see pp.92-93), assess your fitness level, and listen to your body.

Q WHICH PROGRAMME SHOULD I FOLLOW?

A For each distance above 5km, follow a four- to eight-week foundation programme (see pp.94-95), before you start your distance-specific training as you need to build greater running strength and endurance gradually. This way you develop stronger leg muscles and a more efficient technique, which will not only enable you to run for longer, but also greatly reduce your risk of injury when you do. Focus particularly on the base and specific phases of the sample training programmes (see pp.98-103). See opposite and pp.104-105 for specific running session ideas to build endurance.

Q IS THERE A SPECIAL PROGRAMME FOR RUNNING FASTER?

A Everybody wants to go faster. Completing a 5k in under 30mins, a 10k in under an hour, a half-marathon in under two hours or a marathon under four hours are typical targets. As with running further, follow a four- to eight-week foundation programme (see pp.94–95), before starting distance-specific training (see pp.98–103). The base and specific training phases of each programme are still essential, but including an extra performance training phase in the last weeks of your race-specific programme will give you that extra speed (see below and pp.106–107).

Q HOW DO I SET A RACE PACE TARGET?

A Start by setting a new SMART goal (see p.45). Check your training log and look at your pace in previous races, then work out how much you want to increase it – but be realistic. Use a pace calculator (see p.155) to work out a target mile pace and/or finishing time for your next event. Aim to hit your new target pace during your specific-phase tempo runs to see how it feels. When you reach the performance training stage at the end of your programme, run your tempos and short intervals at the target pace (see pp.106–107). This will give you a faster race pace on the day and possibly a fast finish, too.

LAWS OF TRAINING

If you go out for the same type of run day after day, your fitness will improve as explained by the Law of Specificity: the body always adapts to the specific stress placed upon it. The stimulus exerted on the running muscles results in a corresponding increase in your running strength, particularly if you are a first-time runner. As you continue to run, both your muscular strength and your neuromuscular coordination improve, and you'll feel gradually more comfortable (see p.106). When your body reaches its limits with the training, performance will level out and begin to decline as the body is no longer stressed by the training.

BUILDING BLOCKS TO RACING FURTHER

RUNNING MAIN ACTIVITY	
BASE PHASE	BASE RUNS, PROGRESSION RUNS, FARTLEK
SPECIFIC PHASE	LONG RUNS, HILL REPEATS, LONG INTERVAL RUNS
TAPER PHASE	BASE RUNS
NON-RUNNING MAIN ACTIVITY	
YOGA, STRENGTH TRAINING EXERCISES, CORE STRENGTH TRAINING EXERCISES	

BUILDING BLOCKS TO RACING FASTER

RUNNING MAIN ACTIVITY	
BASE PHASE	BASE RUNS, PROGRESSION RUNS, FARTLEK
SPECIFIC PHASE	HILL REPEATS, TEMPO RUNS, SHORT INTERVAL RUNS
PERFORMANCE PHASE	TEMPO RUNS, SHORT INTERVAL RUNS
TAPER PHASE	BASE RUNS, FARTLEK
NON-RUNNING MAIN ACTIVITY	
SWIMMING, CYCLING, YOGA, STRENGTH TRAINING EXERCISES, CORE STRENGTH TRAINING EXERCISES	

KEEPING A TRAINING LOG

How do you know where you're going if you can't see where you've been? Keeping a log is the best way of using your day-to-day training experience to improve your technique and fitness, and of balancing your training with your life.

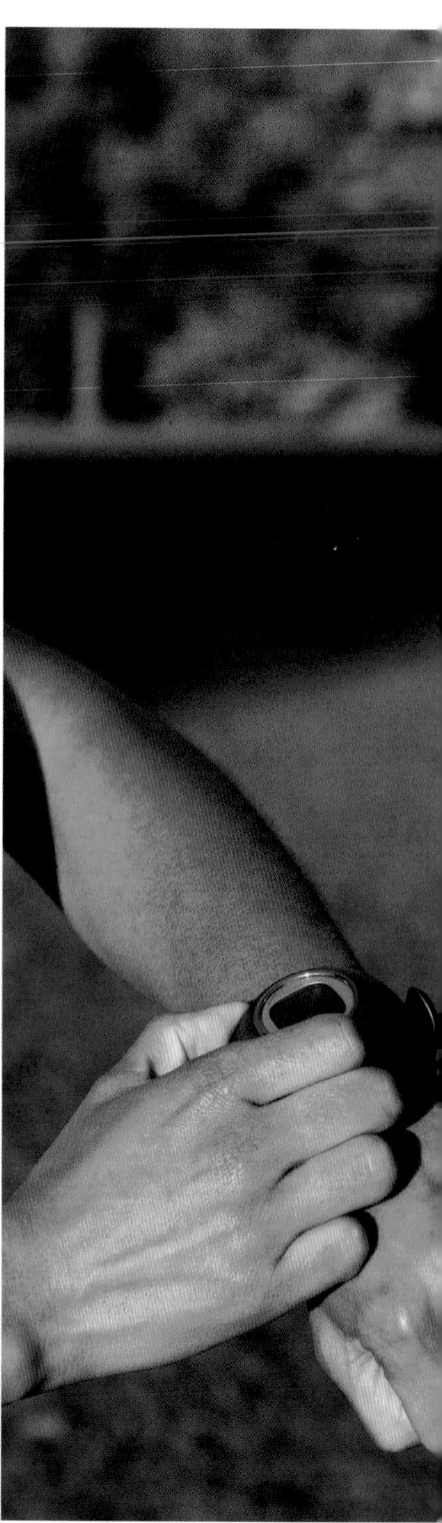

Q WHY SHOULD I KEEP A TRAINING LOG?

A You'll find that you quickly forget what your running was like at the beginning of a training programme. Looking back over a detailed log can jog your memory. The log helps you to identify which training sessions were most effective. You can also monitor your health and mental well-being throughout a training programme, and seeing clear evidence of the progress you've made can help you psychologically. If you look through the log just before a race you'll see what you have achieved, which can really boost your self-confidence.

Q HOW CAN I GET THE MOST OUT OF A LOG?

A Maintain your log alongside your training plan. Describe each session in detail, including everything from the distance covered and injuries sustained to what you ate before and after the session. Check your progress against the plan. The log will help you arrange your schedule to ensure that you are making the best possible use of your training time. It can also help you to make decisions about which sessions to move or drop, and which areas to work on: you might like to try moving a session to before work or focus on a particular muscle group.

RECORDING SPEED, PACE, AND HEART RATE

- Two essentials to have in your running kit are a stop watch, or better still a GPS watch (see p.49), and a heart rate monitor. Use your GPS watch to measure speed and pace. Many GPS monitors can measure heart rate too.
- Measure how long it takes you to run 1km or 1 mile using a stop- or GPS watch. This will give your pace and speed. Get a friend to measure this if you don't want to wear the watch.
- Use a GPS watch to record the distance you ran during a session and the time taken to complete it. You can use this information to work out your average pace (see p.155).
- Wear a heart rate monitor to: check your morning heart rate, calculate your working heart rate (see p.39), and measure how long you spend in each working heart rate running zone during a training session.

WHAT TO RECORD: BEFORE TRAINING

Your log's pre-training notes should contain technical data (date, heart rate, target distance) and general observations such as your mood. This way you can measure your achievements realistically against your overall well-being.

SUBJECT	PURPOSE OF ENTRY
DATE AND DAY	Date and day of the week of the training session.
TARGET	If you are training for a specific run - 10K or marathon - make a note of it. This reminds you of your current aim, and if you return to the same target later it's useful to compare your rate of progress. You can also include your SMART target (see p.45).
SESSION	Make a note of the objective of the session - 8-km (5-mile) interval training, for example, or 13-km (8-mile) base run.
MENTAL AND PHYSICAL WELL-BEING	Describe how you are feeling, for example, whether you feel energized, or you are tired after a long day at work.
MORNING HEART RATE (HR)	Your resting pulse (see p.39) gives an indication of your physical state, and you are most likely to be rested in the morning, after a night's sleep. Also, if your morning pulse rate is seven or more beats faster that your normal resting rate, your body may not have recovered from your previous session, or you may be unwell, so you should rest rather than increase your fatigue further by training.

WHAT TO RECORD: AFTER TRAINING

Take a few moments to record your run data and your observations on conditions. You can compare this information with your pre-run notes and your overall training plan. it is also a good idea to log the mileage on your shoes.

SUBJECT	PURPOSE OF ENTRY
DISTANCE	How far you ran in kilometers or miles.
DURATION	How long the run or training session was.
CALORIES BURNED	If you have a heart rate monitor you can measure this.
SHOES	Which shoes did you wear and what is their cumulative mileage: add the number of miles you ran today to your previous sessions. It's important to change your shoes every six months or around every 500km (300 miles) (see p.163). After a couple of months of training you may feel fitter and stronger, but may not notice that your shoes are not in the best condition.
SESSION DETAILS	Make a note of extra details that can help you analyze your performance. Describe where you ran (track or road) and what it was like (wet, shady, cold, sunny), type of running session (base run, intervals or hill repeats), what you ate before and after, and so on.
RPE	Record your rate of perceived exertion (see p.39)
HEART RATE (HR)	Record your starting HR, the length of time in each working heart zone during the session (see p.39), your average heart rate (AvHR), your maximum heart rate (MaxHR), and the finishing HR.

FOUNDATION PROGRAMME

If you are new to running or you want to start training for a specific race, it is advisable to complete a foundation programme first. This simple programme should build up your fitness and running capability. Over the weeks, you should gradually increase your running distance, while also working on your stability and strength using core and resistance exercises. If you begin a specific plan without first following a foundation programme, your body may not be adequately prepared. As a result, you are less likely to produce your optimum peformance and more likely to suffer an injury.

WHEN TO DO A FOUNDATION PROGRAMME

If your goal is to run 5km (3.1 miles), you don't necessarily need to do the foundation training - the 5k programme on p.97 is sufficient. If your goal is 10km (6.2 miles), do the first four to six weeks of a foundation programme to help develop your running strength and endurance. If you are training for a half-marathon, follow a six- to eight-week foundation programme before you start on the specific race training (see pp 100–101); for a marathon, undertake at least eight weeks before starting the specific plan (see pp.102-103). Stop running for a week between the two programmes and rest or cross-train. This transition week gives your body a recovery break from running.

KEY »

SESSIONS (SEE PP.78-81)
- RECOVERY RUN
- BASE RUN
- FARTLEK
- PROGRESSION RUN
- LONG RUN

CROSS-TRAINING (SEE PP.82-83)
- CYCLE/SWIM
- CORE AND RESISTANCE TRAINING

INTENSITY (SEE PP.38-41)
- RPE
- HEART RATE %

SAMPLE FOUNDATION PROGRAMME

This programme focuses on increasing your weekly mileage through a variety of running sessions, while building your running endurance and economy. Core and resistance training exercises will help your running technique, while other forms of cross-training will give your body a break from high-impact running.

WEEK-BY-WEEK PROGRAMME	DAY-BY-DAY PROGRAMME 1	2	3	4	5	6	7	TOTAL DISTANCE
1	3.2KM (2 MILES) 4-6 70-80%	CORE AND RESISTANCE TRAINING	3.2KM (2 MILES) 3-4 60-70%	REST	CORE AND RESISTANCE TRAINING	3.2KM (2 MILES) 4-6 70-80%	REST	9.6KM (6 MILES)
2	CORE AND RESISTANCE TRAINING	REST	3.2KM (2 MILES) 3-6 60-80%	3.2KM (2 MILES) 3-4 60-70%	SWIM 30-40 MINS 0-2 50-60%	4.8KM (3 MILES) 3-4 60-70%	REST	11.2KM (7 MILES)
3	4.8KM (3 MILES) 3-4 60-70%	CORE AND RESISTANCE TRAINING	REST	3.2KM (2 MILES) 3-4 60-70%	CORE AND RESISTANCE TRAINING	6.5KM (4 MILES) 9-10 85-100%	REST	14.5KM (9 MILES)
4	CORE AND RESISTANCE TRAINING	6.5KM (4 MILES) 3-4 60-70%	4.8KM (3 MILES) 3-6 60-80%	CYCLE 20-30 MINS 0-2 50-60%	REST	6.5KM (4 MILES) 3-4 60-70%	REST	17.8KM (11 MILES)
5	6.5KM (4 MILES) 3-4 60-70%	CORE AND RESISTANCE TRAINING	REST	8KM (5 MILES) 4-6 70-80%	CORE AND RESISTANCE TRAINING	8KM (5 MILES) 3-4 60-70%	REST	22.5KM (14 MILES)
6	CORE AND RESISTANCE TRAINING	6.5KM (4 MILES) 3-4 60-70%	6.5KM (4 MILES) 3-6 60-80%	SWIM 30-40 MINS 0-2 50-60%	REST	9.7KM (6 MILES) 3-4 60-70%	3.2KM (2 MILES) 0-2 50-60%	25.7KM (16 MILES)
7	4.8KM (3 MILES) 3-4 60-70%	CORE AND RESISTANCE TRAINING	8KM (5 MILES) 4-6 70-80%	CORE AND RESISTANCE TRAINING	REST	12.9KM (8 MILES) 3-4 60-70%	4.8KM (3 MILES) 0-2 50-60%	30.5KM (19 MILES)
8	CORE AND RESISTANCE TRAINING	8KM (5 MILES) 3-4 60-70%	6.5KM (4 MILES) 3-6 60-80%	CYCLE 20-30 MINS 0-2 50-60%	REST	16KM (10 MILES) 4-7 70-85%	4.8KM (3 MILES) 0-2 50-60%	35.3KM (22 MILES)

5K PROGRAMME

Three to four running sessions per week will adequately prepare you for a 5k (3.1-mile) race. The runs should be increased gradually, so that you build up to your target distance, and varied to ensure that you remain stimulated and motivated. The inclusion of one cross-training session per week will increase your aerobic capacity and muscular fitness while also giving your running joints a rest. It is also important to give your body time to recover between training sessions, so you should have two or three rest days per week at the start. If you are training for a specific race, it is advisable to reduce your training for the last two weeks before, known as tapering (see pp.146–47).

ADDING A FOUNDATION PROGRAMME

If you have done a 5k race before, or are already an athlete, you might want to focus on increasing your speed. Following the foundation programme on pp.94–95 for four weeks and then undertaking the 5k programme opposite would help you to increase your overall body strength and running endurance, and should lead to better performance and a faster race time. See also pp.104–107 for more information on performance training.

If you are an experienced 5k runner, you could add one or two miles to some of the sessions suggested in this sample programme to improve running fitness and performance over the distance. Use your training logs (see pp.92–93) to make informed decisions about where to adapt your training load and always listen to your body. Don't run more than 40km (25 miles) per week during weeks five and six; it's unnecessary for this event and there's a risk of overtraining, and therefore injury.

KEY »

SESSIONS (SEE PP.78–81)
- RECOVERY RUN
- BASE RUN
- PROGRESSION RUN
- FARTLEK
- HILL REPEATS
- TEMPO RUN
- INTERVALS

CROSS-TRAINING (SEE PP.82–83)
- CYCLE/SWIM

INTENSITY (SEE PP.38–41)
- RPE
- HEART RATE %

SAMPLE 5K PROGRAMME

This programme focuses on building up your distance and is divided into three phases: base, specific, and tapering. It does not include any particular technique, core training, or resistance sessions. You could add some of these exercises to the programme, either on a rest day or before the cross-training.

		DAY-BY-DAY PROGRAMME							TOTAL DISTANCE
		1	2	3	4	5	6	7	
BASE WEEKS	1	REST	3.2KM (2 MILES) 3-4 60-70%	3.2KM (2 MILES) 4-6 70-80%	REST	SWIM 20-30 MINS 0-2 50-60%	4.8KM (3 MILES) 3-6 60-80%	REST	11.2KM (7 MILES)
	2	REST	4.8KM (3 MILES) 3-4 60-70%	3.2KM (2 MILES) 3-6 60-80%	CYCLE 20-30 MINS 0-2 50-60%	REST	3.2KM (2 MILES) 3-4 60-70%	3.2KM (2 MILES) 0-2 50-60%	14.4KM (9 MILES)
	3	REST	4.8KM (3 MILES) 3-4 60-70%	4.8KM (3 MILES) 3.2km (2 miles) tempo 8-9 85-95%	SWIM 20-30 MINS 0-2 50-60%	REST	4.8KM (3 MILES) 3-4 60-70%	3.2KM (2 MILES) 0-2 50-60%	17.6KM (11 MILES)
SPECIFIC WEEKS	4	REST	6.5KM (4 MILES) 3-4 60-70%	4.8KM (3 MILES) 4 × 100m (110yd) hill reps 6-9 85-95%	CYCLE 20-30 MINS 0-2 50-60%	REST	6.5KM (4 MILES) 3-4 60-70%	3.2KM (2 MILES) 0-2 50-60%	21KM (13 MILES)
	5	REST	6.5KM (4 MILES) 3-4 60-70%	4.8KM (3 MILES) 6-8 × 100m (110yd) hill reps 8-9 85-95%	SWIM 20-30 MINS 0-2 50-60%	REST	6.5KM (4 MILES) 3-4 60-70%	4.8KM (3 MILES) 0-2 50-60%	22.6KM (14 MILES)
	6	REST	8KM (5 MILES) 3-4 60-70%	6.5KM (4 MILES) 0.8km on, 0.8km off (0.5 miles) 8-9 85-95%	CYCLE 20-30 MINS 0-2 50-60%	REST	8KM (5 MILES) 3-4 60-70%	4.8KM (3 MILES) 0-2 50-60%	27.3KM (17 MILES)
TAPERING WEEKS	7	REST	6.5KM (4 MILES) 3-4 60-70%	4.8KM (3 MILES) 400m on, 400m off (440yd) 8-9 85-95%	SWIM 20-30 MINS 0-2 50-60%	REST	6.5KM (4 MILES) 3-4 60-70%	3.2KM (2 MILES) 0-2 50-60%	21KM (13 MILES)
	8	REST	4.8KM (3 MILES) 3-4 60-70%	REST	3.2KM (2 MILES) 0-2 50-60%	REST	**RACE DAY 5KM (3.2 MILES)**	REST	8.2KM + 5KM (5 MILES + 3.1 MILES)

10K PROGRAMME

To prepare for a 10k (6.2-mile) race, you will need to do four to five running sessions per week, with two rest sessions to allow your body time to recover. Adding at least one cross-training session every two weeks will give your body a break from running, as well as work on your aerobic and muscular fitness. A two-week taper period at the end of the programme will ensure that your body is prepared for a race (see pp.146-47).

PICKING UP THE PACE

If you have never run a 10k race before, it is advisable to follow the first four to six weeks of the foundation programme on pp.94-95 to develop your running fitness. You should then be sufficiently prepared to progress to this specific 10k programme and avoid the risk of overtraining (see pp.84-85). Experienced 10k runners who want to run faster can benefit from following a full foundation programme before undertaking the 10k programme. If you are an advanced 10k runner, add 3-6km (2-4 miles) to some of the sessions, depending on where you feel you need to improve. Do not exceed 64km (40 miles) per week during weeks five and six, as anything above this is unnecessary for this race distance.

KEY »

SESSIONS (PP.78-81)
- RECOVERY RUN
- BASE RUN
- PROGRESSION RUN
- FARTLEK
- HILL REPEATS
- TEMPO RUN
- INTERVALS

CROSS-TRAINING (SEE PP.82-83)
- CYCLE/SWIM

INTENSITY (SEE PP.38-41)
- RPE
- HEART RATE %

SAMPLE 10K PROGRAMME

This programme has a two-week base phase, followed by a four-week specific training phase. It includes leg-strengthening run sessions allowing you to run for up to one hour. This phase lasts until day two of week six, and finishes with three optional performance training sessions before the two-week taper begins.

		DAY-BY-DAY PROGRAMME							TOTAL DISTANCE
		1	2	3	4	5	6	7	
BASE WEEKS	1	REST	4.8KM (3 MILES) 3-4 60-70%	4.8KM (3 MILES) 4-6 70-80%	3.2KM (2 MILES) 3-4 60-70%	REST	4.8KM (3 MILES) 3-6 60-80%	3.2KM (2 MILES) 0-2 50-60%	20.8KM (13 MILES)
	2	REST	4.8KM (3 MILES) 3-4 60-70%	6.5KM (4 MILES) 4-6 70-80%	SWIM 20-30 MINS 0-2 50-60%	REST	8KM (5 MILES) 3-6 60-80%	4.8KM (3 MILES) 0-2 50-60%	24.1KM (15 MILES)
SPECIFIC WEEKS	3	REST	6.5KM (4 MILES) 3-4 60-70%	4.8KM (3 MILES) 4 × 200m (220yd) hill reps 8-9 85-95%	3.2KM (2 MILES) 3-4 60-70%	REST	6.5KM (4 MILES) 3.2km (2 miles) tempo 8-9 85-95%	4.8KM (3 MILES) 0-2 50-60%	25.8KM (16 MILES)
	4	REST	8KM (5 MILES) 3-4 60-70%	6.5KM (4 MILES) 6 × 200m (220yd) hill reps 8-9 85-95%	CYCLE 20-30 MINS 0-2 50-60%	REST	8KM (5 MILES) 4.8 km (3 miles) tempo 8-9 85-95%	6.5KM (4 MILES) 0-2 50-60%	29KM (18 MILES)
	5	REST	4.8KM (3 MILES) 3-4 60-70%	6.5KM (4 MILES) 6 × 200m (220yd) hill reps 8-9 85-95%	4.8KM (3 MILES) 3-4 60-70%	REST	12.9KM (8 MILES) 2.4km (1.5 miles) on, 0.8km (0.5 miles) off 8-9 85-95%	4.8KM (3 MILES) 0-2 50-60%	33.8KM (21 MILES)
	6	REST	8KM (5 MILES) 3-4 60-70%	8KM (5 MILES) 6.5km (4 miles) tempo 8-9 85-95%	SWIM 20-30 MINS 0-2 50-60%	REST	9.7KM (6 MILES) 1.6km (1 mile) on, 0.8km (0.5 miles) off 8-9 85-95%	6.5KM (4 MILES) 0-2 50-60%	32.2KM (20 MILES)
TAPERING WEEKS	7	REST	REST	8KM (5 MILES) 0.8km on, 0.8km off (0.5 miles) 8-9 85-95%	3.2KM (2 MILES) 3-4 60-70%	REST	9.7KM (6 MILES) 6.5km (4 miles) tempo 8-9 85-95%	4.8KM (3 MILES) 0-2 50-60%	25.7KM (16 MILES)
	8	REST	6.5KM (4 MILES) 3-4 60-70%	REST	3.2KM (2 MILES) 0-2 50-60%	REST	**RACE DAY 10KM (6.2 MILES)**	REST	9.7KM + 10KM (6 MILES + 6.2 MILES)

HALF-MARATHON PROGRAMME

Developing strength and endurance is the key to running a half-marathon. A half-marathon can last from about one and a half hours for advanced runners to three hours for beginners. The main objective of a training programme is to develop your ability to run for long periods of time without stopping.

A STABLE BASE

You will need to run five times per week to build up the required endurance, and it is recommended that, unless you are an experienced distance runner, you follow the foundation programme (see pp.94–95) for six to eight weeks before you begin the half-marathon programme. If you don't prepare your body with a foundation programme, you will struggle with the volume of training and are more likely to suffer an injury.

There are two rest days each week to help your body to recover between training sessions. Cross-training is not necessary, although swimming can be used to promote recovery and increase mobility. You could add some core or resistance exercises to work on strength and stability (see pp.112–27). Experienced runners could add up to 10km (6 miles) to some of the sessions. Do not exceed 89km (55 miles) per week in weeks five and six.

KEY »

SESSIONS (SEE PP.78–81)

- RECOVERY RUN
- BASE RUN
- FARTLEK
- PROGRESSION RUN
- HILL REPEATS
- INTERVALS
- TEMPO
- LONG RUN

INTENSITY (SEE PP.38–41)

- RPE
- HEART RATE %

SAMPLE HALF-MARATHON PROGRAMME

This programme has a one-week base phase followed by a five-week specific training phase that includes hill repeats, tempo runs, and a long run. Performance training sessions are included in the two-week taper: day three of weeks seven and eight focuses on technique and speed.

	DAY-BY-DAY PROGRAMME							TOTAL DISTANCE
	1	2	3	4	5	6	7	
BASE 1	REST	6.5KM (4 MILES) 3-4 60-70%	6.5KM (4 MILES) 8-9 85-95%	3.2KM (2 MILES) 3-4 60-70%	REST	9.7KM (6 MILES) 4-7 70-85%	3.2KM (2 MILES) 0-2 50-60%	29.1KM (18 MILES)
SPECIFIC WEEKS 2	REST	4.8KM (3 MILES) 3-4 60-70%	8KM (5 MILES) 2 × 2.4km (1.5 miles) tempo 8-9 85-95%	3.2KM (2 MILES) 3-4 60-70%	REST	14.5KM (9 MILES) 4-7 70-85%	3.2KM (2 MILES) 0-2 50-60%	33.7KM (21 MILES)
3	REST	6.5KM (4 MILES) 3-4 60-70%	6.5KM (4 MILES) 4 × 300m (330yd) hill reps 6-9 80-95%	3.2KM (2 MILES) 3-4 60-70%	REST	16KM (10 MILES) 3.2km (2 miles) on, 0.8km (0.5 miles) off 9-10 85-100%	4.8KM (3 MILES) 0-2 50-60%	37KM (23 MILES)
4	REST	6.5KM (4 MILES) 3-4 60-70%	9.7KM (6 MILES) 2.4km (1.5 miles) on, 0.8km (0.5 miles) off 9-10 85-100%	4.8KM (3 MILES) 3-4 60-70%	REST	16KM (10 MILES) 4-7 70-85%	4.8KM (3 MILES) 0-2 50-60%	41.8KM (26 MILES)
5	REST	8KM (5 MILES) 3-4 60-70%	8KM (5 MILES) 8 × 200m (220yd) hill reps 9-10 85-100%	6.5KM (4 MILES) 3-4 60-70%	REST	20.9KM (13 MI) 2.4km (1.5 miles) on, 0.8km (0.5 miles) off 9-10 85-100%	3.2KM (2 MILES) 0-2 50-60%	46.6KM (29 MILES)
6	REST	8KM (5 MILES) 3-4 60-70%	8KM (5 MILES) 6.4km (4 miles) tempo 9-10 85-95%	6.5KM (4 MILES) 3-4 60-70%	REST	19.3KM (12 MILES) 4-7 70-85%	4.8KM (3 MILES) 0-2 50-60%	46.6KM (29 MILES)
TAPERING WEEKS 7	REST	6.5KM (4 MILES) 3-4 60-70%	6.5KM (4 MILES) 0.8km on, 0.8km off (0.5 miles) 9-10 85-100%	4.8KM (3 MILES) 3-4 60-70%	REST	14.5KM (9 MILES) 4-7 70-85%	4.8KM (3 MILES) 0-2 50-60%	27.1KM (23 MILES)
8	REST	6.5KM (4 MILES) 3-4 60-70%	4.8KM (3 MILES) 3-6 60-80%	3.2KM (2 MILES) 3-4 60-70%	REST	**RACE DAY 21.2KM (13.2 MILES)**	REST	14.5 + 21.2KM (9 + 13.2 MILES)

MARATHON PROGRAMME

Before starting to train for a marathon for the first time, it is vital that you prepare properly. If you don't, you will struggle with the volume and intensity of training, and you are almost certain to damage or injure your body.

THE BIG RACE

The aim of this programme is to develop your ability to run for long periods of time. Prepare yourself by completing a minimum eight-week foundation programme first. The volume of running will strengthen your upper and lower body, so you do not need to do any resistance training. However, additional core training sessions twice a week and 15- to 20-minute cross-training sessions on the bike or in the pool will aid recovery. Rest is vital, so allow two rest days each week to recuperate. In the last two weeks of your programme, decreasing your training volume, intensity, and frequency (tapering) will ensure you are in the best shape for the race (see pp.146-47).

If you have run a marathon before, you can add up to 6.5km (4 miles) to some sessions; try not to exceed more than 100km (65 miles) per week in weeks five or six to avoid overtraining and injury.

BEFORE RUNNING A MARATHON

- Follow an eight-week foundation programme and even a half-marathon programme to ensure that your body will be able to cope with the marathon.
- Take a break from running for a week between your base programme and your marathon programme. In this transition week, rest completely or cross-train.
- If you are new to distance running, consider running a half-marathon first.
- Incorporate practice races into your programme so you can work on your race pace and strategy, and also experiment with optimum nutrition and hydration.

KEY »

SESSIONS (SEE PP.78-81)

- RECOVERY RUN
- BASE RUN
- TEMPO RUN
- HILL REPEATS
- LONG RUN
- INTERVALS

INTENSITY (SEE PP.38-

- RPE
-  HEART RATE %

SAMPLE MARATHON PROGRAMME

The five-week specific training phase features hill repeats, tempo runs, and long runs to develop endurance, ending with a tempo run and a 10k race to work on performance. Practice races keep you motivated and act as performance indicators. They also help you work out your pace and strategy.

		DAY-BY-DAY PROGRAMME							TOTAL DISTANCE
		1	2	3	4	5	6	7	
BASE	1	REST	9.7KM (6 MILES) 3-4 60-70%	9.7KM (6 MILES) 2 × 3.2km (2 miles) tempo 8-9 85-95%	9.7KM (6 MILES) 3-4 60-70%	REST	24.1KM (15 MILES) 4-7 70-85%	**4.8KM** (3 MILES) 0-2 50-60%	58KM (36 MILES)
SPECIFIC WEEKS	2	REST	9.7KM (6 MILES) 3-4 60-70%	9.7KM (6 MILES) 6 × 300m (330yd) hill reps 8-9 85-95%	9.7KM (6 MILES) 3-4 60-70%	8KM (5 MILES) 3-4 60-70%	REST	**10KM RACE (6.2 MILES)** 0-2 50-60%	47.1KM (29.2 MILES)
	3	REST	9.7KM (6 MILES) 3-4 60-70%	9.7KM (6 MILES) 8 × 300m (330yd) hill reps 6-9 80-95%	9.7KM (6 MILES) 3-4 60-70%	REST	28.9KM (18 MILES) 4-7 70-85%	**4.8KM** (3 MILES) 0-2 50-60%	62.8KM (39 MILES)
	4	REST	9.7KM (6 MILES) 3-4 60-70%	9.7KM (6 MILES) 2.4km (1.5 miles) on, 0.8km (0.5 miles) off 9-10 85-100%	8KM (5 MILES) 3-4 60-70%	6.5KM (4 MILES) 3-4 60-70%	REST	**HALF-MARATHON 21.2KM (13.2 MILES)** 0-2 50-60%	55.1KM (34.2 MILES)
	5	REST	9.7KM (6 MILES) 3-4 60-70%	9.7KM (6 MILES) 3.2km (2 miles) on, 1.6km (1 mile) off 9-10 85-100%	8KM (5 MILES) 3-4 60-70%	REST	32.1KM (20 MILES) 4-7 70-85%	**4.8KM** (3 MILES) 0-2 50-60%	64.3KM (40 MILES)
	6	REST	9.7KM (6 MILES) 3-4 60-70%	9.7KM (6 MILES) 6.5km (4 miles) tempo 8-9 85-95%	9.7KM (6 MILES) 3-4 60-70%	8KM (5 MILES) 3-4 60-70%	REST	**10KM RACE (6.2 MILES) + 3.2KM (2 MILES)** 0-2 50-60%	50.3KM (31.2 MILES)
TAPERING WEEKS	7	REST	8KM (5 MILES) 3-4 60-70%	8KM (5 MILES) 6.5km (4 miles) tempo 8-9 85-95%	6.5KM (4 MILES) 3-4 60-70%	REST	16KM (10 MILES) 4-7 70-85%	**4.8KM** (3 MILES) 0-2 50-60%	43.3KM (27 MILES)
	8	REST	**4.8KM** (3 MILES) 3-4 60-70%	REST	**4.8KM** (3 MILES) 0-2 50-60%	REST	3.2KM (2 MILES) 3-4 60-70%	**RACE DAY 42.5KM (26.4 MILES)**	12.8 + 42.5KM (8 + 26.4 MILES)

STRENGTH AND ENDURANCE

If you want to run further or increase your speed, especially over long distances, you must build up your running strength and endurance. These exercise programmes below will help you maintain strong, powerful, even strides throughout a race.

All of the training programmes on the previous pages include a base phase, then a specific phase, which includes running sessions to develop your strength endurance: long runs, hill repeats, tempo runs, and long interval runs (see pp.80–81). Run your long runs at a comfortable, even pace aiming for a heart rate of between 70 to 85 per cent or RPE of six to nine (see p.39), increasing your distance by 10 to 15 per cent each week.

SHORT HILL REPEATS PROGRAMME

For this type of run (see p.80), choose a hill with a gradient of 10 to 15 per cent, any greater and your running technique may suffer. If you are a beginner to hill running, start at the lower gradient. Look straight ahead when running, not at your feet, so you concentrate on the hill.

LEVEL	RACE GOAL	HILL RUN DISTANCE	REPS	HR	RECOVERY
BEGINNER	5K	50M (55YD)	3-5	90-95%	WALK BACK
INTERMEDIATE	5K	50-75M (55-82YD)	4-6	90-95%	WALK/JOG
ADVANCED	5K	75-100M (82-109YD)	5-7	90-95%	JOG
BEGINNER	10K	100M (109YD)	3-5	90-95%	WALK BACK
INTERMEDIATE	10K	100-150M (109-164YD)	4-6	90-95%	WALK/JOG
ADVANCED	10K	150-200M (164-218YD)	5-7	90-95%	JOG

LONG HILL REPEATS PROGRAMME

For long hill repeats, choose a hill with a smaller gradient - 5 to 8 per cent is ideal. As with short hill repeats, start with the lower gradient if you are a beginner. Don't do hill repeats more than once a week. Hill repeats can be used for speed training too (see pp.106–107).

LEVEL	RACE GOAL	HILL RUN DISTANCE	REPS	HR	RECOVERY
BEGINNER	HALF-MARATHON	200-250M (219-273YD)	3-4	85-90%	WALK BACK
INTERMEDIATE	HALF-MARATHON	250-500M (273-547YD)	4-5	85-90%	WALK/JOG
ADVANCED	HALF-MARATHON	500-750M (547-820YD)	5-6	85-90%	JOG
BEGINNER	MARATHON	250M (273YD)	3-4	85-90%	WALK BACK
INTERMEDIATE	MARATHON	250-500M (273-547YD)	4-5	85-90%	WALK/JOG
ADVANCED	MARATHON	500-750M (547-820YD)	5-6	85-90%	JOG

INFO DASHBOARD

SLOW- AND FAST-TWITCH MUSCLES

Muscle is made up of bundles of fibres (see p.12). There are two types of fibre - slow-twitch and fast-twitch. The overall ratio of fast- to slow-twitch fibres determines muscle function and which sports an athlete is likely to excel at. Muscles that contain more slow-twitch fibres are redder as they rely on a steady energy supply of oxygenated blood so contain more blood vessels. Fast-twitch muscle fibres use oxygen to make ATP - a substance that transports energy within cells - to fuel them, and are better for generating short bursts of strength or speed.

SLOW-TWITCH MUSCLES	FAST-TWITCH MUSCLES
USE OXYGEN FOR ENERGY	USE ATP AND GLYCOGEN FOR ENERGY
SLOW MUSCLE-FIRING	FAST-FIRING; BEST FOR EXPLOSIVE MOVEMENTS
DO NOT FATIGUE EASILY	TIRE OUT QUICKLY
EFFICIENT AT RUNNING FURTHER	EFFICIENT AT RUNNING FASTER

TEMPO RUN PROGRAMME

A tempo run (see p.80) should be comfortably hard rather than an all-out effort. You should ensure you are fully warmed up before beginning. A 10-15 minute session before an easy run will be sufficient; perform a cool-down of the same length afterwards.

LEVEL	RACE GOAL	TEMPO RUN DISTANCE	PACE	HR	RPE
BEGINNER	5 OR 10K	6.4-8KM (4-5 MILES)	15-30 SECONDS SLOWER THAN YOUR 5KM PACE	85%	8
INTERMEDIATE	10K OR HALF-MARATHON	8-14KM (5-9 MILES)	30-45 SECONDS SLOWER THAN YOUR 10KM PACE	85%	8
ADVANCED	HALF-MARATHON OR MARATHON	14-21KM (9-13 MILES)	25-35 SECONDS SLOWER THAN YOUR 5KM RACE PACE	85-95%	8-9

LONG INTERVAL RUN PROGRAMME

High-intensity interval training (see p.81) is one of the best ways to improve your race performance. These sessions are usually reserved for building strength for half- and full marathons. Running faster than your normal race pace for short periods of time helps to build vital running strength endurance.

LEVEL	RACE GOAL	DISTANCE	INTERVALS	PACE	HR	RPE
BEGINNER	HALF-MARATHON AND MARATHON	1.2-1.6KM (0.75 -1 MILE)	6-8	5-7.5% FASTER THAN YOUR 10KM RACE PACE	85-100%	9-10
INTERMEDIATE	HALF-MARATHON AND MARATHON	1.6-2KM (1-1.25 MILES)	4-6	2-2.5 % FASTER THAN YOUR 10KM RACE PACE	85-100%	9-10
ADVANCED	HALF-MARATHON AND MARATHON	2-3.2KM (1.25-2.0 MILES)	3-4	2-2.5% FASTER THAN YOUR 10KM RACE PACE	90-100%	9-10

INCREASING YOUR SPEED

If you want to run faster, you need to train fast. Speed work is an essential part of any running training programme if you want to break your all-important personal best.

Running at a set pace for a specific distance is the simplest way to train for speed. Adding fast tempo runs and short intervals (see pp.80-81) towards the end of your race-specific programme will leave you feeling faster, fresher, and more confident in your running. Listen to your body, however, as you're either ready or you're not. If you feel you're pushing your body too hard, adjust your training.

INFO DASHBOARD

LAW OF TRAINING IN PRACTICE

To improve in any activity you need to practice. The law of training (see p.90) states that if you perform the same training session or run in the same way, at the same distance, and the same level each time, your fitness will continue to improve until your body reaches its physical limits. This is because when you overload the body, it continues to adapt, and therefore progress. Once the limits are reached performance levels off, and starts to decrease as the body is no longer stressed by the training session - reversing the law of training.

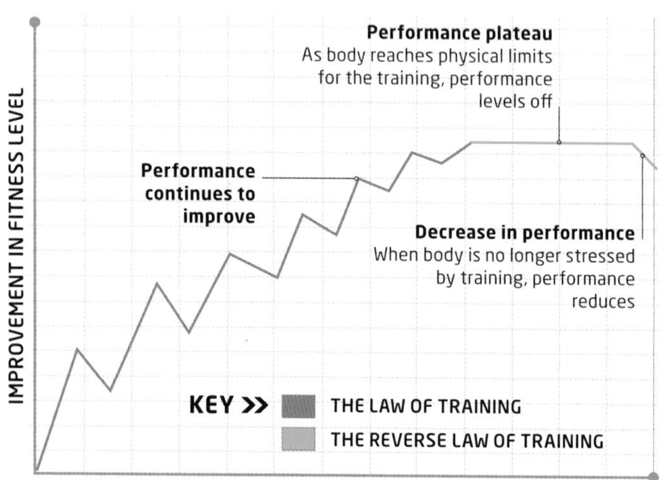

FACTS ABOUT RUNNING FASTER

IT BURNS!

Running fast takes effort and requires quick supply of energy to the muscles. After a session you will feel out of breath and your leg muscles will feel like they're burning. Don't panic, this is all part of the body supplying energy to the muscles and then dealing with the build up of lactic acid (see p.81). Learning how your body responds to running faster is part of your training.

LEG SPEED IS KEY

To run faster you need to increase leg speed, or turnover. Focus on your running cycle (see pp.30-31) and ensure that all your limbs are working through the correct running technique and to their maximum capacity.

REST DAYS ARE IMPORTANT

You can't run every day, especially for long distances, and you shouldn't attempt more than one or two speed sessions a week. The body takes time to adapt to the stresses of training and your muscles need time to recover no matter how elite you are. All of the training programmes in the book (see pp.96-103) include at least two rest days a week.

FAST TEMPO RUN PROGRAMME

Tempos (see p.80) used to develop speed are run at a faster pace over a shorter distance than for strength endurance training (see p.105). Use the instant feedback you get by attempting fast tempos to calculate your ideal running pace. Fast tempos are physically taxing as you are training close to your limits.

LEVEL	RACE GOALS	RUN DISTANCE	PACE	HR	RPE
BEGINNER	5 TO 10K	1.6-3.2KM (1-2 MILES)	45-60 SECONDS SLOWER THAN YOUR 5KM RACE PACE	90-95%	9
INTERMEDIATE	10K TO HALF-MARATHON	3.2-4.8KM (2-3 MILES)	45-60 SECONDS SLOWER THAN 10KM RACE PACE	90-95%	9
ADVANCED	HALF-MARATHON TO MARATHON	4.8-6.4KM (3-4 MILES)	60-75 SECONDS SLOWER THAN 10KM RACE PACE	90-95%	9

SHORT INTERVAL RUN PROGRAMME

Short intervals (see p.81) help you get into your stride quickly and improve your running technique as you need an effective toe-off phase to propel you forward. Leg and arm drive also contribute to forward momentum. Performing core-training exercises (see pp.112-27) will give you more power in your stride.

LEVEL	RACE GOALS	DISTANCE	INTERVALS	PACE	HR	RPE
BEGINNER	ALL DISTANCES	200-300M (219-328YD)	8-10	MAXIMUM EFFORT	90-100%	9-10
INTERMEDIATE	ALL DISTANCES	300-400M (328-437YD)	6-8	MAXIMUM EFFORT	90-100%	9-10
ADVANCED	ALL DISTANCES	400-600M (437-656YD)	4-6	MAXIMUM EFFORT	90-100%	9-10

POST-RACE PROGRAMMES

Completing a race is a great feeling, but don't rush back into training – instead, follow the appropriate recovery programme. Additionally, it is a good idea to go for a walk the day after a race – it will ease your stiff joints and tight muscles tremendously. Mobility and stretching sessions (see pp.58–59) promote recovery and help return your muscles to their full range of motion and elastic length. Low-level full-body activities such as yoga and swimming increase total recovery, as does cycling.

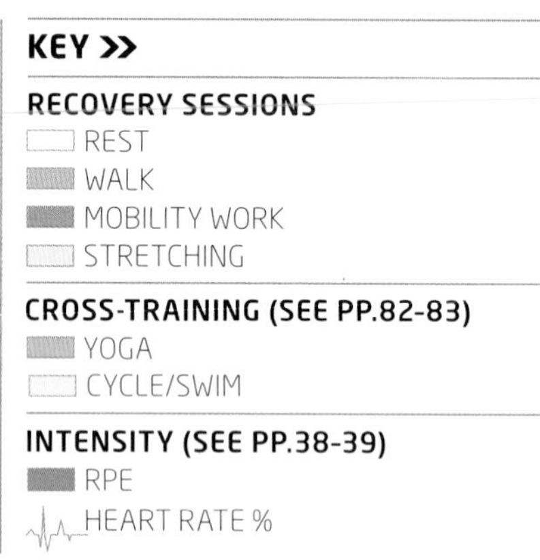

SAMPLE 5K RECOVERY PROGRAMME

Allow yourself a week to recuperate after a 5-km (3.1-mile) race. If you have followed your training programme correctly, your body should only need a short programme to rebuild itself.

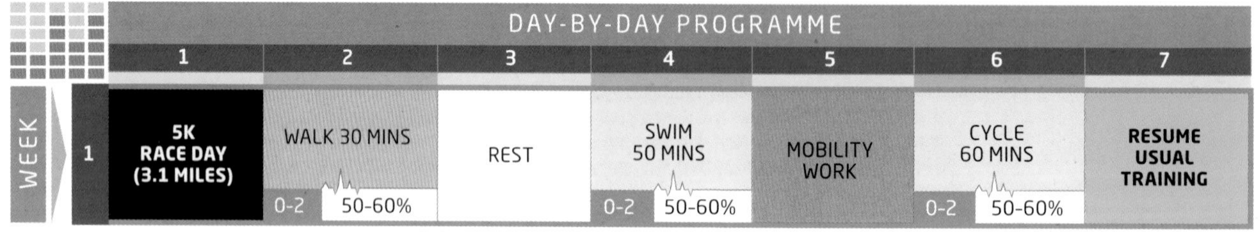

WEEK	DAY-BY-DAY PROGRAMME						
	1	2	3	4	5	6	7
1	**5K RACE DAY (3.1 MILES)**	WALK 30 MINS (0-2, 50-60%)	REST	SWIM 50 MINS (0-2, 50-60%)	MOBILITY WORK	CYCLE 60 MINS (0-2, 50-60%)	**RESUME USUAL TRAINING**

SAMPLE 10K RECOVERY PROGRAMME

If you have completed a 10-km (6.2-mile) event, your body will need a more substantial break before restarting training. This slightly longer recovery programme introduces stretching.

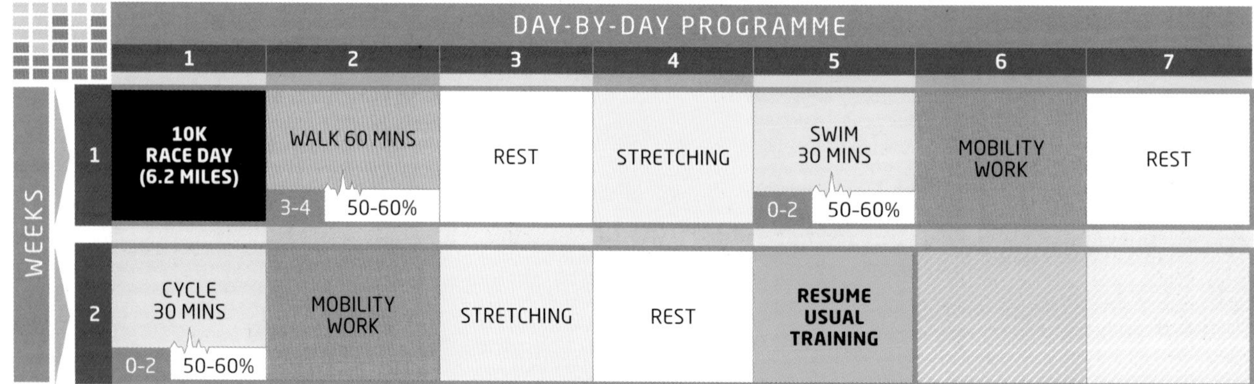

WEEKS	DAY-BY-DAY PROGRAMME						
	1	2	3	4	5	6	7
1	**10K RACE DAY (6.2 MILES)**	WALK 60 MINS (3-4, 50-60%)	REST	STRETCHING	SWIM 30 MINS (0-2, 50-60%)	MOBILITY WORK	REST
2	CYCLE 30 MINS (0-2, 50-60%)	MOBILITY WORK	STRETCHING	REST	**RESUME USUAL TRAINING**		

SAMPLE HALF-MARATHON RECOVERY PROGRAMME

Once you have progressed to longer races such as the half-marathon, your recovery takes on even more importance. This programme introduces yoga, which consists of demanding but low-impact exercises.

WEEKS	DAY-BY-DAY PROGRAMME 1	2	3	4	5	6	7
1	**HALF-MARATHON RACE DAY**	WALK 60 MINS 3-4 60-70%	REST	SWIM 40 MINS 0-2 50-60%	STRETCHING	YOGA	REST
2	MOBILITY WORK	REST	YOGA	STRETCHING	SWIM 50 MINS 0-2 50-60%	YOGA	REST
3	CYCLE 60 MINS 0-2 50-60%	MOBILITY WORK	**RESUME USUAL TRAINING**				

SAMPLE MARATHON RECOVERY PROGRAMME

Allow yourself at least four weeks for recovery after competing in a marathon – extend the programme if you feel your body has not returned to full strength by the end of it.

WEEKS	DAY-BY-DAY PROGRAMME 1	2	3	4	5	6	7
1	**MARATHON RACE DAY**	WALK 60 MINS 3-4 60-70%	REST	WALK 60 MINS 3-4 60-70%	REST	SWIM 40 MINS 0-2 50-60%	STRETCHING
2	YOGA	REST	YOGA	STRETCHING	SWIM 50 MINS 0-2 50-60%	REST	YOGA
3	MOBILITY WORK	CYCLE 60 MINS 0-2 50-60%	STRETCHING	REST	MOBILITY WORK	CYCLE 60 MINS 0-2 50-60%	YOGA
4	MOBILITY WORK	SWIM 50 MINS 0-2 50-60%	REST	YOGA	MOBILITY WORK	REST	**RESUME USUAL TRAINING**

BUILD YOUR STRENGTH

AS YOUR RUNNING BECOMES MORE ADVANCED, YOUR STRENGTH IS INCREASINGLY IMPORTANT FOR GETTING THE BEST OUT OF YOUR TRAINING AND YOUR PERFORMANCE. THIS CHAPTER CONTAINS A SELECTION OF CORE STRENGTH AND RESISTANCE TRAINING EXERCISES TAILORED TO RUNNERS – USE THESE TO DEVELOP YOUR STRENGTH AND TAKE YOUR RUNNING TO THE NEXT LEVEL.

CORE TRAINING

A WELL-BALANCED TRAINING PROGRAMME SHOULD INCLUDE SOME WORK ON STRENGTHENING THE MUSCLES OF YOUR CORE.

Although it may not seem the most obvious area of the physique for runners to train, the core is important for running as well as for other sports. Introducing core strength training into your schedule helps your overall strength, power, and stability, as well as providing some much-needed variety.

KEY »

SETS
A pre-defined number of repetitions separated by a short period of rest - for example, two sets of five repetitions.

REPETITIONS
The number of times an exercise should be repeated, usually within a single set - "reps" for short.

REST
The suggested length of recovery period between individual sets.

Q WHAT IS THE CORE?

A The core consists of the spine and the muscles of the hips, abdomen, and back (see pp.16-19). These muscles interact to stabilize the spine, providing a solid base for the legs and arms. It holds internal organs in place and creates pressure in the abdominal cavity.

Q WHY TRAIN MY CORE?

A Strong core muscles generate the power, stability, and mobility that are crucial in demanding, dynamic sports such as running. A strengthened core will also aid the transfer of power through the kinetic chain (see p.11) and help reduce your susceptibility to injury.

BEGINNERS' PROGRAMME

This introductory programme is suitable for runners with less than 2 months of resistance or core training experience. It is made up of exercises of low to medium intensity, and is intended to build a foundation of core strength on which to base more advanced exercises, and to create a strong base to aid running performance.

AIM OF PROGRAMME	DEVELOP BASIC MUSCULAR STRENGTH AND POWER
DURATION OF PROGRAMME	2-3 TIMES PER WEEK FOR 2-4 WEEKS

	EXERCISE	SETS	REPS	REST
1	BREATHING DRILL (P.127)	1	20-30 BREATHS	NONE
2	LOWER BODY ROLL (P.114)	2-3	3 EACH SIDE	30-60 SECS
3	DEAD BUG (P.115)	2-3	20 ALTERNATING SIDES	30-60 SECS
4	GLUTE BRIDGE (P.116)	2-3	12-15	30-60 SECS
5	BREATHING DRILL (P.127)	1	20-30 BREATHS	NONE

INTERMEDIATE PROGRAMME

The intermediate programme is targeted at runners with 2-12 months of resistance or core training experience. The featured exercises are mostly of medium intensity and will help build your core stability to a greater level. It is suitable for runners competing in medium-distance events.

AIM OF PROGRAMME	DEVELOP STATIC STABILITY AND DYNAMIC CORE STABILITY
DURATION OF PROGRAMME	2-3 TIMES PER WEEK FOR 4-6 WEEKS

	EXERCISE	SETS	REPS	REST
1	HALF KNEELING CHOP (P.124)	1	12-15 EACH SIDE	30-60 SECS
2	SINGLE LEG GLUTE BRIDGE (P.117)	2-3	12-15 EACH SIDE	30-60 SECS
3	BIRD DOG (P.115)	2-3	20 ALTERNATING SIDES	30-45 SECS
4	REVERSE BACK EXTENSION (P.121)	2-3	12-15	30-45 SECS

ADVANCED PROGRAMME

You should undertake this programme if you are an experienced runner with more than 1 year of resistance or core training experience, and can complete similar exercises with good form (correct movement and body position). It is intended to give you a high level of core stability suitable for running over races of longer distances.

AIM OF PROGRAMME	DEVELOP STRENGTH, POWER, AND DYNAMIC CORE STABILITY
DURATION OF PROGRAMME	2-3 TIMES PER WEEK FOR 4-6 WEEKS

	EXERCISE	SETS	REPS	REST
1	MEDICINE BALL SLAM (P.123)	3-5	5-7	90 SECS
2	BARBELL GLUTE BRIDGE (P.117)	3	6-10	60-90 SECS
3	STANDING CHOP (P.124)	2-3	10-12	60 SECS
4	STICK CRUNCH (PP.126-27)	2	10-12	45-60 SECS
5	SPRINTER CRUNCH (P.118)	2	12-20 ALTERNATING SIDES	45-60 SECS

01/ LOWER BODY ROLL

This lower body rolling pattern aims to enhance your hip mobility and stability, while working your core. Increased control of your pelvis and spine will improve your overall running efficiency, and stronger core muscles will help to make your breathing more effective when you run.

TARGET MUSCLES

- Transverse abdominis
- Obliques
- Pelvic floor

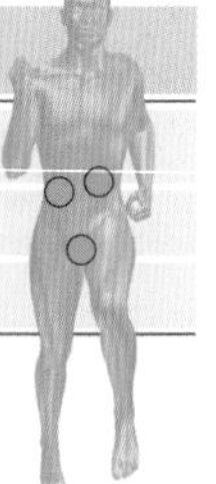

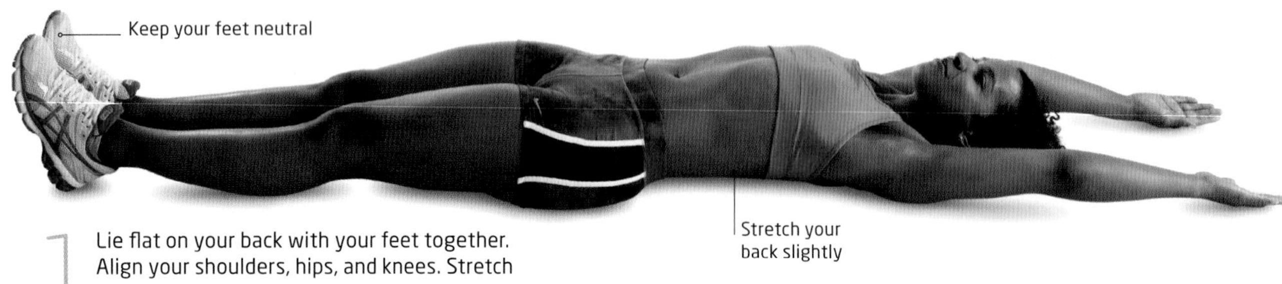

1 Lie flat on your back with your feet together. Align your shoulders, hips, and knees. Stretch your hands up over your head.

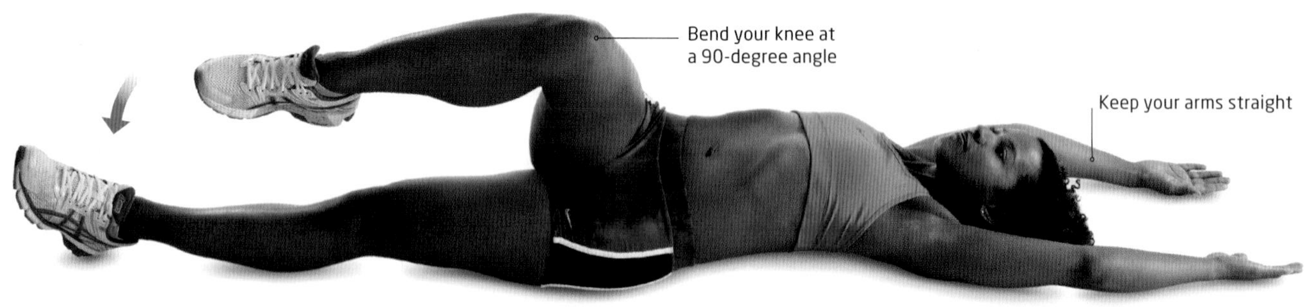

2 Bend your right leg up towards your chest until the knee is level with your hips. Reach your leg across your body, rotating your hips in the direction of the roll. Let your upper body follow your hips until you roll over.

3 To continue the roll, extend your left leg upwards and diagonally across the back of your body. Let your upper body remain on the floor until your lower body pulls it over. Rest, then roll in the opposite direction.

02/ **BIRD** DOG

This exercise works on strengthening and stabilizing your lumbar spine. It is essential to maintain good form – do not exceed your ability to control movement in the lower back.

TARGET MUSCLES
- Transverse abdominis
- Obliques
- Gluteals

1 Kneel on all fours, with your knees directly below your hips and your hands below your shoulders. Keep your spine in a neutral position and align your head with your back. Engage your core.

2 Raise your left arm straight in front of you, palm-down. Stretch out your right leg and raise it behind you until it is parallel to the floor, using your core to keep your body stable. Hold briefly, then return your arm and leg to the floor and repeat on the other side.

03/ **DEAD** BUG

This exercise works your abdominals at the same time as developing arm and leg coordination. It is essential to keep your core engaged as you alternate arms and legs.

TARGET MUSCLES
- Transverse abdominis
- Obliques
- Iliopsoas

1 Lie flat on your back with your legs extended and your feet hip-width apart. Stretch your arms out above your head. Tighten your abdominals so that your lower back pushes down into the floor.

2 Raise your left arm and your right leg, keeping both arm and leg straight, until they are at 90 degrees to the floor. Lower both at the same time and repeat on the other side.

04/ GLUTE BRIDGE

This exercise is an important core-stabilizing movement, which activates the large gluteal muscles of your buttocks. There is a range of variations, including the Single Leg Glute Bridge and Barbell Glute Bridge (see opposite), making it very versatile.

TARGET MUSCLES

- Gluteals
- Pelvic floor
- Quadratus lumborum
- Multifidus
- Erector spinae
- Rectus abdominis
- Transverse abdominis

1 Lie flat on your back with your knees bent up at a 90-degree angle and your feet flat on the floor, hip-width apart. Place your arms at your sides, with your hands palms-down.

2 Engage your core. Slowly lift your buttocks off the floor until your body is in a straight line from your knees to your shoulders. Hold briefly, then slowly reverse the movement to return to the start position.

05/ **SINGLE LEG** GLUTE BRIDGE

Performing the bridge on one leg forces you to control the rotation and tilt of your pelvis. Ensure that you keep your hips level throughout.

TARGET MUSCLES

- Gluteals
- Pelvic floor
- Quadratus lumborum
- Multifidus
- Erector spinae
- Rectus abdominis
- Transverse abdominis

Keep your foot flat on the floor

Engage your core

1 Lie flat on your back with your feet hip-width apart and your knees at a 90-degree angle. Place your hands palms-down by your sides and raise your left knee towards your chest, until your thighs are at a 90-degree angle to each other.

2 Lift your buttocks off the floor until your hips are fully extended and your body is in a straight line from your right knee to your shoulders. Hold briefly, then slowly reverse to the start position and repeat on the other side.

06/ **BARBELL** GLUTE BRIDGE

The weight of the barbell makes this bridge more challenging, working your glutes harder. Place a foam pad or towel under the bar for comfort.

TARGET MUSCLES

- Gluteals
- Pelvic floor
- Quadratus lumborum
- Multifidus
- Erector spinae
- Rectus abdominis
- Transverse abdominis

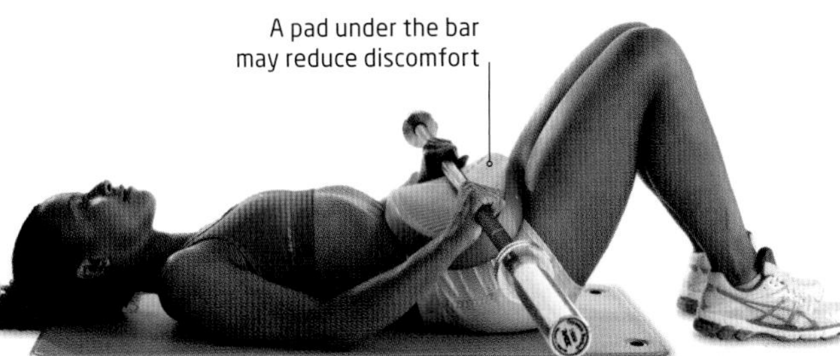

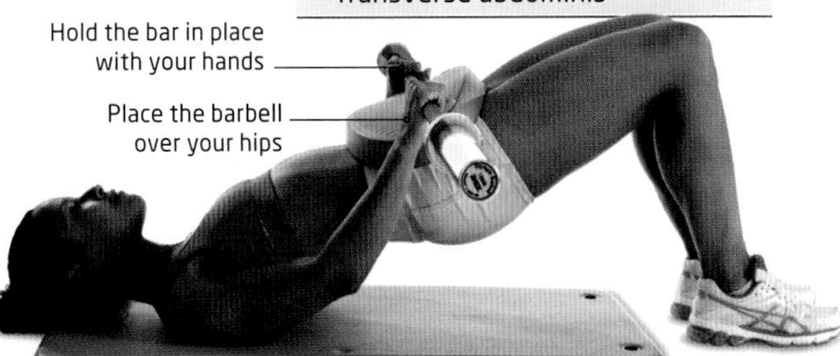

1 Lie on your back with your feet hip-width apart and your knees bent at a 90-degree angle. Roll the barbell so that it is directly over your hips and grasp it with your hands, using an overhand grip.

2 Engage your core and slowly lift your hips off the floor until your body is in a straight line from your knees to your shoulders, holding the bar in place with your hands. Hold briefly, then reverse the movement to return to the start position.

07/ SPRINTER CRUNCH

The basic abdominal crunch is one of the simplest and most popular of all exercises, helping you to develop a strong core and improve your posture. This more advanced crunch builds rotational strength as well as the core strength you need to run.

TARGET MUSCLES

- Transverse abdominis
- Rectus abdominis
- Obliques
- Iliopsoas

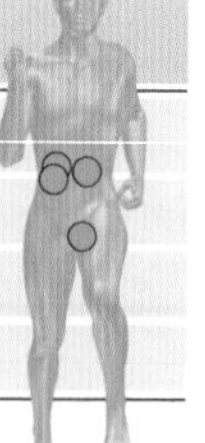

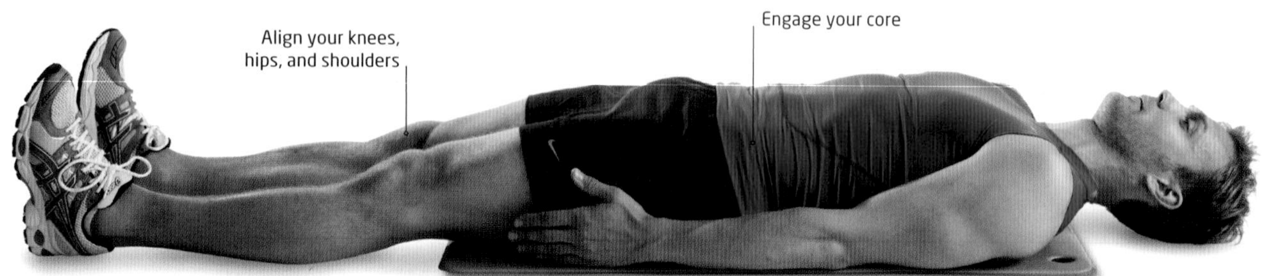

1 Lie flat on your back on the floor with your legs extended and your arms by your sides. Turn your palms in towards your body. Tighten your abdomen and engage your core.

2 Crunch up and lift your shoulders off the ground. Bring your left knee up towards your chest. Bend your right arm and bring your elbow up, reaching across to touch your left knee with your right elbow. Hold briefly, then uncrunch and repeat on the other side.

08/ **STABILITY BALL** CRUNCH

Doing crunches on a stability ball helps you to keep your abdominals contracted, as you need to work constantly using your deep core muscles to balance yourself on the inherently unstable ball. Make sure not to "flop" back as you lower your upper body.

TARGET MUSCLES

- Transverse abdominis
- Rectus abdominis
- Obliques

Support your lower back on the ball

Keep your feet flat on the floor

Maintain tight core control

1 Sit on a stability ball. Walk your feet forwards until you are horizontal, with your knees at a 90-degree angle. Bend your elbows and place your hands at the sides of your head.

2 Lift your shoulders off the ball and crunch your abs towards your hips, pushing your lower back into the ball. Hold briefly, then lower your upper body back to the start position.

09/ **STABILITY BALL** CRUNCH WITH MEDICINE BALL

Incorporating a medicine ball into the basic Stability Ball Crunch (see above) works your abdominals harder. You can substitute a football or even a heavy bag for the medicine ball.

TARGET MUSCLES

- Transverse abdominis
- Rectus abdominis
- Obliques

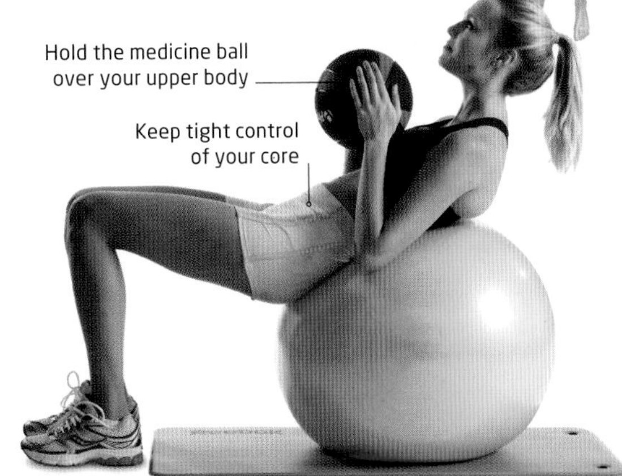

1 Hold a medicine ball in front of your chest, with your elbows bent. Sit on a stability ball and walk your feet forwards until you are balanced horizontally on the ball with your knees at 90 degrees.

2 With your core engaged, lift your shoulders and crunch your abs towards your hips, pushing your lower back into the ball. Hold briefly, then lower your upper body to the start position.

10/ GHD BACK EXTENSION

Using a glute-hamstring developer (GHD) machine, this advanced movement targets the muscles of your spine, your lower back, and your glutes. It demands a high level of flexibility in your hips and hamstrings. When not in the gym, you can also perform it on a table, with a partner holding your legs.

TARGET MUSCLES

- Gluteals
- Hamstrings
- Erector spinae

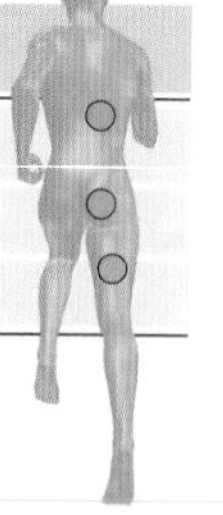

1 Position yourself face down on the GHD machine. Anchor your feet in the foot supports and rest your thighs on the leg pad. Bend your elbows and place your hands at the sides of your head. Flex at your hips and lower your upper body towards the floor until your hamstrings restrict further movement.

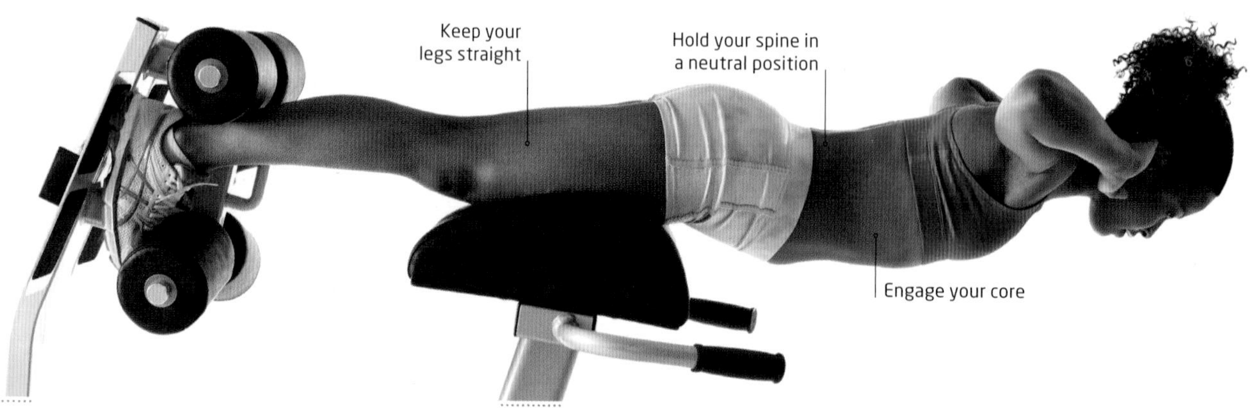

2 Using your core to control the movement, raise your upper body parallel to the floor, in a straight line with your legs. Hold briefly. Keeping your core engaged, return to the start position, with your upper body at 90 degrees to the floor.

11/ **REVERSE** BACK EXTENSION

This exercise uses a GHD machine to work your spine, your glutes, and your hamstrings, and to develop strength in your upper back. You can also perform it on a table with a partner.

TARGET MUSCLES

- Gluteals
- Hamstrings
- Erector spinae

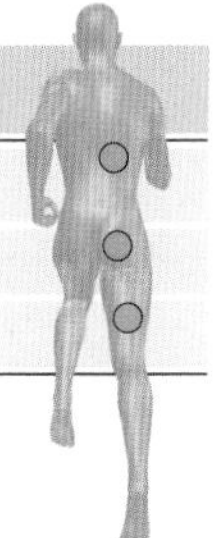

1 Hold onto the foot pad of the GHD machine and rest your upper body on the leg pad. Allow your legs to hang down from your hips at around a 90-degree angle.

2 Engage your core, flex your glutes, and raise your legs until they are in line with your upper body. Hold briefly. Maintain core control and lower your legs back to the start position.

12/ **STABILITY BALL** GLUTE EXTENSION

This glute extension works all your main core muscle groups. You have to work constantly using your deep core muscles to balance yourself on the inherently unstable ball.

TARGET MUSCLES

- Gluteals
- Hamstrings
- Erector spinae
- Transverse abdominis
- Quadratus lumborum
- Obliques

1 Lie forwards over the ball. Rest your toes and your hands on the floor. Lengthen your legs and walk yourself forwards over the ball until your hips are on top of it. Engage your core.

2 Lift your left leg off the floor until it is in line with your upper body, parallel to the floor but no higher. Hold briefly, then lower your leg back to the start position, keeping your core engaged. Repeat with your right leg.

13/ STABILITY BALL ROTATION

This exercise is a rotational movement that makes your core stabilizers work hard to keep your upper body balanced and stable. Make sure you brace your core throughout. Use a lightweight ball until you have perfected your technique.

TARGET MUSCLES

- Transverse abdominis
- Obliques
- Gluteals
- Rectus abdominis

1 Hold a medicine ball. Lie back against a stability ball, with your upper body supported by the ball. Bend your knees at a 90-degree angle, with your feet flat on the floor. Hold the medicine ball directly above your chest.

Keep your arms straight

Keep your feet flat on the floor

Keep your core tight

2 Pivoting from your waist, rotate your arms, shoulders, and upper body as far as you can to the left. Control the movement with your core. Keep your feet flat on the floor, your hips aligned, and your arms straight.

3 Hold briefly, then rotate your upper body, shoulders, and arms back to the start position, keeping your core engaged. Repeat the movement to your other side.

14/ **MEDICINE BALL** SLAM

This is a powerful, dynamic exercise that works your core hard and strengthens your shoulders. Focus on keeping your body balanced throughout. Start with a light ball, until you can carry out the movement with good form and confidence.

TARGET MUSCLES

- Rectus abdominis
- Transverse abdominis
- Obliques
- Quadratus lumborum
- Erector spinae
- Multifidus
- Latissimus dorsi

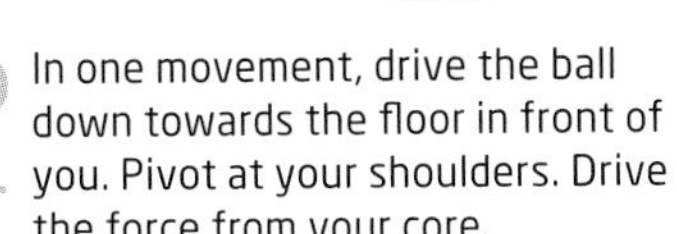

1 Hold a medicine ball in both hands. Stand with your feet hip-width apart. Engage your core. Raise the medicine ball above your head and rise up on your toes.

2 In one movement, drive the ball down towards the floor in front of you. Pivot at your shoulders. Drive the force from your core.

3 Release the ball at the bottom of the downwards movement, bending your knees as if going into a squat position (see p.131). Retrieve the ball and repeat.

15/ HALF-KNEELING CHOP

This chop works the muscles of your core as you try to maintain your balance. It is an anti-rotational exercise, which develops hip, ankle, and knee stability while improving mobility. It targets your abdominal muscles, in conjunction with your lower back muscles.

TARGET MUSCLES

- Rectus abdominis
- Transverse abdominis
- Quadratus lumborum
- Obliques
- Multifidus

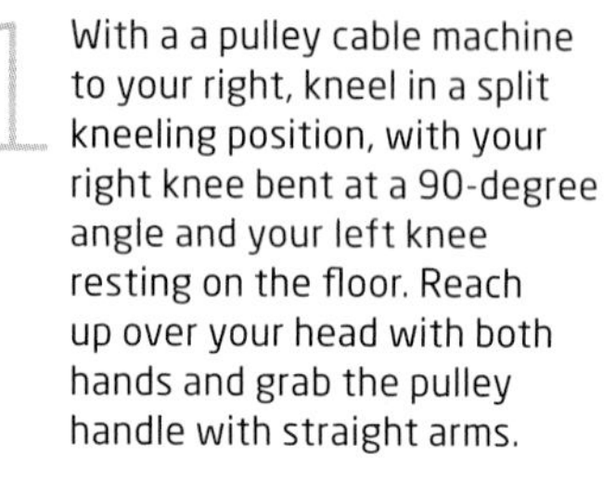

1 With a a pulley cable machine to your right, kneel in a split kneeling position, with your right knee bent at a 90-degree angle and your left knee resting on the floor. Reach up over your head with both hands and grab the pulley handle with straight arms.

PROGRESSION

STANDING CHOP
Your body is less supported in a standing position, so performing the chop while standing works your core harder, improving your strength and stability. Stand with your feet wider than hip-width. Keep your shoulders straight and your hips fixed throughout the movement.

Keep your shoulders straight

Place your foot flat on the floor

2 Engage your core and pull the cable down and across your body in one fluid motion. As you lower your arms, bend your elbows to pull the cable in to your chest.

3 Keeping the cable close to your body, straighten your arms and push down to finish the movement. Hold briefly, then reverse the move to the start position and repeat on the other side.

16/ HALF-KNEELING LIFT

This exercise works to strengthen your shoulders, upper back, and arms, helping to improve your core stability while keeping your spine still. If you find it too hard to begin with, try kneeling on both legs rather than just one.

TARGET MUSCLES

- Rectus abdominis
- Transverse abdominis
- Quadratus lumborum
- Obliques
- Multifidus

1 With a pulley cable machine to your left, kneel in a split kneeling position with your right knee bent at a 90-degree angle and your left knee resting on the floor. Keep your back straight. Reach down and grasp the pulley handle with both hands. Keep your arms straight.

PROGRESSION

STANDING LIFT
Performing the lift in a standing position works your core harder, improving strength and stability. It develops your leg muscles too. Stand with your feet wider than shoulder-width apart, your back straight, and your shoulders, hips, knees, and ankles aligned.

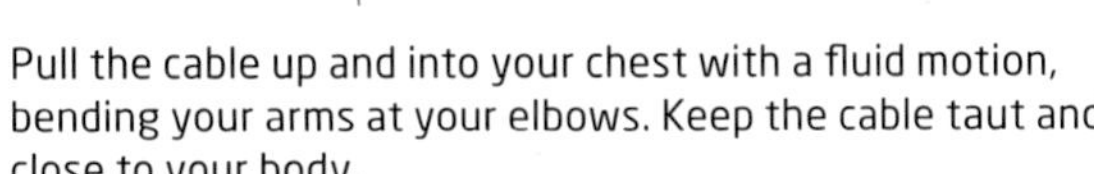

2 Pull the cable up and into your chest with a fluid motion, bending your arms at your elbows. Keep the cable taut and close to your body.

3 Turn your shoulders and upper body away from the machine and push up with your hands until your arms are extended. Hold, reverse, and repeat on the other side.

17/ STICK CRUNCH

This challenging exercise requires a high level of core stability, strength, and hip mobility to perform correctly. Take the stick as far down your shins towards your toes as you can before attempting the full crunch. Focus on developing good form and movement. A broomstick is ideal for the exercise.

1 Lie flat on your back. Grasp the stick with an overhand grip, with your hands slightly wider than shoulder-width apart. Engaging your core, lift the stick.

2 Keeping your core tight and your feet together, raise your knees towards your chest and crunch up with your upper body. Bring the stick over your head to your knees and down your shins as you do so. Keep your arms straight.

3 Continue the crunch with a smooth, controlled movement, pulling your knees in to your chest. Bring the stick down and around the soles of your feet without touching them.

5 Continue the movement until your upper body and head are on the floor, and the stick is beneath your buttocks. Keep your legs straight. Rest briefly, then reverse the sequence to the start position.

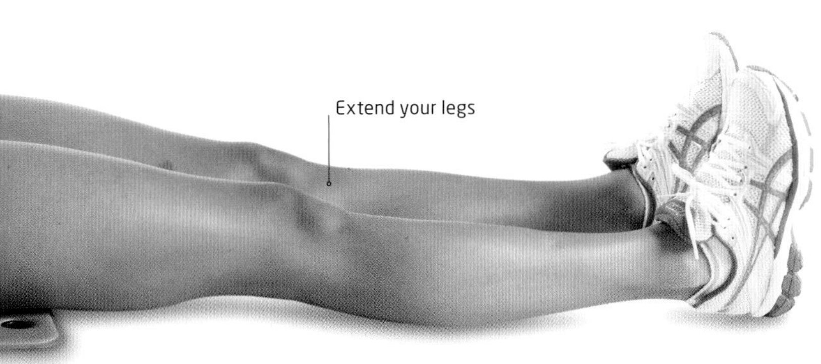

4 Bring the stick back under your legs with a smooth movement controlled with your core. Straighten your knees and lean back with your torso as you do so. Make sure you keep your back straight.

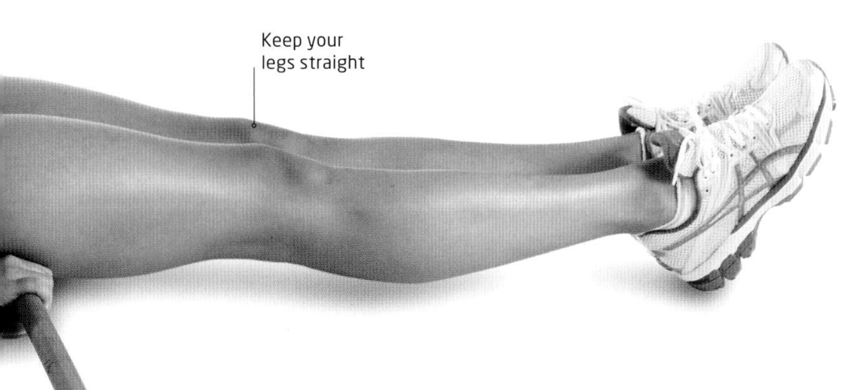

TARGET MUSCLES

- Rectus abdominis
- Transverse abdominis
- Pelvic floor
- Hip flexors
- Erector spinae
- Gluteus maximus

BREATHING TECHNIQUE DRILL

Breathing technique is often neglected by runners. This drill will help you to improve your breathing patterns, so that more oxygen enters your bloodstream when you are running, improving your efficiency.

1 Lie flat on your back with your legs raised so that your hips and knees are bent at right angles. Place your hands palms-up by your sides. Breathe in through your nose and count to two. Breathe out through your mouth and count to four. Let your abdomen expand before your chest, using your diaphragm to pull air in to your lungs.

RESISTANCE TRAINING

GOOD FOUNDATIONS FOR MUSCULAR STRENGTH CAN BE DEVELOPED THROUGH RESISTANCE TRAINING.

Although distance runners do not generally need a large amount of muscle bulk, it is still important to have strong musculature and good overall power. Resistance training is an extremely effective way of achieving this, and is also good for your overall fitness.

Q WHAT IS RESISTANCE TRAINING?

A Resistance training is any type of training in which your muscles work against resistance. This might be provided by a weight, a rubber band, or your own bodyweight.

Q WHAT ARE ITS BENEFITS?

A The main focus of this training is to build your overall strength, and it is good for toning some of the key muscles for running. It also burns fat and helps improve your general fitness; you may enjoy the variety it brings to your training schedule.

KEY »

SETS
A pre-defined number of repetitions separated by a short period of rest - for example, two sets of five repetitions.

REPETITIONS
The number of times an exercise should be repeated, usually within a single set - "reps" for short.

REST
The suggested length of recovery period between individual sets.

BEGINNERS' PROGRAMME

This programme is aimed at runners with less than 2 months of resistance or core training experience. It is intended to provide an introduction to the basics of resistance training, and to give you a solid foundation of strength that can be built upon with more advanced exercises later in your training.

AIM OF PROGRAMME	DEVELOP BASIC MUSCULAR STRENGTH AND POWER
DURATION OF PROGRAMME	2-3 TIMES PER WEEK FOR 4-6 WEEKS

	EXERCISE	SETS	REPS	REST
1	HIP HINGE DRILL (P.135)	3	10-15	30-60 SECS
2	SQUAT TECHNIQUE DRILL (P.131)	2	10-15	30-60 SECS
3	KETTLEBELL DEADLIFT (P.140)	3	12-15	30-45 SECS
4	WALKING LUNGE WITH DUMBBELLS (P.132)	2-3	16-20 ALTERNATING SIDES	30-45 SECS
5	SUSPENDED ROW (STANDING) (P.141)	2-3	12-15	30-45 SECS
6	PRESS-UP, KNEES OR FEET (P.138-39)	2-3	12-15	30-45 SECS
7	CALF RAISE + DUMBBELL VARIANT (P.136)	2-3	10-15	30-45 SECS

INTERMEDIATE PROGRAMME

The intermediate programme is designed for runners with 2-12 months of resistance or core training experience. It includes exercises of medium intensity that will increase your strength and familiarize you with the correct movement patterns. It can be incorporated into a training schedule for moderate-distance races.

AIM OF PROGRAMME	BUILD FOUNDATIONAL MOVEMENT PATTERNS/ENDURANCE
DURATION OF PROGRAMME	2-3 TIMES PER WEEK FOR 4-6 WEEKS

	EXERCISE	SETS	REPS	REST
1	KETTLEBELL SWING (P.140)	3	8-10	90 SECS
2	BARBELL DEADLIFT (P.134)	3	8-10	90 SECS
3	SINGLE-LEG SQUAT (P.131)	2-3	10-12 EACH SIDE	60-90 SECS
4	SINGLE-ARM SUSPENDED ROW (P.141)	2-3	8-10	60-90 SECS
5	PRESS-UP (BOSU BALL VARIATION) (P.139)	2-3	8-10	60-90 SECS
6	CALF RAISE + DUMBBELL VARIANT (P.136)	2-3	10-15	30-45 SECS

ADVANCED PROGRAMME

You should undertake this programme if you are a runner with more than 1 year of resistance or core training experience. The exercises are generally more demanding than the intermediate programme and are designed to help you build a high level of muscular strength.

AIM OF PROGRAMME	DEVELOP ADVANCED MUSCULAR STRENGTH AND POWER
DURATION OF PROGRAMME	2-3 TIMES PER WEEK FOR 4-6 WEEKS

	EXERCISE	SETS	REPS	REST
1	HANG POWER CLEAN (P.143)	3-5	3-5	120-180 SECS
2	BACK SQUAT (P.130)	3-4	6-8	120-180 SECS
3	SINGLE-LEG DEADLIFT(P.135)	2-3	6-10	90 SECS
4	SINGLE-ARM SUSPENDED ROW (ROTATION) (P.141)	2-3	6-10	90 SECS
5	PRESS-UP (SINGLE-ARM VARIATION) (P.139)	2-3	6-10	90 SECS
6	ECCENTRIC CALF RAISE (P.137)	2	8-10 EACH SIDE	90 SECS
7	TOE RAISE (P.137)	2	10-15	60-90 SECS

01/ BACK SQUAT

This advanced multi-joint exercise is extremely effective for developing the muscles of your legs for running. A great foundation exercise for building overall power and strength, it is best performed inside a power rack for safety. Be sure to maintain good form to avoid risk of injury.

TARGET MUSCLES

- Gluteals
- Quadriceps
- Hamstrings
- Erector spinae

1 Stand at arms-length in front of a power rack. Take a balanced overhand grip (see p.143) on the bar in the rack. Duck under it, step back, and stand upright, with your feet directly under the bar. Rest it on the upper part of your back.

2 Tensing your abs and glutes, slowly start to descend. Ease your hips back and bend your knees. Keep your feet pointing slightly outwards and ensure that your knees follow the angle of your feet.

3 Continue bending at your knees, easing your hips back until your thighs are parallel to the floor. Your upper body should now be at a 45-degree angle. Slowly reverse the movement to the start position, maintaining tight control.

WARNING!

Don't round your back or lean forwards when performing the squat; this places too much stress on the lower back and can cause injury.

02/ SINGLE LEG SQUAT

Single leg squats work several muscle groups in the legs at the same time as improving core balance. This is an excellent lower-body strength exercise, which is used to enhance leg strength and stability.

Face forwards with a level gaze

Engage your core

1 Stand with your feet hip-width apart and your arms extended directly out in front of you. Bending your right knee, raise your right foot off the ground behind you. Engage your core to stabilize your spine.

Hold your arms in front of you for balance

Keep your hips aligned

2 Bend your left knee and bend forwards from your hips until your upper body is at a 45-degree angle. Bend your right knee and lift your right foot behind you. Reverse the movement and repeat on the other side.

Keep your foot firmly on the floor

TARGET MUSCLES

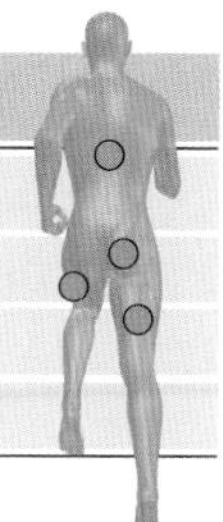

- Gluteals
- Quadriceps
- Hamstrings
- Erector spinae

SQUAT TECHNIQUE DRILL

Correct technique is essential to perform squats effectively and without risk of injury, especially if using weights.

1 Stand with your feet a little wider than hip-width apart. Grasp a broomstick with an overhand grip and rest it on your upper back.

2 Bend your knees and ease your hips back until your thighs are parallel to the floor. Hold briefly, then reverse the movement.

03/ WALKING LUNGE WITH DUMBBELLS

This is an excellent way to mobilize your hips and thighs, testing both your balance and coordination. The dumbbells increase resistance, building strength in your leg muscles and upper body that can increase running speed and diminish the risk of injury.

TARGET MUSCLES

- Gluteals
- Quadriceps
- Hamstrings
- Gastrocnemius
- Soleus

1 Stand with your feet hip-width apart and a good posture. Hold a dumbbell in each hand, with your arms by your sides. Take a step forwards with your left leg, bending at your hips, knees, and ankles. Hold your upper body upright.

2 Drop down until both knees reach a 90-degree angle, with your front knee over the foot and your back knee under your hips. Hold briefly, then raise yourself, step forwards with your right foot, and repeat on the other side.

04/ OVERHEAD WALKING LUNGE WITH DUMBBELLS

This advanced lunge mobilizes your thoracic spine and emphasizes the mobility of your hips and lower back. Adding a weight also works the stabilizers in your shoulders.

1 Stand with your feet hip-width apart and a good posture. Align your shoulders, hips, and knees and keep your spine neutral. Hold the dumbbells overhead.

2 Step forwards with your right leg and bend your knees at a 90-degree angle. Step back into the upright position with your left leg and repeat on the other side.

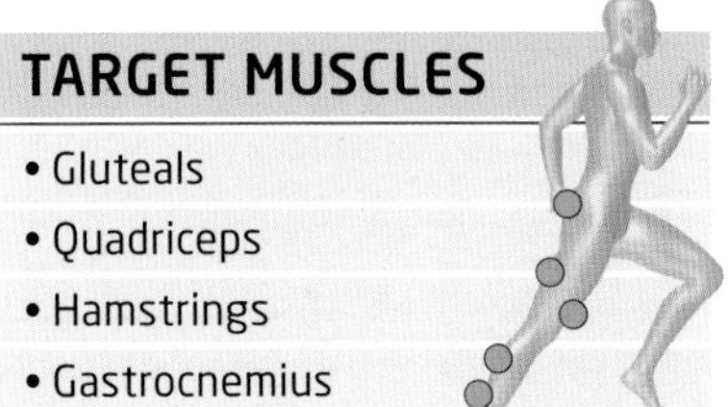

TARGET MUSCLES

- Gluteals
- Quadriceps
- Hamstrings
- Gastrocnemius
- Soleus

05/ WALKING LUNGE WITH ROTATION (MEDICINE BALL)

This is another good mobility exercise for your hips and thighs. It stretches your hip flexors and glutes. The rotation engages your upper body too.

1 Stand with your feet hip-width apart. Hold a medicine ball in front of you. Step forwards into a lunge with your left leg and extend your arms.

2 Rotate your upper body to the right, holding the medicine ball in front of you with extended arms. Hold, then reverse the rotation. Step back into the upright position with your right leg and repeat on the other side.

TARGET MUSCLES

- Gluteals
- Quadriceps
- Hamstrings
- Gastrocnemius
- Soleus
- Obliques

06/ BARBELL DEADLIFT

Sometimes called the "king of exercises" because it is so effective at building leg and back strength, the deadlift can help you to build power for running, enhancing your speed and efficiency. Correct technique is essential to avoid risk of back injury.

TARGET MUSCLES

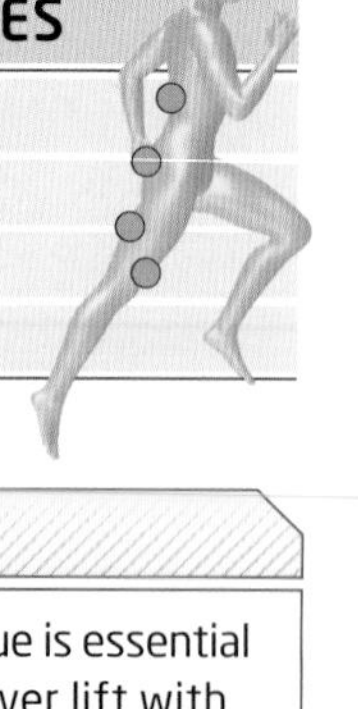

- Gluteals
- Quadriceps
- Hamstrings
- Erector spinae

1 Stand with your feet a little wider than hip-width apart. Following the hip hinge drill (see opposite), squat down so that your feet are under the bar and it rests against your shins. Grip the bar with an overhand grip (see p.143).

WARNING!

Correct lifting technique is essential in this movement. Never lift with your spine flexed forwards: not only will the exercise be ineffective, but you also risk spinal injury.

2 Begin lifting the bar with a long, strong leg push, extending your knees and hips. Your knees should be bent as you lift the bar past them.

3 Continue the lift until you stand up straight with your knees locked, then start to lower the bar back to the start position under tight control. Do not drop the bar.

07/ SINGLE LEG DEADLIFT

This exercise strengthens your lower back and hips, and develops your glutes, thigh muscles, and hamstrings. It also works your core muscles. Performing the exercise with one leg helps to improve balance and stability.

TARGET MUSCLES

- Gluteals
- Quadriceps
- Transverse abdominis
- Hamstrings
- Erector spinae
- Quadratus lumborum
- Obliques

1 Stand with your feet hip-width apart and position your right foot about half a step in front of your left foot. Hold a dumbbell in each hand, using an overhand grip (see p.143).

2 Bend from your waist and push your hips backwards to lower the dumbbells towards your right foot. Bend your right leg and lift your leg leg behind you for balance.

3 Lower the dumbbells down your shin as far as you can. Hold the position, then push your hips forwards to bring your upper body back to the start position and lower your leg. Repeat on the other side.

HIP HINGE DRILL

The hip hinge is an important technique to develop the correct form for a deadlift. It works on efficient hip and spine mechanics. Practise it with a broomstick.

1 Stand with your feet hip-width apart. Hold the broomstick with one hand behind your lower back and the other behind your neck. Bend your legs, push your hips backwards and your chest forwards. Hold, then reverse the movement to the start position.

08/ CALF RAISE

This exercise strengthens your calf muscles and helps to protect your Achilles tendon from injury. You can perform it with the balls of your feet on a low step to allow maximum range of motion.

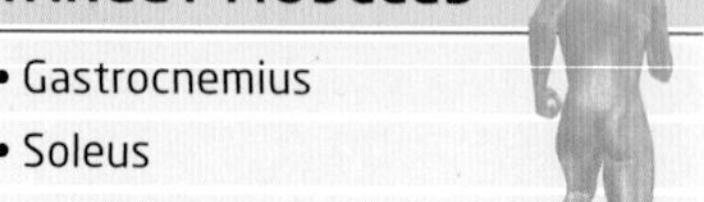

TARGET MUSCLES
- Gastrocnemius
- Soleus
- Achilles tendon

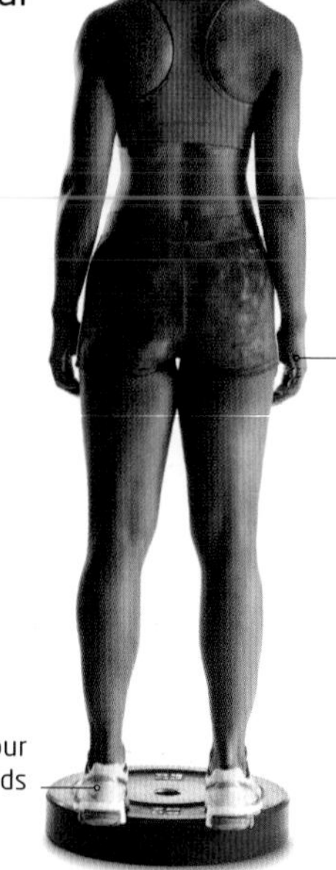

1 Stand with your feet hip-width apart and flat with your heels placed over the edge of a low step. Point your toes straight in front of you to work all your calf muscles equally. Let your arms hang down by your sides.

2 With your head facing forwards, engage your core and raise both your heels up until you are standing on the balls of your feet, with your ankles fully extended. Lower your heels to return to the start position.

Engage your core muscles

Extend your ankles

09/ CALF RAISE WITH DUMBBELLS

A progression of the basic Calf Raise (see above), performing the exercise with dumbbells works your calf muscles harder. You can also perform variations with a barbell or other free weights for increased resistance.

TARGET MUSCLES
- Gastrocnemius
- Soleus
- Achilles tendon

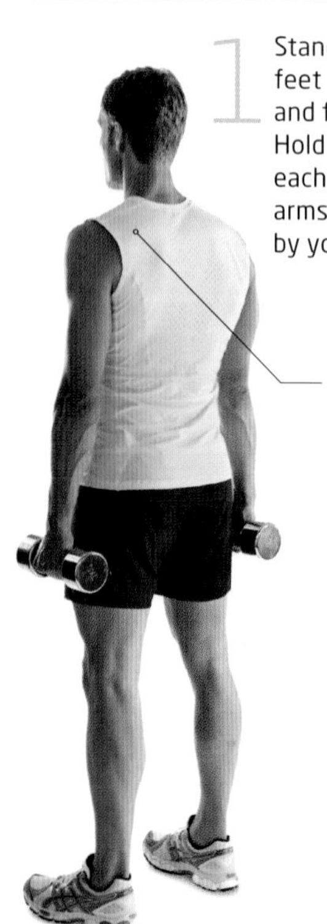

1 Stand with your feet hip-width apart and flat on the floor. Hold a dumbbell in each hand. Let your arms hang straight by your sides.

2 Engage your core. Raise your heels up until you are standing on the balls of your feet, with your ankles extended. Lower your heels to return to the start position.

10/ **ECCENTRIC** CALF RAISE

Another progression of the basic Calf Raise (see left), this move works on the lowering movement to improve eccentric strength. It is effective for the prevention of calf muscle strains and Achilles tendon injuries.

TARGET MUSCLES

- Gastrocnemius
- Soleus
- Achilles tendon

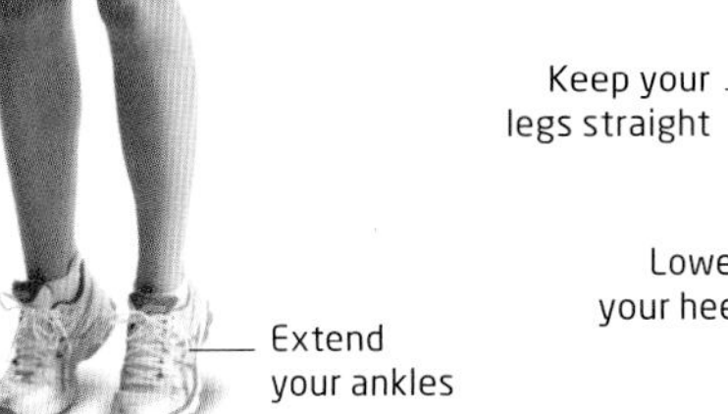

1 Stand with your feet hip-width apart and raise both your heels up until you are standing on the balls of your feet with your ankles fully extended. Shift your weight onto your right foot.

2 Raise your left foot off the ground and bring the heel down, focusing on the lowering phase of the movement. Shift your weight back to both feet. Raise your right foot off the ground and bring the heel down. Return to the start position.

11/ **TOE** RAISE

This exercise improves strength and stability around your feet and ankles. It is a good stretch to perform alongside the calf raises, as it works the opposing shin muscles.

TARGET MUSCLES

- Tibialis anterior
- Foot extensors

1 Sit on a bench with both feet on the ground. Cross your right leg over your left leg. Pass a resistance band under the toe of your left foot and over the toe of your right foot.

2 Stretch the toe of your right foot up against the resistance band, pushing down with your heel. Hold, then relax your toe. Repeat on the other side.

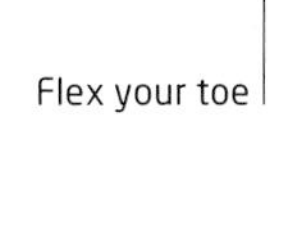

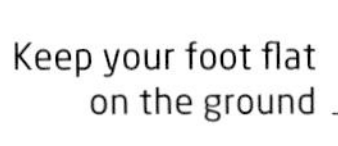

12/ PRESS-UP (FEET)

This is one of the simplest but most effective exercises for developing strength in your shoulders, arms, chest, and core. Its added benefit is that it requires no apparatus to practise – just your own body weight. Keep your body straight throughout.

TARGET MUSCLES

- Pectorals
- Triceps brachii
- Rotator cuff
- Serratus anterior
- Obliques
- Transverse abdominis

1 Lie face-down on the floor, tuck your toes under, position your hands under and a little wider than your shoulders, and raise your body up off the floor, with your arms straight and your fingers extended. Keep your legs, upper body, and head in a straight line throughout.

Engage your core

Keep your head, upper body, and legs in a straight line

Place your hands a little wider than your shoulders

2 Lower your body slowly and under control until your upper body almost touches the floor. Hold the position briefly, then push your upper body up from your elbows until your arms are straight and you are back in the start position.

Push up from your elbows

Keep the angle of your neck constant

Your upper body should almost touch the floor

13/ **PRESS-UP** (KNEES) VARIATION

Support your weight on your knees

1 If you find the Press-Up (Feet; see opposite) too hard at first, support your body weight on your knees, with your arms straight and hands a little wider than your shoulders.

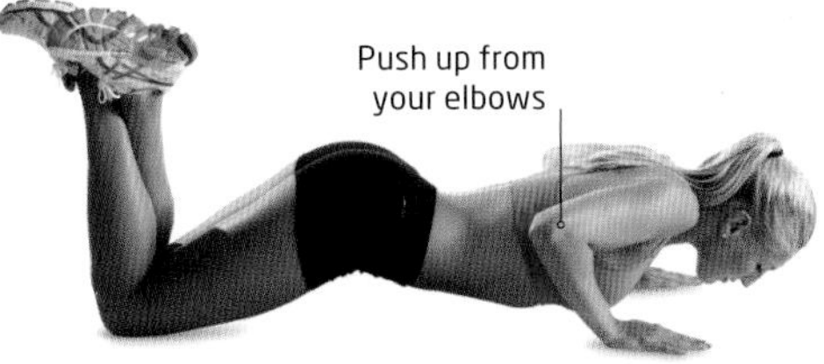

2 Lower your body slowly and under control until your upper body almost touches the floor. Hold briefly, then push up until you are back in the start position.

14/ **BOSU** PRESS-UP VARIATION

1 The Bosu adds instability to the basic Press-Up (Feet; see opposite), engaging the stabilizers of your core. Support your body weight on your toes. Position your hands under and just a little wider than your shoulders on a Bosu balance trainer. Bend your elbows, lowering your body almost to the ground, and push up again as before.

15/ **SINGLE LEG** PRESS-UP VARIATION

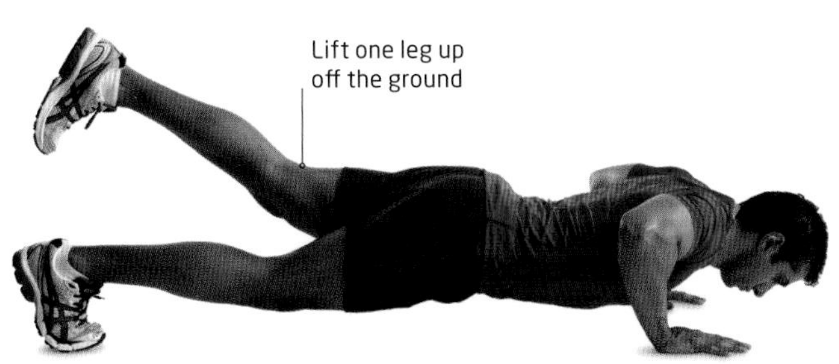

1 The Single Leg Press-Up is a challenging variation on the basic Press-Up (Feet; see opposite), with core stabilizing benefits. Support your body weight on your hands and toes, but raise one leg off the ground. Bend your elbows, lowering your body almost to the ground, and push up again.

16/ **SINGLE ARM** PRESS-UP VARIATION

1 The Single Arm Press-Up is the most challenging variation on the basic Press-Up (Feet; see opposite), working the core by resisting rotation. Place your feet wider than shoulder-width and raise one arm off the ground. Bend your elbow, lowering your body almost to the floor, and push up again.

17/ KETTLEBELL DEADLIFT

The deadlift is the safest way to pick up a kettlebell and is the basis for all kettlebell exercises. It builds leg and back strength. Keep your back straight, bending from your hips to avoid straining your lower back.

TARGET MUSCLES

- Gluteals
- Quadriceps
- Hamstrings
- Erector spinae

1 Stand with your feet shoulder-width apart and the kettlebell between your feet. Bend at your hips and knees, keeping your spine straight, and grip the kettlebell with both hands.

2 Following the hip hinge drill (see p.135), lift from your legs and hips. Lift the kettlebell off the floor and straighten to a standing position. Hold, then lower the kettlebell again under tight control.

18/ KETTLEBELL SWING

This whole-body exercise works the muscles of your glutes, lower back, and thighs. Generate the force of the movement from your hips, rather than trying to lift the weight up using the muscles of your upper body.

TARGET MUSCLES

- Gluteals
- Quadriceps
- Hamstrings
- Erector spinae

Drop your buttocks backwards

1 Stand with your feet a little wider than hip-width apart. Lift the kettlebell using a deadlift (see above), and allow it to hang loosely. Bend your knees and drop your buttocks backwards, leaning your upper body forwards from the hips.

2 Drive forwards with your hips to stand up straight, so that the kettlebell swings forwards and upwards. As it swings back, drop your hips, lean your upper body forwards, and lower it.

19/ **SUSPENDED** ROW (STANDING)

This is an excellent exercise for increasing upper back strength, helping to enhance running posture and breathing control. Walk your feet forwards to increase difficulty.

TARGET MUSCLES

- Trapezius
- Latissimus dorsi
- Biceps brachii
- Obliques
- Transverse abdominis

1 Suspend the straps of a pulley cable at chest height. Stand with your feet hip-width apart. Grasp the pulley handles and lean back so that your arms are fully extended. Keep your head, body, and legs straight.

2 Flex your elbows and pull yourself up. Keep your body straight and your shoulders back. Extend your arms and lower yourself back down to the start position.

20/ **SINGLE ARM** SUSPENDED ROW WITH ROTATION

Performing the Suspended Row with one arm develops your core strength and coordination, while the rotation works on your thoracic mobility and shoulder strength.

TARGET MUSCLES

- Trapezius
- Latissimus dorsi
- Biceps brachii
- Obliques
- Transverse abdominis

1 Start as in the Suspended Row (Standing; see above), but grasp the pulley handle with only your right hand. Flex your elbow and pull yourself up.

2 Extend your right arm and lean back, keeping your body straight. Extend your left arm out to the side and open up your chest. Return to the start position and repeat on the other side.

24/ HANG POWER CLEAN

Though technically difficult, this explosive power exercise is a fantastic all-round performance enhancer. Performed with lighter weights, it also makes an excellent warm-up. It can help runners to increase speeds by building both upper- and lower-body strength.

1 Squat with your feet hip-width apart and take a shoulder-width overhand grip on the bar. Your hips should be higher than your knees, and your shoulders in front of the bar. Lift the bar above your knees and hold it with straight arms, resting gently on your thighs. This is the starting "hang" position for the exercise.

Shrug your shoulders up high

Keep the bar close to your body

Fully extend your body, rising up onto your toes

2 Keeping your arms straight at first, drive your hips towards the bar and explosively straighten your legs to give the bar upwards momentum.

Rotate your arms around the bar

Your toes may leave the floor as you drive up explosively

3 Continue the pull on the bar, giving it as much upwards momentum as possible. As the weight rises, start to dip your body below the bar.

4 As the bar reaches shoulder height, punch your elbows through and catch the bar on the top of your shoulders. Extend your legs and stand up straight.

5 To return to the start position, rotate your wrists and elbows around the bar. Lower it slowly and under control to rest on your thighs and then the floor.

TARGET MUSCLES

- Gluteals
- Quadriceps
- Hamstrings
- Erector spinae
- Trapezius
- Gastrocnemius
- Soleus

GRIPS

When lifting weights, several different grips are commonly used, changing the muscle emphasis of the exercise.

NEUTRAL GRIP
Stand with your hands by your sides and your palms turned in. Grip the bar with your thumbs up.

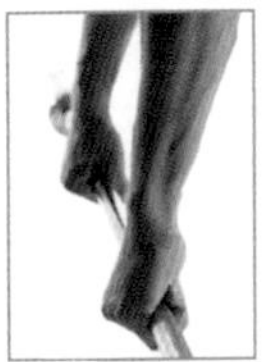

OVERHAND GRIP
Stand with your hands by your sides and your palms facing backwards. Grip the bar from above and lift.

UNDERHAND GRIP
Stand with your hands by your sides and your palms facing forwards. Grip the bar from below and lift.

WARNING!

This is an advanced exercise that places high loads on your lower back, so you should always warm up before attempting it. Maintain good technique and work within your capabilities. Do not pull with your arms first - your hips and legs should do the work.

THE RACE

IF YOU'RE AIMING TO RUN COMPETITIVELY, YOU'LL NEED TO PULL OUT ALL THE STOPS ON THE BIG DAY – THIS CHAPTER SHOWS YOU HOW. FROM MAKING SURE THAT YOU'RE AT YOUR MENTAL AND PHYSICAL PEAK, TO GIVING YOURSELF THE BEST CHANCE BY FUELLING YOUR BODY CORRECTLY, YOUR TRAINING WILL PAY OFF ONLY WITH A WELL-PLANNED RACE STRATEGY.

TAPER YOUR TRAINING

You might think that some last-minute hard training would be good race preparation, but in fact you should peak two to three weeks before a race. After that, you should reduce your training load and optimize your nutrition. Known as tapering, this will ensure that you are in the best possible shape for the race.

REASONS TO TAPER

- Reduces training fatigue
- Allows muscle repair
- Stores up glycogen in muscles
- Increases aerobic capacity by raising number of red blood cells
- Strengthens immune system by increasing white blood cell count
- Focuses your mind
- Reduces the risk of injury

Q WHY DO I NEED TO TAPER?

A Tapering can feel a little counter-intuitive – many runners worry that they will lose fitness and decrease their race speed if they don't train hard. In fact, you could stop training completely two weeks before a race without adversely affecting your performance. Reducing your training in the build-up to the event allows your body and mind time to recover from your training programme, ensuring that you feel fresh for the race. Tapering also gives your muscles time to build up glycogen stores as well as repair themselves, so you are less likely to pick up last-minute injuries. You can reverse the taper after the race to build up your training again.

Q HOW CAN I TAPER MY PROGRAMME?

A A tried-and-tested tapering method is to reduce your training volume gradually by about 60 per cent or more, over a period of up to three weeks (see opposite). You should keep the intensity of your training high in these sessions to stay sharp, but reduce the frequency of your training by up to 20 per cent to help your recovery time. There are other ways to taper too – you could reduce the number of training sessions you do, the intensity of your workouts, the amount of training performed in a session, or the length of time that you train. As you become more experienced, you will find discover your own optimum taper technique.

Q SHOULD I EAT LESS WHEN I'M TAPERING?

A No, even though your training volume decreases, you should continue with your normal diet (see pp.50–53). The calories that you would usually burn in training will be stored as extra glycogen and the nutrients will be used by the body to build up other systems, such as the blood cell volume (see box, left). Effective tapering almost doubles your glycogen stores, thereby providing you with enough fuel for your run. If you will be running for longer than 90 minutes, you need to saturate your muscles with carbohydrates just before the race (see carb-loading, p.53).

BOOSTING YOUR BLOOD

Tapering leads to an increase in the number of new red blood cells and an increase in the volume of the existing cells. The haemoglobin in red blood cells carries oxygen around the body so an increase in the number and volume of cells raises your aerobic capacity. White blood cell count is also increased, which helps reduce inflammation and boosts immunity therefore decreasing the chance of any unwanted injury or illness leading up to the big race.

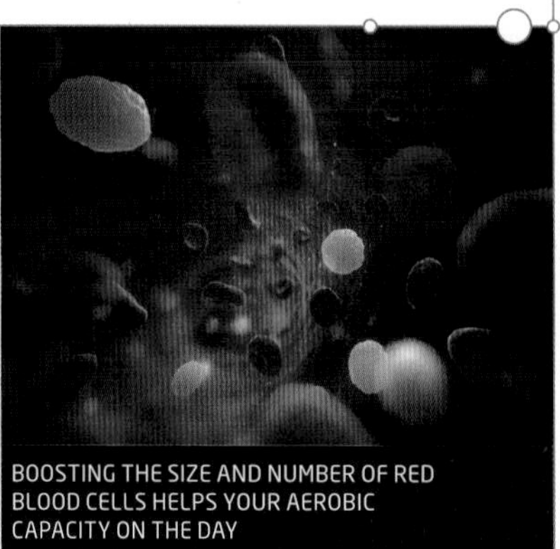

BOOSTING THE SIZE AND NUMBER OF RED BLOOD CELLS HELPS YOUR AEROBIC CAPACITY ON THE DAY

INFO DASHBOARD

TAPERING

The amount of tapering you should introduce into your training depends on the distance of your race – the further the race, the greater the reduction in training.

GET INTO THE MIND ZONE

Your psychological approach to a race is just as important as meticulously following your training schedule and nutrition programme. Pre-race anxiety is very common, but channelling it positively into your performance can help focus your mind and enable your body to reach its optimum performance.

PRE-RACE CHECKLIST

- Make sure you have your running kit and race documents
- Plan your race strategy, nutrition, and hydration
- Confirm your travel arrangements and the race start time. If the race is over two hours from home, stay nearby overnight
- Try to relax and have a good night's sleep before the race

YOUR ROUTE TO SUCCESS »

BE POSITIVE

The key to a good race is a positive mental attitude, according to most sports psychologists. If you enter a race alongside someone of a similar level, who has followed the same training, nutrition, and recovery schedule, the runner who has also prepared mentally will perform better. You should start every race feeling confident that you will achieve your goals.

SET GOALS

Setting yourself race goals will help focus your mind on the task ahead and guide your performance during the race. If you are a beginner, just finishing the race could be your primary goal, but you still need to work out how you will achieve that. Set your goals by focusing on elements that you can control, such as your pace. Setting a target finish time is a great way to motivate yourself and will also help you work out your race strategy (see pp.154-55). Remember that during the race your performance can also be affected by factors such as the weather, which are beyond your control. If you acknowledge that fact and you are well prepared, then these elements won't throw you off course.

BE CONSISTENT

Don't be tempted to change anything before your race. Keep your training consistent, plan your tapering programme (see pp.146-47), and stick to your regular diet (see pp.50-53) and sleep patterns. Avoid testing out new running clothing or footwear – a marathon is no time to break in new trainers. Any changes to your normal routine could actually undo all your hard work in training, or at least have an adverse effect on your performance.

INFO DASHBOARD

WHILE YOU SLEEP
Your body needs at least 7½ hours of uninterrupted sleep a night, and ideally up to 9 hours in the tapering phase. The body goes through several different sleep stages. During stages three and four it releases a hormone that repairs muscle tissue and speeds recovery from injury.

100% SLEEP CYCLE

STAGE 1
4–5%
Light sleep. Muscle activity slows down. Occasional muscle twitching

STAGE 2
45–55%
Breathing pattern and heart rate slow down. Slight decrease in body temperature

STAGE 3
4–6%
Deep sleep begins. Brain begins to generate slow delta waves

STAGE 4
12–16%
Very deep sleep. Rhythmic breathing. Limited muscle activity. Brain produces delta waves

STAGE 5
20–25%
Rapid eye movement. Brainwaves speed up and dreaming occurs. Muscles relax and heart rate increases. Breathing is rapid and shallow

RESEARCH THE COURSE

Familiarize yourself with the course route and terrain so that you know what is coming throughout the race. This can really boost your confidence, which is especially helpful during the later stages of the race when physical and mental fatigue set in. Try identifying some key landmarks along the route that you can use to count yourself towards the finish line.

For races of up to 10k (6.2 miles), walk or cycle the whole course a few days beforehand. For longer distances, such as a half-marathon or marathon, it's best to cover just the last 10k (6.2 miles). Never walk or drive the whole of a marathon course – the realization of just how long it is can have a negative effect on your mental preparation. If you don't live near enough to the race course to be able to walk all or part of it, study a map or research online.

GET PLENTY OF SLEEP

Rest and relaxation are key to performance and a positive mental attitude. In particular, make sure that you get enough sleep. In the two weeks leading up to the race, you should aim for between 7½ and 9 hours sleep per night. Not only does this help your mental approach, but the body also repairs itself while you sleep (see above).

CONTROL YOUR NERVES

Even the most experienced runners feel nervous before a race. If you accept that this is part of the competition experience, then you can feed off the anxiety to boost your performance - learn to recognise the feeling of adrenaline, and channel it towards the finish line. You can also try repeating a mantra to yourself, or doing breathing exercises before the race.

If you are in control of your nerves, you are less likely to let uncontrollables throw you off your plan, or to be wound up if they do. Above all, knowing that you have trained well, fuelled efficiently, and planned your race strategically should give you confidence that you can reach your goals. Be positive – you have completed your training and are ready for the big race.

FUEL YOUR PERFORMANCE

Fuelling your body is one of the most important parts of your race preparation. What you eat, how much you eat, and when you eat it can make a big difference to your performance on the day. Experiment with what suits you during your training.

TRAINED ATHLETES STORE UP TO 720G (23OZ) OF CARBS IN THEIR MUSCLES. NON-ATHLETES ONLY STORE 280G (10OZ)

Q WHY SHOULD I EAT BEFORE A RACE?

A Your body needs energy to function and it gets this from carbohydrates (see p.53). When you run, you are pushing your body to its limits and burning energy quickly. Eating before a race has two important functions:

ENERGY GELS

During running, your body's primary fuel source is carbohydrate, stored in the muscles as glycogen (see p.51). However, you can only store a limited amount, so on longer races you may need to replenish – energy gels are designed to do just this. However, while they can help refuel you, they are not a direct replacement for glycogen stored in your muscles, as this has already been digested – when you consume a gel, most of the glucose will go directly to your blood, as your stomach takes time to digest it. As a result, you will "feel" more energized as your brain responds to glucose in the blood. However, your muscles may remain tired while you digest a proportion of the carbohydrates from the gel. For best results, take gels with water – never on their own or with sports drinks.

1. FUELLING YOUR MUSCLES
Eating enough carbohydrates in the days before a race builds up stores of glycogen in the muscles. Eating easily digested food hours before a race adds to this. If you don't eat enough, your blood sugar levels will fall too early and your body will start to convert its stored glycogen in order to meet energy demands. This can lead to extreme fatigue, known as "hitting the wall". If you don't replenish supplies, you might not be able to finish the race. Energy gels can help with this (see box, left).

2. FUELLING YOUR BRAIN
Low glycogen levels can also adversely affect your brain. You will start to feel weak, dizzy, and unable to focus on running – known by runners as "brain drain".

Q WHAT FOODS SHOULD I BE EATING?

A Eat high-starch, low-fat foods such as bread, pasta, or bagels. Avoid high-fat proteins, such as cheese and red meat, as these take a long time to digest, so your body won't feel the benefit until after the race. Choose easily digestible foods that have formed part of your nutrition plan during training - the stress of trying new foods can lead to stomach cramps.

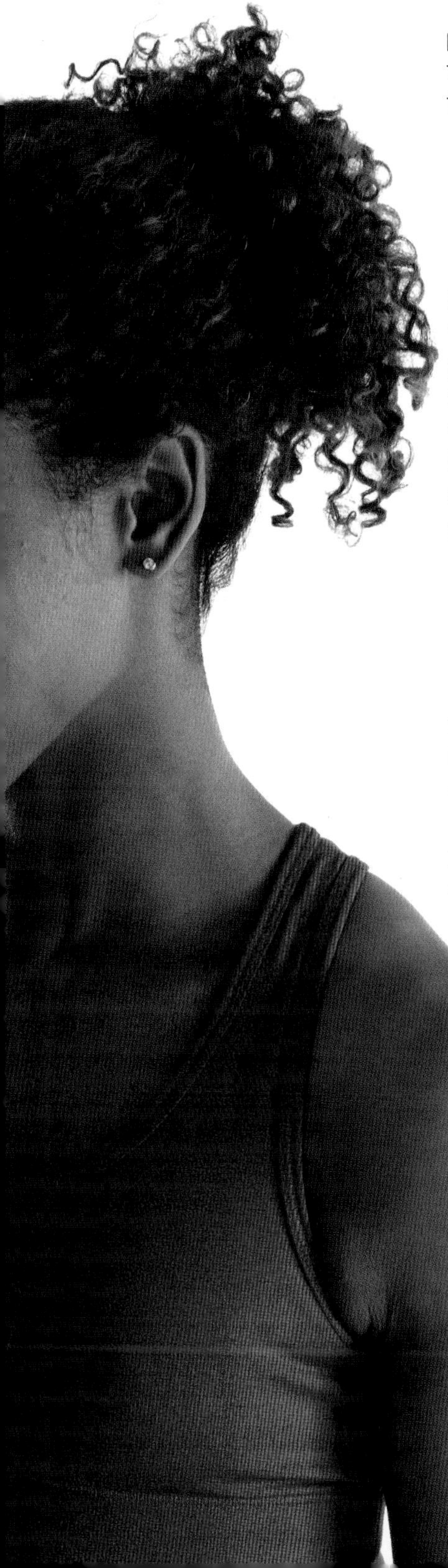

Q HOW MUCH SHOULD I EAT BEFORE A RACE?

A This can vary according to your age, sex, and fitness level, as well as the race distance. Your individual metabolism and preferences will also be a factor. See pp.50-53 for advice on nutrition and the basics of carb-loading. Make sure that you experiment with your optimum portion size during training.

Q WHEN IS THE BEST TIME TO EAT?

A This depends on what time your race starts. Never eat a big meal close to the start time. During a race your muscles will be working at near maximum capacity. Blood needs to prioritize supplying your muscles with glucose and oxygen, and so your body will reduce the blood flow to your stomach by up to 80 per cent. As a result, any food in the stomach is digested very slowly, and your body won't benefit from the nutrients.

INFO DASHBOARD

FUELLING YOUR RACE

The guide below is for races starting in the late morning, afternoon, or evening. For an early morning race you should eat a high-carbohydrate meal the night before and then a small, high-carbohydrate breakfast 2-4 hours before the race. This will top up your glycogen stores, which will have depleted slightly while you slept.

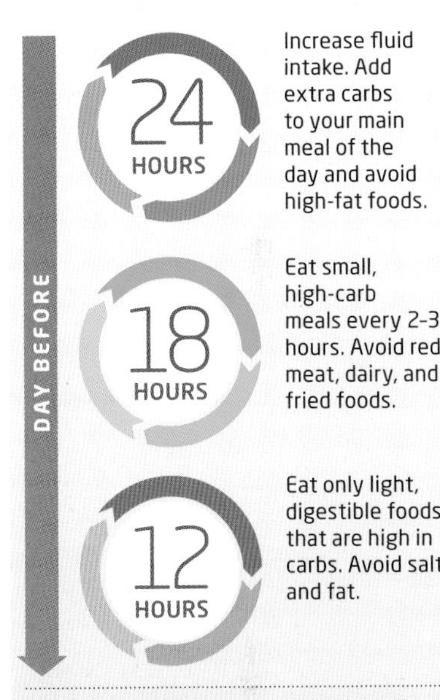

Increase fluid intake. Add extra carbs to your main meal of the day and avoid high-fat foods.

Eat small, high-carb meals every 2-3 hours. Avoid red meat, dairy, and fried foods.

Eat only light, digestible foods that are high in carbs. Avoid salt and fat.

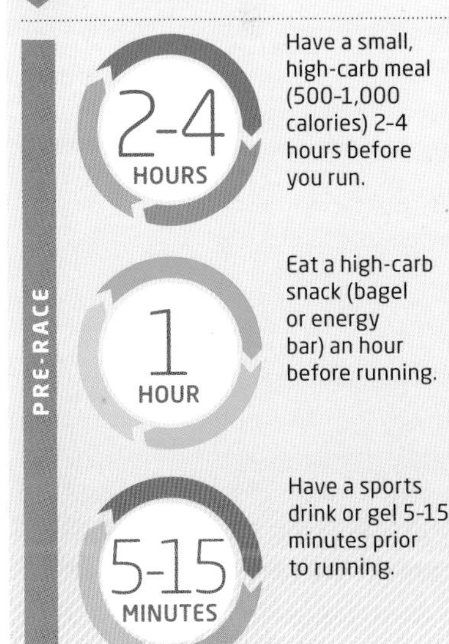

Have a small, high-carb meal (500-1,000 calories) 2-4 hours before you run.

Eat a high-carb snack (bagel or energy bar) an hour before running.

Have a sports drink or gel 5-15 minutes prior to running.

BOOST YOUR FLUID LEVELS

Hydration is an essential part of your race strategy. Fluid and body salts are lost through sweating and need to be replaced – start the race with your fluid levels topped up, and maintain them throughout. Staying properly hydrated during your run will reduce the strain on your body and lower your perception of exertion.

HYDRATE TO WIN

You will be pushing your body to its limits during the race, so you need all the help you can get. Staying hydrated will help your body work at maximum efficiency and is an easy and effective way to get the most out of your performance. Your water intake affects many of the physical processes that enable you to compete at your best: sweating helps stabilize body temperature, while drinking enough fluid also helps balance your blood plasma volume. Blood plasma is vital for transporting nutrients to your muscles as they work, and moving waste products such as lactic acid away from them. Both your physical performance and mental clarity will be detrimentally affected as soon as you start to become dehydrated. Experiment with your fluid intake during training (see pp.54–55), so that you are familiar with your body's needs and know how to hydrate effectively during your race.

TOO LITTLE OR TOO MUCH

If you don't replace fluids lost through sweat, your blood thickens, reducing your heart's efficiency, and increasing the time it takes for oxygen to be delivered to cells. This is known as **hypernatraemia**. It raises your body temperature and increases the concentration of salts in the blood, causing dehydration.

Rarely, drinking too much fluid too quickly can over-dilute your blood. This is called **hyponatraemia**, and can lead to dizziness, confusion, and, in severe cases, seizures and respiratory failure. If you follow a good race hydration strategy, the chances of either occurring are small.

PICKING UP DRINKS FROM THE LEFT DURING A RUN CAN BE QUICKER, AS MOST PEOPLE GO TO THE RIGHT

INFO DASHBOARD

RACE HYDRATION

Runners' hydration needs vary, so use this chart below as a guide. It is best to drink water before a race, but sports drinks can be better during and after a race as they also replace glucose and body salts. If you pick up a drink while running, it is best to drink it in small sips, slow to a walk for a few steps, and don't consume more than the recommended amounts to avoid excess fluid causing discomfort in your stomach, or hyponatraemia (see box above). Don't forget that it is equally important to replace lost fluid at the end of the race.

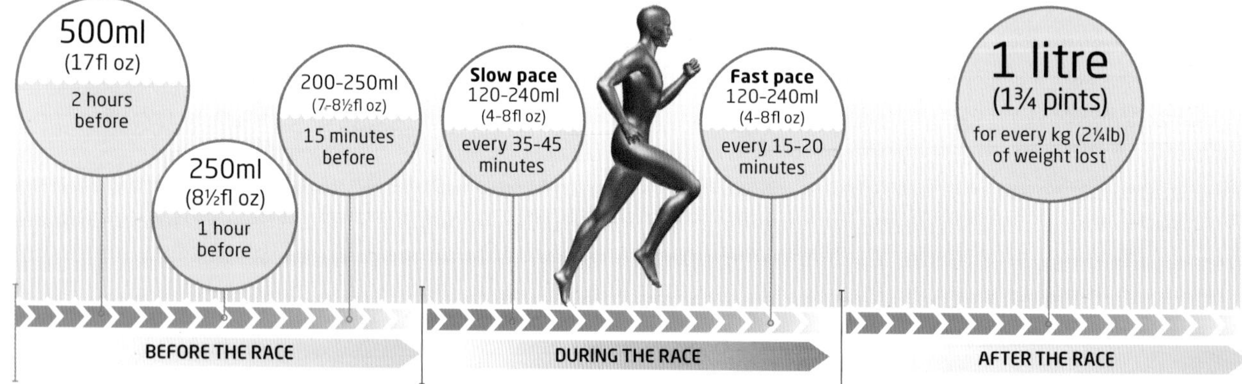

YOUR ROUTE TO SUCCESS »

BEFORE THE RACE

You need to be properly hydrated before you run. Runners who have sufficient fluid intake before a race will have lower heart rates and body temperatures than those who are not adequately hydrated. Drinking water around 2 hours before your race will generally ensure you are properly hydrated – see chart, opposite. If you do not feel the need to urinate within an hour of this, then you can top up with additional liquid. About 15 minutes before the start, try to consume some more water to boost levels.

DURING THE RACE

Feeling thirsty is the brain's way of telling you that you are already dehydrated and must drink immediately. So if you wait until you feel thirsty, it will be too late. Fluid needs vary from runner to runner, and are also determined by weather conditions and the amount you sweat, but it is vital to drink enough on runs over 10km (6 miles), or if it is very hot. Both water and sports drinks (hypotonic or isotonic) can be drunk while running. Sports (or energy) gels are a good way of maintaining blood-sugar levels, but need to be washed down with water.

AFTER THE RACE

When restoring your hydration levels after a race, it is important to replace the body's electrolytes (salts and glucose) too, as they regulate your hydration levels. Sports drinks (see p.54) can help with this: isotonic drinks contain the same levels of salts and glucose as your body while hypertonic drinks have a higher concentration, so should not be drunk during a run but are ideal for drinking afterwards. If you are drinking water, then try to eat some easily digestible source of carbohydrate, such as a banana, or take a sports glucose tablet.

TACTICS FOR THE RACE DAY

You've spent weeks training hard, eating well, and mentally preparing for the big race. Now you need to make sure that all your hard work is rewarded on the day. The best way to achieve this is to plan a sensible, achievable strategy and pace, then follow it during the race.

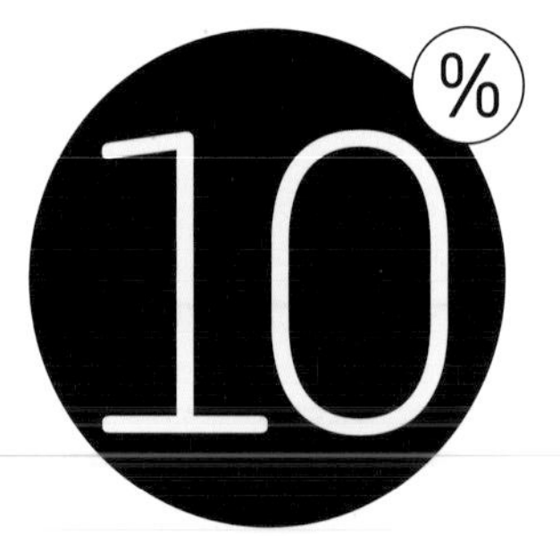

ESTIMATED INCREASE IN THE SUCCESS RATE OF SPORTING COMPETITORS WHO WEAR RED

YOUR ROUTE TO SUCCESS »

PLAN YOUR STRATEGY

Decide how to approach the race. The three most common tactical strategies are: try to run against yourself, aiming to beat your previous best; set yourself a time target, then run against the clock; or run against runners of a similar ability and try to beat them. If you choose either of the first two options, you are in complete control of your race strategy. The third option can be very motivating, but it is also risky as it depends on the pace and performance of others, so you are not in control.

SET YOUR PACE

Working out your pace, setting a target, and then sticking to it is a smart way to ensure that you achieve your planned race time, as it will help you conserve your energy. For example, running too fast, too soon, can lead to a build-up of lactic acid in the muscles and a sense of fatigue before you've even had a chance to get into your stride. Use the formula opposite to calculate your pace per km/mile over the race distance, then use your GPS watch or stopwatch to measure it during the race. When planning your race pace, always take into account the course terrain and set a realistic pace – remember you will run slower during uphill sections, but also faster on the downhill sections. Some larger races have official event runners who run at a set pace, which can help you stick to your plan.

A GOOD START

Getting off to a good start is important, but that doesn't mean it has to be a quick one. Do your warm-up programme before you get to the start line so that your muscles and joints are ready for the race (see pp.56–57). Then focus on starting at a steady pace from a good position. Aim to set off with runners slightly above your ability; this can be very motivating and will also help you keep up the necessary race pace. If you start with slower runners, you may get blocked in or held up during the race.

INFO DASHBOARD

CALCULATING YOUR RUNNING PACE

Knowing your current running pace is the first step to making yourself a more efficient and successful runner. Whether you are training with a specific goal in mind - for example, beating your previous best - or running your first race, it is essential to work out what pace you are able to run at. You will need two pieces of information to calculate your pace: the distance of the run and the time it takes you to complete it.

1. Choose a route and measure it using a map, GPS monitor, or milometer.
2. Go for the run and time yourself accurately with a stopwatch or GPS watch.
3. Divide your time by the distance of the route.

$$\frac{\text{TIME}}{\text{DISTANCE}} = \frac{\text{RUN}}{\text{RATE}}$$

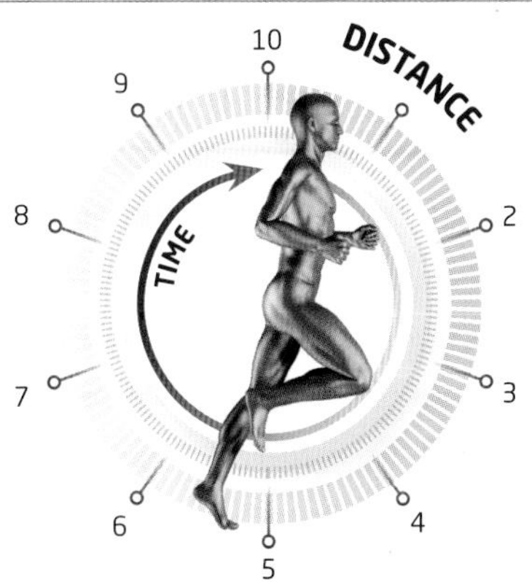

MOST IMPORTANT MILES

The middle section of the race can be the toughest. This is when physical and mental fatigue set in and you might start to question your race strategy and ask yourself negative questions: Have I trained enough? Can I keep this pace up? Should I be speeding up, slowing down, or overtaking the person in front of me? This is where your mental preparation comes into its own. Put the doubts out of your mind: believe in your training, maintain your target pace, and stick to your strategy. Use the landmarks you identified when studying the course to see how far you are progressing.

A STRONG FINISH

If you follow your strategy, you should be in good shape as you approach the finish. If you have paced yourself correctly, you might even have enough left in the tank for a strong finish. Don't save energy for the end, as there's nothing more frustrating than finishing a race with energy left over that you feel you could have used during the race.

Remember that the race finishes as you cross the line, not before, so don't slow down as you approach the end; vital seconds will be added to your time. If you have been timing yourself, don't worry about stopping your watch immediately. A GPS watch can give you an accurate time, but your race chip will have recorded an official race time.

RUN A SMART RACE

DO »

- Plan your strategy in advance
- Wear broken-in shoes
- Have a hydration plan
- Get a good start position
- Pace yourself during the race
- Stick to your strategy
- Trust your training
- Finish fast if you can

DON'T »

- Run without any strategy or race plan
- Go too fast at the start of the race
- Exceed your planned race pace
- Get blocked in by slower runners
- Change your strategy during the race
- Run with a friend, staying at his or her pace
- Slow down before the finish line

AFTER THE BIG RACE

You did it. Your hard work paid off and you crossed the finish line. Your body aches and you're mentally exhausted, but you've achieved your goal. So, what happens now? Don't stop just yet. It's important to do your cool-down, replenish your body's supplies, and give yourself some recovery time.

GLYCAEMIC WINDOW: **15-30 MINS** AFTER THE RACE. USE THIS TIME TO EAT HIGH GLYCAEMIC INDEX FOODS THAT ARE EASILY ABSORBED

YOUR ROUTE TO SUCCESS »

HELP YOUR RECOVERY

As soon as you finish the race you might be tempted to sit down, but you must keep moving for just a little while longer. Follow your cool-down programme (see pp.64-67) to stretch out your tired muscles and reduce potential post-race stiffness. After that a shower and fresh clothes will also help your body and mind to begin their recovery. Then you can relax and finally enjoy a well-deserved feeling of accomplishment.

REHYDRATE AND REFUEL

Even if you keep your hydration and nutrition levels topped up during a race, you will still deplete your reserves. It is very important to start rehydration and refuelling as soon as possible, during what is known as the glycaemic window (see above).

A sports drink or some water with a banana or sports gel within 15 minutes of finishing will start the refuelling process. You will need to drink about 1 litre (1.8 pints) of fluid for every 1kg (2.2lb) of body weight lost (see p.153).

Start to restore your muscle glycogen levels over the next four to five hours by consuming small carbohydrate snacks. Eat a little protein, too - around a third as much - as this stimulates the action of insulin, the hormone that converts the glucose in carbohydrates into a form that can be picked up by the blood and used by the body.

REST TO REPAIR

After a race you deserve a break from running, and your body needs it. You should avoid exercise for at least two days to allow your muscles time to begin to repair themselves, your body time to replenish its energy stores, and to reduce your chance of injury or illness. You will not lose fitness by resting. In fact, if you run with muscle pain or stiffness, it can lead to poor biomechanics, which will not only affect your technique but may cause injury.

RECOVERY AND REBOOT PROGRAMME (POST-MARATHON)

WEEK PROGRAMME	DAY-BY-DAY PROGRAMME						
	1	2	3	4	5	6	7
1	RACE DAY	WALK 20 MINS	REST	SWIM 20-30 MINS	BIKE 30-40 MINS	REST	WALK 30 MINS
2	JOG 15 MINS	SWIM 30-40 MINS	REST	BIKE 40 MINS	REST	JOG 20 MINS	REST
3	CORE TRAINING	JOG 20 MINS	RESISTANCE TRAINING	REST	CORE TRAINING	REST	JOG 25 MINS
4	RESISTANCE TRAINING	JOG 20 MINS	CORE TRAINING	RESISTANCE TRAINING	REST	JOG 25 MINS	REST
5	CORE TRAINING	JOG 30 MINS	RESISTANCE TRAINING	REST	CORE TRAINING	JOG 30 MINS	REST
6	RESISTANCE TRAINING	JOG 35 MINS	CORE TRAINING	RESISTANCE TRAINING	REST	JOG 40 MINS	REST
7	CORE TRAINING	JOG 45 MINS	RESISTANCE TRAINING	REST	CORE TRAINING	JOG 50 MINS	REST

REBUILD TRAINING GRADUALLY

You might be keen to get straight back into training to build on your performance, but you need to listen to your body. The best way to start training again is to reverse your taper programme (pp.146–47) and build up gradually. The length of this "rest" period will depend on the length of your race. Some people recommend taking one easy, or recovery, day for every 1.6km (1 mile) of your race. During the first week, you should run only at a low intensity, if at all. Build some non-weight-bearing exercises such as swimming and cycling into your programme. They place less stress on your joints, while at the same time enabling your muscles to start working again safely. Swimming in a heated pool will also help to relax your tired muscles. Use the chart above as a guide to rebuilding your training programme over the next few weeks, or try one of the four-week recovery programmes on pp.108-109 before starting to build up to your choice of training regime again. Keep your heart rate at 50-60 per cent during recovery training – any runs or jogs should be done at an easy pace.

INFO DASHBOARD

POST-RACE CARBOHYDRATES

This chart shows the average amount of carbohydrate found in one serving of effective post-race foods. Have them with some protein: the ideal ratio of carbohydrate to protein in a post-race meal is 3:1.

225G (8OZ) PORRIDGE: 108G (4OZ)

112G (4OZ) PRUNES: 49G (1½OZ)

112G (4OZ) DRIED APRICOTS: 36G (1¼OZ)

LARGE BANANA: 31G (1OZ)

FIG ROLL: 12G (½OZ)

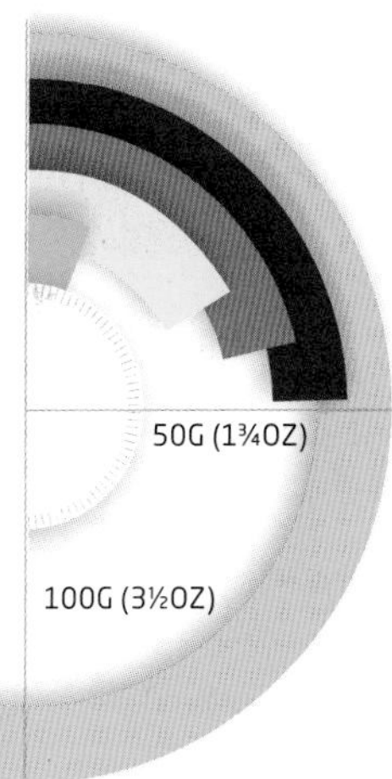

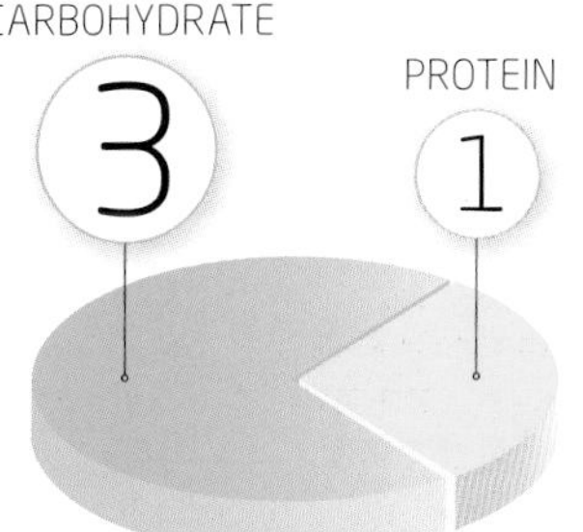

ESSENTIAL MAINTENANCE

RUNNING IS AN INTENSIVE, HIGH-IMPACT SPORT, AND RUNNERS' INJURIES ARE ALL TOO COMMON – TAKING CARE OF YOUR BODY SHOULD BE A HIGH PRIORITY. THIS CHAPTER GIVES YOU ADVICE ON THE BEST WAYS TO AVOID HURTING YOURSELF, AND INFORMATION ON HOW TO DEAL WITH A SELECTION OF COMMON RUNNERS' COMPLAINTS AND INJURIES.

AVOIDING INJURY

The repetitive nature of running, and the high impact of the forces placed upon the body, means that runners are prone to a range of injuries. Most result from lack of preparation, poor technique, or overtraining. You can reduce your risk significantly by looking after your body.

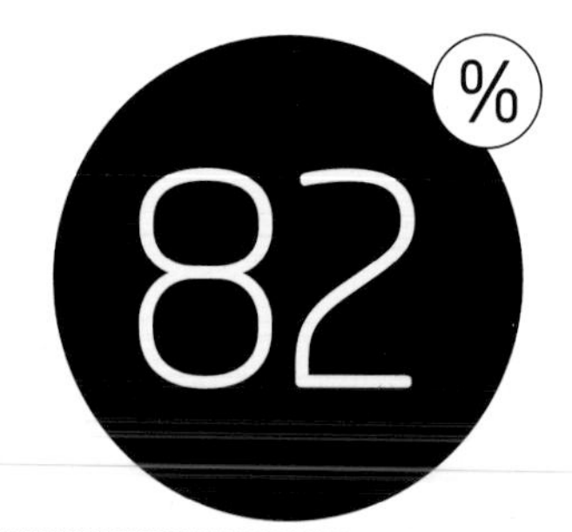

THE PERCENTAGE OF RUNNERS WHO WILL SUFFER AN INJURY AS A RESULT OF OVERTRAINING

YOUR ROUTE TO SUCCESS »

PREPARE YOURSELF

Wear shoes designed for running (see pp.46–47) and make sure that your clothing is comfortable, unrestrictive, and appropriate to the weather conditions; keep warm in winter and cool in summer (see pp.48–49). Keep your skin moisturized in winter to prevent dry skin and chapped lips, and wear sunscreen in summer to protect against the UVA and UVB rays that cause sunburn (p.173).

Complete a thorough warm-up before every run to prepare your body for exercise, and a cool-down afterwards to help you recover (see pp.60–67). You can also use the foam roller exercises before or after a run to loosen tight muscles or help reduce physical imbalances (see pp.164–69).

FUEL AND HYDRATE

Good nutrition plays a major role in preparing your body for sport and in recovery afterwards (see pp.50–53). Before a run, eat foods rich in complex and simple carbohydrates that provide the energy to fuel your actvity. Don't overload on foods too close to a run because of the risk of nausea and cramp: eat a light snack one to two hours before you set out. Within 30 minutes of completing a run, eat a meal made up of a 3:1 ratio of carbohydrates to protein to aid recuperation. Recovery supplements can also be used to boost energy levels.

Fluid intake is equally important before, during, and after your run, to prevent dehydration (see pp.54–55), cramps, and possible heat exhaustion (see p.171). Make sure you drink enough water in the few hours before a run. After a run, drink either water containing mineral replacements or a sports drink (see p.54) to replace the fluids and body salts lost through sweating.

BUILD UP GRADUALLY

Doing too much, too often, too soon is a sure way to sustain an injury. Plan a training regime that consists of both hard, easy, and rest days (see pp.86–87). Whatever your level of fitness, don't increase your training by more than five to 10 per cent a week. In addition, always start an activity off gradually and ease yourself into it to prevent sudden and excessive stresses being placed on your body.

Keep your training log up-to-date and describe how hard or how easy each activity felt (see pp.92–93). Balance high-impact running with low-impact cross-training (see pp.82–83) that strengthens your non-running muscles and allows your running muscles to rest. The combination helps you build your all-round fitness.

INFO DASHBOARD

ACTIVITIES THAT REDUCE RISK OF INJURY

If you look after your body and prepare for exercise, you are less likely to be injured and more likely to achieve your training goals. There are many low-impact non-running activites that can strengthen your muscles, tendons, ligaments and joints, keep your body balanced, and build aerobic fitness.

ACTIVITY	BENEFIT FOR THE BODY
Warm-up sessions	Prepares body for exercise, prevents sudden and excessive stresses on the muscles and joints (see pp.60-63)
Strength and core training	Corrects muscular imbalances, aligns the spine, increases the strength and stability of major joints (see pp.112-43)
Stretching and mobility exercises	Maintains flexibility and range of movement in major muscle groups; reduces risk of muscle, tendon, and ligament injuries (see pp.58-67)
Sports massage or self-massage with foam rollers	Loosens tight muscles, preventing imbalances that result in injury (see pp.164-69)
Low-impact sport (swimming, cycling, and rowing)	Builds aerobic fitness, strengthens muscles, allows muscles and joints to recover from high-impact running sessions (see pp.82-83)
Cool-down sessions	Prevents muscle soreness, improves flexibility, and aids recovery (see pp.64-67)

WATCH YOUR TECHNIQUE

Good posture is vital for runners. Bad posture can lead to poor technique – a major cause of injury as it places increased stress on your back, hips, knees, ankles, and feet. Skipping with a rope is a great way to practice maintaining an upright posture (and it helps cardiovascular fitness).

The wrong stride length can also lead to injury. Over-striding places unwanted stress on your joints (see pp.36–37) and over time can alter your running mechanics, which leads to overuse injuries.

Regular road running unbalances the body as roads are cambered (curved), which places stress on one side of the body. Some road running is unavoidable, and concrete is the most unforgiving surface (tarmac is better). Help posture by interspersing road running with training on softer level surfaces such as cycle paths, dirt tracks, and grass.

RECOVERY IS KEY

Making time for rest within your training programme is just as important as the training itself. You should never run every day, as the repetitive motion of running places physical stress upon the body, which leads to minor tissue damage. Rest days allow your body to recover and repair itself; without them, the risk of injury is increased.

Non-running activities such as swimming and cycling also allow your body to recover from the stresses of running. Core and resistance excercises are an important and often overlooked aspect of training (see pp.112–43).

Muscles that become tight or imbalanced through insufficient recovery time will not function as well as required on a run, which puts extra stress on your body. Regular stretching and mobility exercises help maintain flexibility. Massage will also reduce muscle tightness, and can even identify and correct areas of imbalance before they lead to injury.

LISTEN TO YOUR BODY

Pain is your body's way of telling you that something is wrong. Never try to "run on" through aches and pains, however slight. Depending on the level of discomfort, you may need to reduce your training load, or stop altogether for a few days. Apply the RICE treatment (see p.165) to reduce swelling: rest the injured area and put an ice pack on it for at least 10 minutes every two hours and if necessary support it with a compression bandage. Restart training gradually – if you rush it, a minor injury can become a long-term problem. If in doubt, consult a medical professional for a diagnosis (see p.165).

LOOK AFTER YOUR FEET

Foot care is very important for runners. Your feet absorb forces of several times your body weight as you run (see pp.30–33). This repetitive load causes a range of foot complaints, and it can affect other parts of the body further up the kinetic chain – the ankles, knees, hips, and lower back.

TOO SMALL OR TOO BIG?

Check every so often that your shoes fit, as feet can expand as much as two sizes if you run a lot.

- Shoes that are too small can cause bunions, corns, runner's toe, numbness, or pins and needles (see pp.170–71).
- Shoes that are too big can cause friction that results in blisters and calluses (see pp.170), and plantar fasciitis (see p.182).

YOUR ROUTE TO SUCCESS »

CHOOSE THE RIGHT SHOES

Foot care starts with the correct footwear. Running in ill-fitting shoes is a major cause of foot complaints and other injuries. Wearing properly-fitted shoes designed for running (see pp.46–47) significantly reduces the risk of problems with your feet. Ask for your feet to be measured every time you buy new shoes as feet do change size. Keep your running shoes only for running; wearing them for walking around or for other forms of exercise reduces the support they provide when you run. Have a separate pair of shoes for your other sporting activities. Running shoes have a shock absorbent sole to help reduce excessive forces exerted upon the feet, but this gradually wears out with use so shoes need to be replaced more often than you might think (see opposite).

WEAR THE RIGHT SOCKS

The right running socks are as important to runners as the right shoes. The wrong socks can lead to an uncomfortable run, blisters, and sweaty, even cold, feet. The first rule is never wear cotton socks; they will rub your feet. Wear double-skinned running socks that minimize friction between your foot and shoe, which helps prevent blisters. Socks made from a moisture-wicking material, or with a wicking inner layer, absorb sweat, which keeps the skin dry. This not only reduces the risk of fungal infections such as athlete's foot, but also prevents cold injuries such as frostbite in the winter. Some socks have additional cushioning around the heel and toe that helps alleviate the pressure on these areas. So-called compression socks have an extra thread running from top to toe and act like a support bandage for the lower leg muscles, foot, and ankle joints (see p.49).

LOOK AFTER YOUR SHOES

Untie your laces before you take your shoes off – levering them off with your other shoe damages the heel counter, which reduces the support it can provide. Don't run in wet shoes; a wet midsole loses 40 to 50 per cent of its shock absorbency, which can cause injury. If you buy two pairs of running shoes, you should always have a dry pair when you need them. Never wash your shoes in the washing machine, it can deform them; wash them by hand if you need to. Always air dry your shoes – exposing them to direct heat by putting them on a radiator or out in the sun can cause them to shrink.

INFO DASHBOARD

ORTHOTIC INSOLES

The tendency to roll your heel outwards or inwards (pronate), can affect your running, which can result in heel, knee, and lower back pain. If you can't find comfortable shoes, consult a foot specialist who may prescribe shoe inserts that can correct your gait and improve your biomechanics. Allow three weeks of running to adjust to them, and if after six weeks they are still causing problems, discard them.

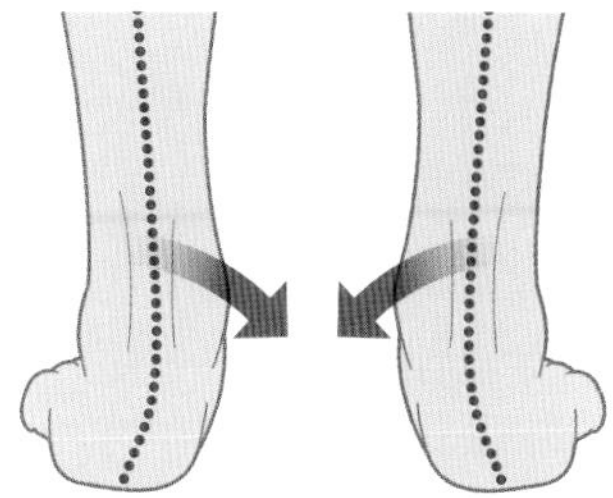

EXCESSIVE PRONATION
Overpronation is very common and causes the foot arch to drop or flatten as your feet and ankles roll inwards.

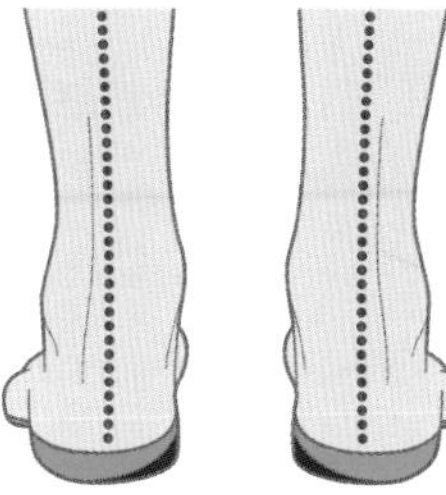

CORRECTED PRONATION
Inserting orthotic insoles realigns the foot and ankle, lifting fallen foot arches, and relieving knee and back problems.

REPLACE YOUR SHOES OFTEN

It is recommended that you replace running shoes about every 480–800km (300–500 miles) or every six months, whichever is sooner, and ideally before the shoes show signs of wear. However, this can also depend on the quality of the footwear as well as your running style, running surface and bodyweight. Heavier runners are harder on shoes and will need to replace their shoes sooner than lighter runners. Running shoes gradually lose their shock absorption and supportive properties and if the support is no longer adequate, the impact of running on your joints is increased, leading to a greater risk of heel pain, muscle fatigue, and overuse injuries such as shin splints (see p.180) and stress fractures (see p.179).

WATCH FOR SIGNS OF WEAR

The first part of any running shoe to show signs of wear is the midsole (see p.47). Press down on the midsole with your thumb: if it is too hard or too soft it may have become too compressed and will have lost its cushioning ability. Creases along the sock liner also indicate that the midsole is worn. Change your shoes if there are holes or tears in the fabric of the upper shoe or signs of wear on the outsole, commonly at the heel, forefoot and front of the shoe. If you are suffering from more aches and pains in your joints, or greater muscle tightness than usual, the shoe's shock absorption may be reduced, so it's time to change them. Running for too long in worn shoes can ultimately alter the way you run (see pp.46–47).

DAY-TO-DAY FOOTCARE

Even with the right shoes, foot complaints such as aches, blisters, calluses, cracked skin, and fungal infections are all common amongst runners. In order to maintain healthy feet:

- Cut your toenails regularly to prevent conditions such as runner's toe (see p.170) and in-growing toenails that can result if the nail bed presses against your shoe during running.
- Moisturize your feet everyday to prevent dry, cracked skin and calluses, which can develop especially at the heel and the inner side of the big toe.
- Massage your feet regularly to relieve tension, maintain mobility, and reduce the risk of injury. Have a professional massage, do it yourself, or try rolling your foot over a golfball (see plantar fascia band exercise, p.169).

FOAM ROLLER EXERCISES

Massage should form a key part of your maintenance programme. Foam roller exercises are a useful form of self-massage. With rollers you can use your own body weight to apply controlled pressure to specific muscle groups and give yourself a deep-tissue massage. This helps loosen tight tissues, reduce physical imbalances, and increase your mobility.

Q ARE THE EXERCISES EASY TO DO?

A Some of the foam roller exercises are easier than others. They can be uncomfortable at first because tight, sensitive muscles are pressed against the roller under your body weight. Foam rollers come in a variety of lengths, diameters, and densities, see below. If you have never used one, start with a low-density roller while you learn the exercises as they are softer against your tight muscles. As you become used to the exercises, progress to higher-density rollers, which can give a deeper massage.

Q WHEN SHOULD I DO THE EXERCISES?

A Roller exercises are especially useful for releasing "knots" in muscles that need mobilization. You don't need to do all the foam roller exercises for every workout - instead, use them to work on specific areas of muscle tightness. You can do roller exercises before a training session to loosen and mobilize particular muscles, or after a run to help break down the lactic acid that can accumulate in them. Alternatively, incorporate them into your balance and mobility maintenance programme. The exercises can also be used as part of an injury recovery programme, but always consult your doctor or physiotherapist first (see pp.172-83).

TOP TIPS FOR FOAM ROLLER EXERCISES

- Roll forwards and backwards over the target area for at least 30 seconds if exercises are part of your maintenance programme (less if you are using them in your warm-ups)
- Pause at any sensitive points and hold the position until discomfort has eased – allow the targeted muscle to relax completely
- Always repeat the process on both sides to prevent muscle imbalances – even if the muscle tightness is only on one side
- Breathe normally as you carry out each exercise
- Avoid rolling over any bony areas, (ankle, knee, and hip joints)
- Make sure your body does the work, not the roller
- Use an exercise mat for additional comfort

CHOOSING A FOAM ROLLER?

Rollers come in a variety of lengths from 30-90cm (1-3ft) long and on average are about 15cm (6in) in diameter. The ideal length is about 45cm (18in) as these rollers are easier to store, but you may want a longer one if you are planning a lot of back exercises. Most foam rollers are colour-coded according to firmness. White rollers are the softest, blue or green rollers tend to be medium density, and black rollers are the hardest. Rollers with a smaller diameter, and/or a ridged surface can be used to increase the pressure applied to the muscles and progress the exercises.

As an alternative to the rollers, try using a tennis ball or even a golf ball to work on smaller muscle "knots".

NECK AND UPPER TRAPEZIUS MUSCLES

Use this exercise to loosen up the muscles at the base of your skull and around your neck. These muscles can become very tight especially if you have a tendency to run with your head forward. The neck tightness can cause headaches.

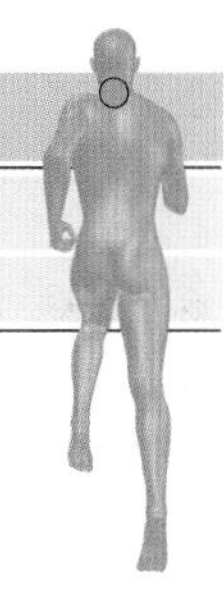

TARGET MUSCLES

- Neck muscles
- Upper trapezius

1 Lie on your back with your feet flat on the floor. Position the roller at the top of your neck, just beneath the base of your skull. Slowly turn your head from left to right over the roller for at least 30 seconds. Return your head to centre.

2 Move the roller down to the bottom of your neck and roll your head over it for another 30 seconds, working on the lower neck muscles. If you want to increase the pressure on your neck, try lifting your hips up slightly.

THORACIC SPINE

This exercise reduces tightness and improves movement in the muscles of your mid and upper back, known as the thoracic spine. Mobility through the upper back and ribs helps you maintain an upright posture and to breathe correctly.

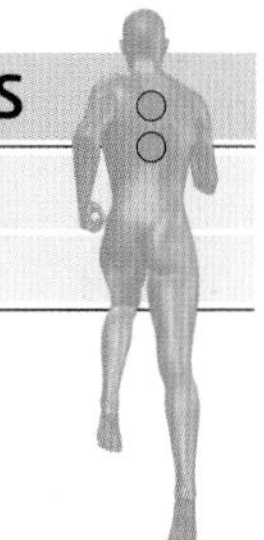

TARGET MUSCLES

- Mid back
- Upper back

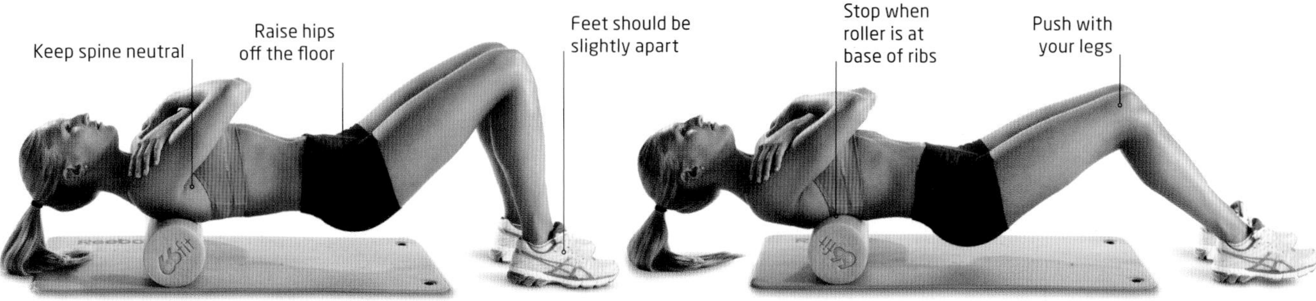

1 Sit down with knees bent and feet on the floor. Position the roller so that it will be level with your shoulder blades. Place your arms across your chest, lie back onto the roller, and lift your hips. Keep your back and neck in a straight line.

2 Breathe normally and, using your legs and feet, push your body over the roller until it reaches the bottom of the ribs, then work back to your shoulder blades again – repeat for 30 seconds.

LUMBAR SPINE

This exercise reduces muscle tightness and imbalance in your lower back. Correct tension across your lower back allows a more even distribution of force through this part of the spine when you are running, minimizing the likelihood of back pain.

TARGET MUSCLES

- Muscles of the lower back

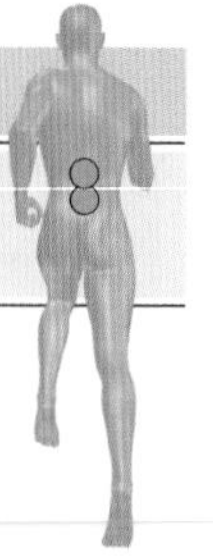

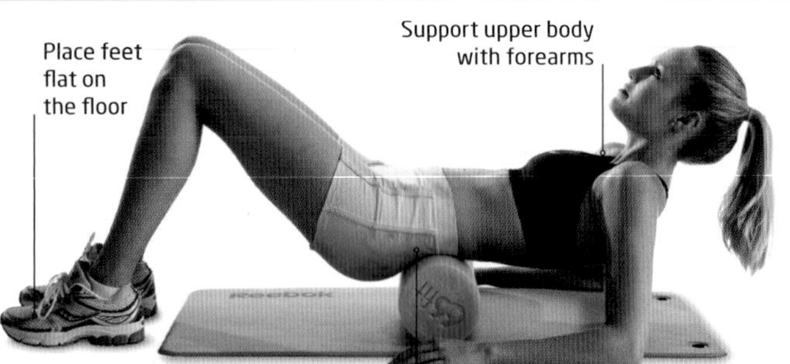

1 Sit on the floor with knees bent and feet on the floor. Position the roller so that it is level with the top of your pelvis. Lie back over the roller supporting your upper body with your arms. Keep your spine neutral.

2 Push your body over the roller as far as the base of your ribs, then back to top of your pelvis. Rotate your body towards your left side and repeat the exercise, targeting the muscles on the outer side. Turn towards your right side and repeat.

GLUTEAL AND **PIRIFORMIS** MUSCLES

This exercise focuses on the gluteal and piriformis muscles on the outer side of your buttocks. These muscles help with hip and leg stability and can over-tighten with running.

TARGET MUSCLES

- Gluteals
- Piriformis

1 Sit on the foam roller with your left buttock and cross your left leg over your right leg. Push your buttock backwards and forwards over the roller for 30 seconds. Sit on your right buttock, cross your legs, and repeat.

2 Rotate sideways to shift your weight on to the outer side of your left buttock. Cross your left leg over the right and push backwards and forwards over the roller. Turn to sit on the outer side of the right buttock, cross your legs, and repeat.

TFL MUSCLE AND ITB BAND

This exercise loosens the tensor fasciae lata (TFL) muscle of the upper leg and the iliotibial band (ITB), a band of fibrous tissue on the outer side of the leg (see p.22). Runners are especially prone to tightness in this area.

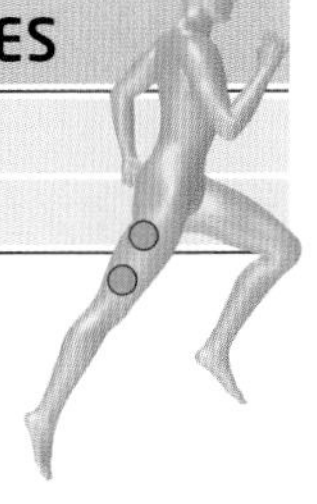

TARGET MUSCLES

- Tensor fasciae lata
- Iliotibial band

1 Lie on your left side, with the roller just above your knee. Support your upper body on your left forearm and place the other hand on your hip. Cross your right leg over the left, and put your right foot flat on the floor.

2 Using your left arm, gently push down over the roller, until the it is level with the top of your thigh, then pull back up until it is above your knee again. Repeat for 30 seconds. Turn over and massage your right leg.

HAMSTRING MUSCLES

This exercise helps to reduce muscle tension and imbalances in the hamstring muscles at the back of the thigh. Muscle tension is particularly common in runners who have a tendency to over-stride, or anyone with a misaligned pelvis.

TARGET MUSCLES

- Hamstring group of muscles

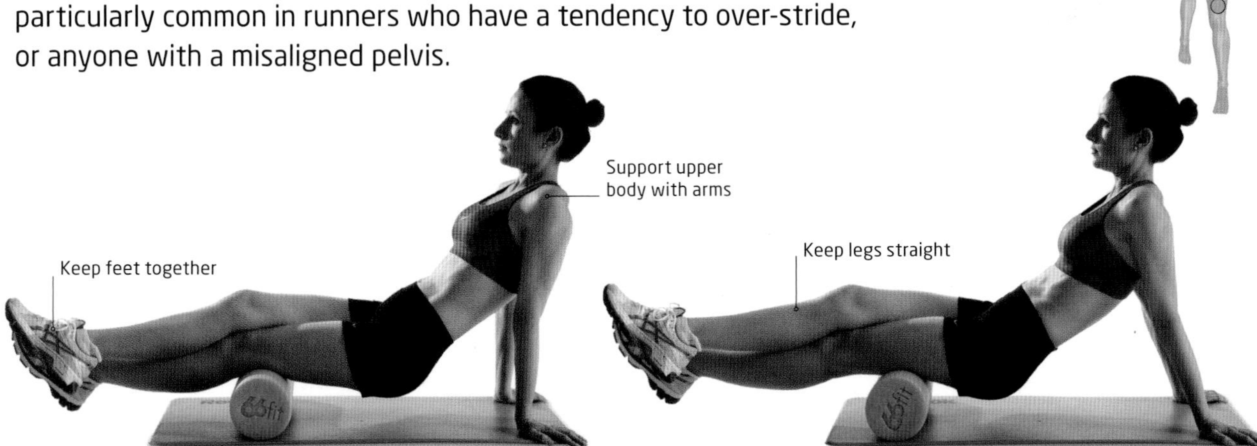

1 Sit with your legs straight out in front and place the roller under the back of your knee. Cross your right leg over the left one at the knees. Raise your buttocks off the mat, keeping head, neck, and spine aligned.

2 Using your arms, push yourself over the roller, working from your knee to the base of your buttocks, then back to the knee. Repeat for at least 30 seconds. Cross your left leg over the right and massage your right leg.

QUADRICEPS MUSCLES

This exercise helps to reduce muscle tightness and imbalance at the front of the thigh. These muscles become tight due to repetitive muscle contraction, especially during long runs. Tightness in these muscles can also affect knee mechanics.

TARGET MUSCLES

- Quadriceps group

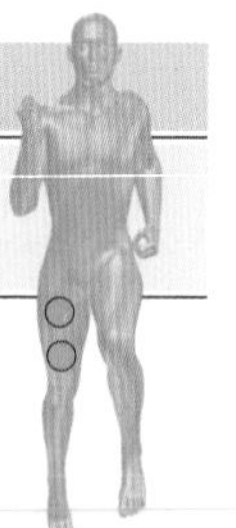

1 Lie on your front with the roller beneath the top of your thighs. Keep your head, neck, body, and legs aligned. Support your upper body with your arms and make sure your toes are on the ground to support your legs.

2 Move your body up over the roller until it is just above your knee, then work back to the top of your thighs again. Repeat for 30 seconds. Crossing your legs at the ankles adds extra pressure, but always repeat on each leg.

GASTROCNEMIUS AND SOLEUS MUSCLES

This exercise reduces tension in the calf muscles, to help ankle mobility. Tightness in these muscles can lead to pain in the Achilles tendon, heel, or foot arch.

TARGET MUSCLES

- Gastrocnemius
- Soleus

1 Sit with your legs straight, cross your right leg over the left, and place the roller under the back of your ankles. Support your upper body with your arms and lift your hips off the mat.

2 Push your legs over the foam roller, working from your ankle to the back of the knee and back to the ankle again; repeat for 30 seconds. Cross your left leg over the right leg and repeat to massage the muscles of your right leg.

TIBIALIS ANTERIOR AND PERONEAL MUSCLES

This exercise massages the muscles of the shin and the outer side of the lower leg. These muscles help to stabilize your ankle and, if overworked, they are prone to tightness and injury.

TARGET MUSCLES

- Tibialis anterior
- Peroneal

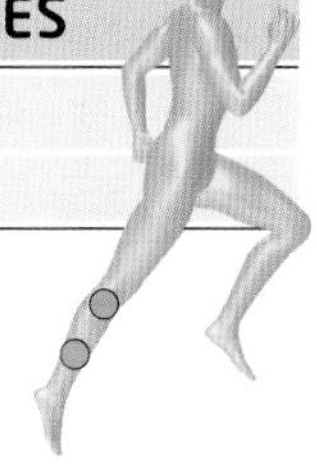

1 Lie on your left side and with the roller just above your ankle. Raise your upper body and support your body with your left forearm. Put your right foot on the floor in front of you to help with balance.

2 Using your forearm and foot, push your leg down over the roller, to massage from the ankle to just below the knee, and then back to the ankle. Turn over onto your right side and repeat to massage your right leg.

PLANTAR FASCIA BAND

The plantar fascia is a band of tissue that supports the arch of the foot and it is particularly prone to tension from the repetitive stress caused by running long distances. Use a golf ball so you can target smaller points of tension.

TARGET MUSCLES

- Plantar facscia

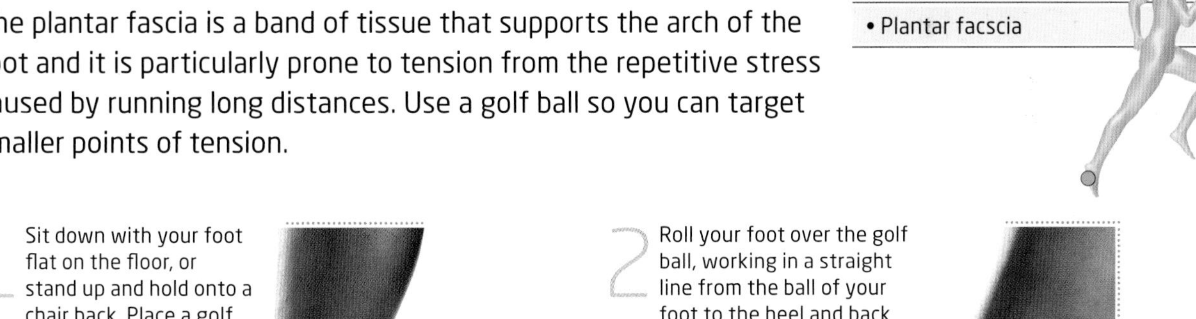

1 Sit down with your foot flat on the floor, or stand up and hold onto a chair back. Place a golf ball on the floor and rest your foot on it.

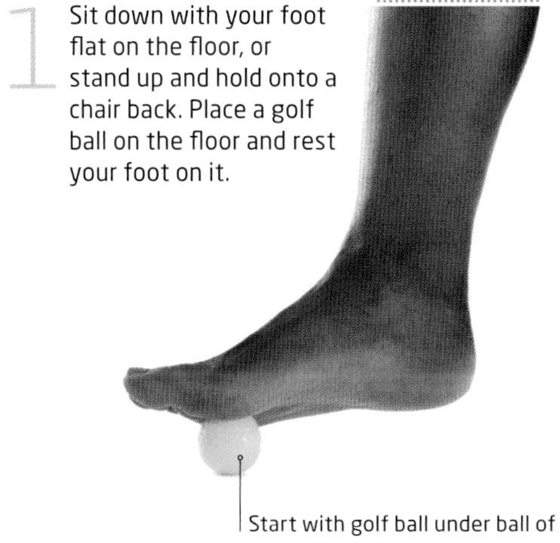

2 Roll your foot over the golf ball, working in a straight line from the ball of your foot to the heel and back again. Increase the pressure through your foot as required. Repeat exercise with your other foot.

Roll foot over golf ball

COMMON COMPLAINTS

When participating in a busy running programme, you may experience a number of common runners' complaints. Most of them are nothing to worry about, and good preparation can prevent many of them, but you should familiarize yourself with basic first aid procedures just in case.

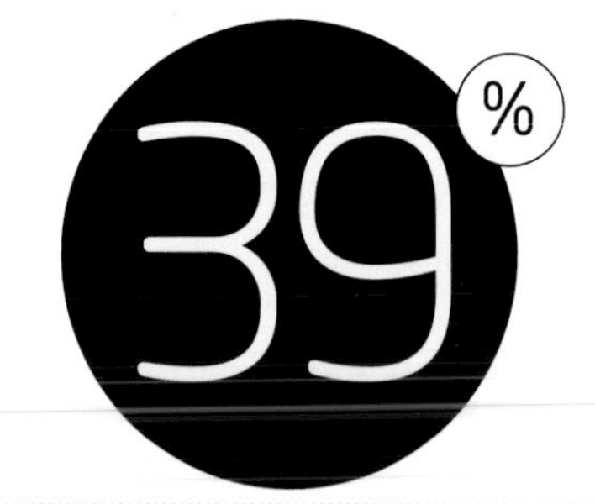

PERCENTAGE OF RUNNERS WHO EXPERIENCE DISABILITY DURING A RACE DUE TO BLISTERS

COMPLAINT	PREVENTION	FIRST AID
RUNNER'S NIPPLE Soreness, irritation, and even bleeding around one or both of the nipples commonly results from repetitive friction or chafing from loose-fitting running shirts, especially if they are made of cotton. Runner's nipple is more common in men.	Wear a light, well-fitting sports vest, preferably made of synthetic material, close to your skin. Apply petroleum jelly to the nipple and/or cover with a plaster. Women should wear a supportive sports bra (see p.49).	If you get runner's nipple during a run, clean it with warm water when you get back, and air dry. Apply antiseptic cream to prevent infection and dryness, and cover with a plaster.
BLISTERS Painful, fluid-filled blisters typically occur around the heel and ball of the foot if the skin is pinched or compressed by repetitive friction from unsuitable socks or footwear. Although not usually serious, blisters are painful and may become infected if left untreated.	Apply petroleum jelly to susceptible areas and wear double-skinned socks to minimize friction.	Do not break a blister. If possible, wash the area with clean water and pat dry. Cover a blister with a cushioned gel blister plaster for protection and comfort.
RUNNER'S TOE Also called black toenail, this is a blackening of the toenail caused by bleeding under the nail, often as a result of compression against the nail bed from ill-fitting or unsupportive footwear. Although not serious, runner's toe may be very painful and can prevent you from running.	When selecting new running shoes, make sure you factor in swelling of the feet during running – you may need bigger shoes. Keep your toenails trimmed so that they are not in contact with the inside of the shoes.	Stop running for a few days. Keep the toe clean and dry to protect it from infection. It is possible that all or part of the affected nail will drop off altogether, but it should soon grow back.
DELAYED ONSET MUSCLE SORENESS Also known as DOMS, delayed onset muscle soreness is caused by microtrauma in the muscle fibres as a result of physiological adaptations to exercise. It usually develops 24–72 hours after exercise, and is most common in beginners or those starting a new exercise programme.	To reduce the risk of DOMS, complete a warm-up prior to running and a cool-down afterwards (see pp.60–67). Work on specific muscles with foam-roller exercises (see pp.164–69) and have a regular post-run massage.	Rest the affected area and place an ice pack on it for 20–30 minutes every few hours. Anti-inflammatory medication may also help.
CRAMP An involuntary over-contraction of a muscle, cramp can be very painful. It tends to occur towards the end of a run when your muscles are tired. Heat exhaustion, dehydration, excessive loss of body salts through sweating, and/or a diet that is low in sodium, potassium and/or magnesium can cause a muscle to cramp.	You can reduce the likelihood of cramp with regular stretching and massage of the areas most commonly affected, and by maintaining hydration and a well-balanced diet.	Sit down, rest, and stretch the affected muscle to relieve the contraction. Massage the affected area.

COMPLAINT	PREVENTION	FIRST AID
PINS AND NEEDLES Numbness, tingling, and pins and needles in the feet and toes when running can occur if your shoes are too small, or the laces are tied too tightly, as this compresses the nerves around the ankle and foot.	Check to make sure your shoes are the right size (see pp.46–47) – your feet may have swollen. Check that your laces are not too tight or too loose before you set out.	If you experience pins and needles when running, stop and undo your laces, and re-tie them more loosely. If numbness persists after running, or you are in pain, seek medical advice.
NECKACHE AND HEADACHES Tightness around the neck is common amongst runners with a tendency to run with their head too far forward. The head position places additional stress on the muscles of the neck that stabilize the head, and it can lead to headaches.	Check your running posture. Practise regular stretching, mobilization, breathing, and strengthening exercises to help you maintain good posture.	Use a foam roller exercise to massage your neck – see p.165. Take one to two tablets of your normal, over-the-counter pain relief medication.
NAUSEA Runners can experience nausea during or after a run. It can be caused by dehydration, eating foods before a run that are difficult to digest, eating too close to a run, low blood sugar levels, and/or loss of body salts through sweating.	Don't overload on food or fluids before a run. Eat snacks or a light meal no less than 1–2 hours before setting out so that the body has time to digest them. Hydrate little and often before, during, and after a run (see pp.54–55).	If this happens during a run, try slowing down and stay as hydrated as possible. After a run, re-hydrate, ideally with a sports drink or water containing rehydration salts. Be careful not to drink too much too quickly.
CHEST PAIN This is not uncommon amongst inexperienced runners. It can occur due to incorrect breathing or running technique, indigestion caused by eating too close to a run, or simply by not being used to the cardiorespiratory demands of running. Associated breathing problems may also be the result of an underlying medical condition.	Build up your training programme gradually (see Chapter 5). Allow for rest and recovery time to help your cardiovascular fitness.	Stop your activity and rest. If chest pain is severe or persistent, seek urgent medical attention.
ABDOMINAL PAIN Cramp in the abdomen, commonly known as a "stitch", may be experienced when running. It often occurs in the trunk or the sides of the chest. The exact cause is still open to debate – it is thought to be due to tiredness, reduced blood flow to the diaphragm (the sheet of muscle below the lungs), which causes it to over-tighten, or a build-up of lactic acid in the abdominal muscles. Eating too close to a run and inefficient breathing patterns are also thought to contribute.	Practise a controlled diaphragmatic breathing pattern when running to help reduce abdominal pain.	Sit down and rest – the pain should ease within a few minutes. If it does not ease, seek medical advice.
SUNBURN This is reddening or burning of the skin caused by exposure to the sun's UV (ultraviolet) rays. Remember that sunburn can occur even on an overcast day in the summer; severe sunburn can cause blisters.	Cover exposed skin with high-factor sunscreen or sun block, and run in the shade whenever possible. Wear protective clothing and sunglasses.	Cover any affected skin and move into the shade. Cool the affected areas with cold water and dab aftersun or calamine lotion on the skin. Stay out of the sun. If there is any blistering, seek urgent medical advice – never break the blisters.
HEAT-RELATED ILLNESS Dehydration can occur when body fluids lost through sweating are not replaced. In severe cases, too many body salts will be lost, leading to heat exhaustion. You may have a headache, and pale, clammy skin, feel dizzy and confused, and experience cramps (see above). If untreated, this can lead to heatstroke, a life-threatening medical emergency in which the body's thermostat system fails altogether.	Make sure you are properly hydrated before you start your run. Sip water during the run.	Stop and rest in the shade, and drink plenty of water (although be careful not to drink too much too quickly). If dehydration is severe, add oral rehydration salts to the water, or have a sports drink.

RUNNERS' INJURIES

AT SOME POINT, YOU'RE LIKELY TO PICK UP ONE OR TWO INJURIES DURING TRAINING. AVOID SERIOUS SETBACKS BY READING THE SIGNS.

No matter how fit you are, injuries are a common by-product of the stress placed on the body by intense physical activity. Knowledge of first aid is likely to come in handy when you're out on a run, where blisters, sprains, and even broken bones can occur. It's also important to be aware of your body's limits in order to avoid minor injuries that may be less obvious, but can develop into long-term problems.

Q WHAT HAPPENS WHEN I INJURE MYSELF?

A We build muscle through exercise, with the stress of the workout causing minute tears in the tissue. The muscle grows stronger as it repairs itself. An injury occurs when a part of the body is stressed so much it is no longer able to function normally. Pain is your body's way of telling you that something is wrong; it's important to listen to the messages your body is sending you. If you ignore them, the injury is likely to worsen.

Q WHAT KIND OF INJURIES MIGHT I SUSTAIN?

A Injuries can be divided into two types: acute, or sudden onset, and chronic, or long-term. Acute injuries result from a specific event, or trauma, and can be minor, for example blisters, or more serious, like a torn ligament. Chronic, or "overuse", injuries result from wear and tear, for example Achilles tendinopathy (see p.182), and develop over an extended period of time. In either case, it's essential to identify the injury and find out what treatment is needed.

Q HOW DO I DEAL WITH AN ACUTE INJURY?

A Sharp pain is likely to accompany an acute injury. Injuries to soft tissue such as muscles, tendons (bands of tissue that attach muscles to bones), and ligaments (bands of tissue that support joints), are also accompanied by swelling as a result of internal bleeding from ruptured blood vessels (bruising). Stop your training and apply the RICE procedure, opposite.

Q WHAT SHOULD I DO IF SOMEONE BREAKS A LEG?

A If a person is in significant pain, movement increases the pain, and/or he or she cannot bear weight on the injured leg, a bone may be broken. Don't attempt to move or straighten the person's leg. Support the joints above and below the injury by hand, and place rolled clothes on either side to immobilize it. Call an ambulance and continue the support until help arrives.

Q HOW DO I DEAL WITH A CHRONIC INJURY?

A The majority of injuries and conditions experienced by runners in training for a marathon are overuse injuries caused by running many miles and pounding on hard surfaces. Chronic injury often results in a dull, nagging

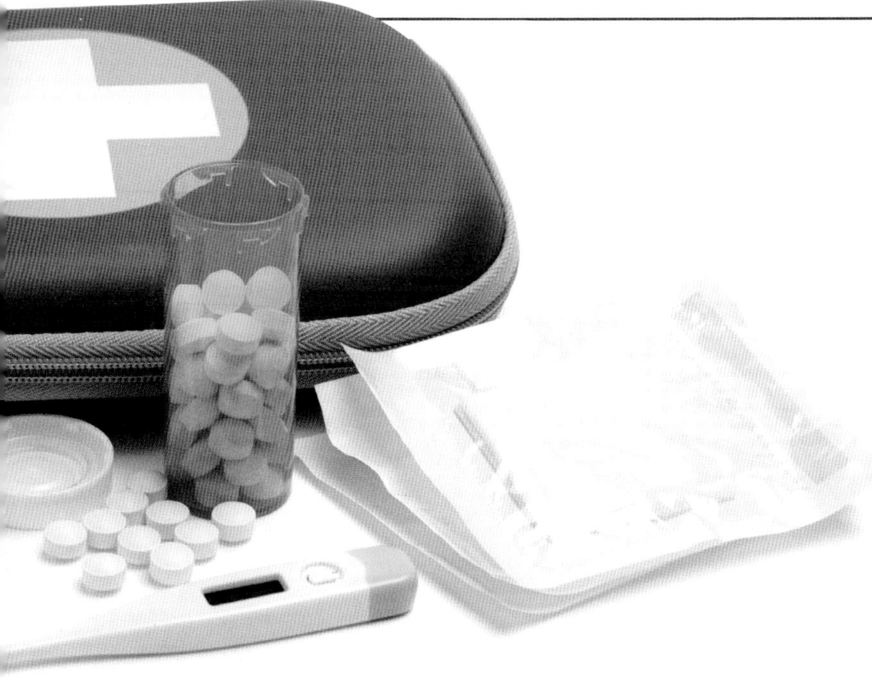

pain. If you suspect you have any of the muscle or joint conditions described on the following pages, stop training, apply RICE treatment, and consult a medical professional.

Q HOW DO I GET BACK TO RUNNING AFTER AN INJURY?

A Returning to running before an injury has healed completely will lead to recurrence, or worsen the injury. Listen to your doctor or physiotherapist. Follow any exercises you have been given and re-apply load gradually. After a minor injury, aim to bear weight and walk with the correct technique within two or three days; serious injury will take much longer. Try low-impact exercise like swimming to maintain your fitness until you can run. When you start running training again, build up slowly.

REDUCE YOUR RISK OF INURY BY WEARING THE RIGHT KIT AND TAKING TIME TO WARM MUSCLES AND JOINTS UP GENTLY BEFORE EXERCISE AND COOL DOWN AFTERWARDS

FIRST AID FOR SOFT TISSUE INJURIES

A strain is a "pulled" or torn muscle or the tendon that attaches a muscle to a bone. A sprain occurs when the ligaments around a joint are damaged or torn. If a strain or sprain occurs, treat the injury as described below to reduce the swelling and alleviate the pain. An easy way to remember what to do is the mnemonic RICE (Rest, Ice, Compression, and Elevation). Consult a medical professional before you start training again.

ACTION	EXPLANATION
REST (R)	Sit or lie down to REST the injured part.
ICE (I)	Wrap an ICE pack (a bag of ice cubes or frozen peas) in a towel and leave it on the injury for 20-30 minutes; don't put ice directly on the skin. Repeat every two hours for the first three days.
COMPRESSION (C)	Apply a COMPRESSION bandage that extends from the joint below the injured part to the joint above (bandage from the toes to the knee for a sprained ankle).
ELEVATE (E)	ELEVATE the injured part. Support it in a raised position and and seek medical advice. If the injury is severe and you cannot move, you may need to call an ambulance.

MUSCLE STRAIN OR TEAR

The term "strain" refers to the over-stretching of fibres within a muscle. Muscle injury can vary in severity from minor or moderate strains to the more serious tear, or rupture, of part of a muscle. Strains or tears are usually caused by a sudden forceful stretching or contraction (for example, an abrupt change of direction or speed), fatigue, poor running technique, over-training, and/or an inadequate warm-up programme before you set out. For runners, the muscles in the lower leg (gastrocnemius and soleus), thigh (quadriceps and hamstring groups of muscles), and buttocks (gluteus muscles) are most susceptible to this type of injury.

WHAT ARE THE SYMPTOMS?

There will be swelling, possible redness around the area, and reduced movement of the affected muscle. You may feel twinges of pain in the affected area during exercise, and/or when you apply pressure. If you have torn a leg muscle, pain will be severe and you won't be able to move or stand up – you may also hear a "pop" in the muscle at the moment of injury.

WHAT IS THE TREATMENT?

Stop the activity. Follow the RICE procedure (see p.173) and seek medical attention. If you have strained your hamstrings at the back of the leg, or your calf muscles, apply RICE over a straight leg; if your quadriceps are affected, bend your leg if possible. If the pain is severe, and/or you suspect a tear, immobilize the leg and seek urgent medical help. A doctor will carry out a physical examination and perhaps an ultrasound or MRI scan. You will be advised to rest until the pain has subsided. For a minor or moderate strain, your doctor may prescribe pain relief and suggest treating the injury with ice for a few days, followed by a gentle return to exercise. You may be referred to a physiotherapist, who will advise on exercises to strengthen the affected muscle(s). Left untreated, the injured muscle may become very tight, you will experience loss of mobility, and scar tissue will develop. If a strain is severe, you may need to use crutches to prevent overloading the muscle during recovery. A complete rupture of the muscle is likely to need surgery, followed by a rehabilitation programme.

WHEN CAN I RETURN TO RUNNING?

With a minor strain you can return to gentle exercise after a few days, but you must stop again if the activity causes any pain. A moderate strain may need one to two months' recovery depending on the muscle affected. A rupture that requires surgery will need four to six months' recovery post surgery. A moderate strain of the calf muscles may need up to three months' rehabilitation but a ruptured muscle will need from six to nine months recovery.

QUADRICEPS INJURIES

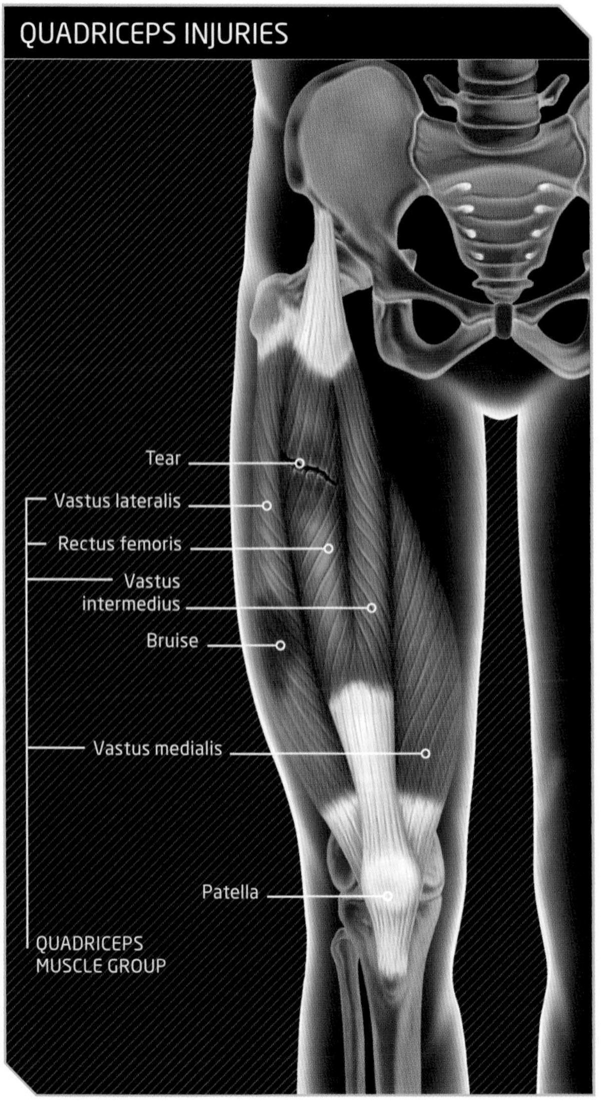

BURSITIS

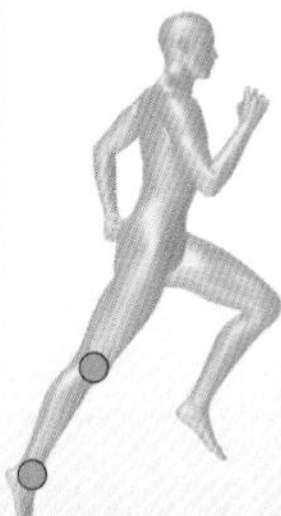

Bursae are small fluid-filled sacs that act as cushions between tendons and bones at a joint to aid smooth movement. Overuse and repetitive friction can cause a bursa to be become inflamed and movement of the associated joint will be painful – a condition known as bursitis. The bursae most susceptible to inflammation in runners are the trochanteric bursa at the hip, the patellar bursae in the knee (see below), and the retrocalcaneal bursa at the ankle. Poor running technique, biomechanical abnormalities, and unsuitable footwear can all cause bursitis. Bursae can also become infected, which can lead to chronic, or long-term, bursitis.

WHAT ARE THE SYMPTOMS?

There will be localized pain and tenderness of the bursa and surrounding area. There may be swelling and the skin may feel hot. Walking may be difficult, and running will aggravate the pain; if you continue running, you will experience ongoing pain. The pain may stay at the same level of intensity, or it may worsen. If any of the knee bursae are affected, kneeling is likely to be painful.

WHAT IS THE TREATMENT?

Stop any activity that causes pain. Apply the RICE treatment (see pp.173) to the affected area and seek medical advice. Rest and pain-relief medication will be recommended, and you should continue applying ice to the injury for a few days. Your doctor may also suggest an X-ray to rule out other potential injuries and you will be referred to a physiotherapist for treatment to build strength in the affected joint and prevent a recurrence. The physiotherapist may suggest insoles or orthotics in your shoes if a biomechanical abnormality is the cause. If bursitis does not respond to rest, corticosteroid injections and/or surgery may be needed. If the skin over the joint is broken, bacteria can enter, spread to the inflamed bursa, and infection may develop. If infection is suspected, fluid may need to be drained from the bursa for analysis and antibiotics will be prescribed if it is confirmed.

WHEN CAN I RETURN TO RUNNING?

If the bursitis is in the hip or knee, you should be able to return to your training programme within one or two weeks, as long as there are no complications. Start with a reduced training programme and build up again; always stop if exercise causes pain. Recovery from retrocalcaneal bursitis can take up to three months. The recovery period for an infected bursa is unpredictable, and it can be up to two months before you can run again. If you have had surgery, you can expect to be fully fit within one to two months of the operation following a prescribed rehabilitation programme.

PATELLAR BURSITIS

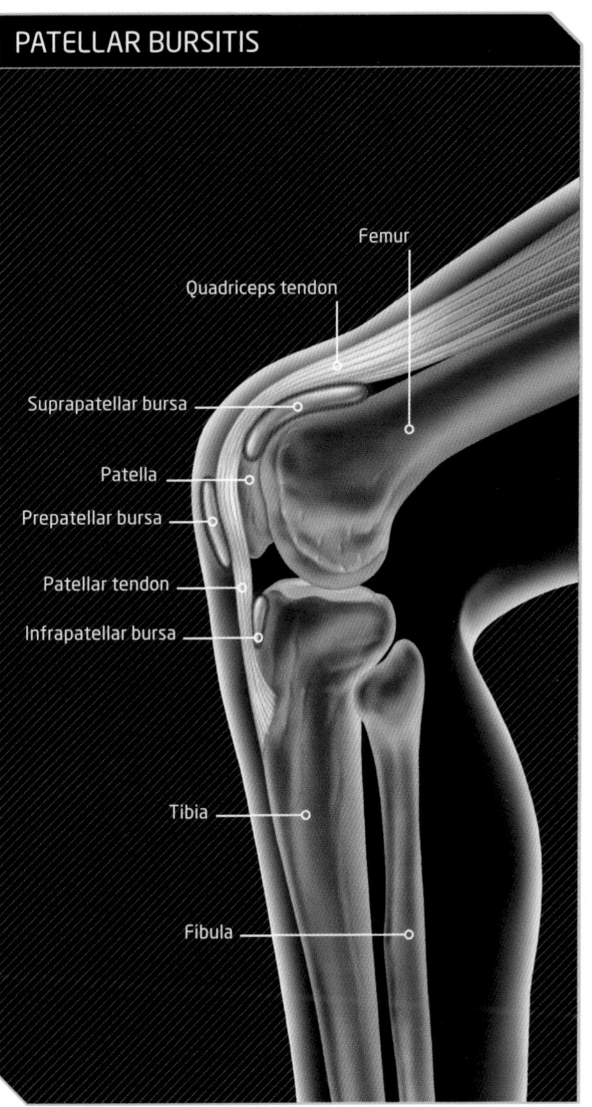

LOWER BACK PAIN

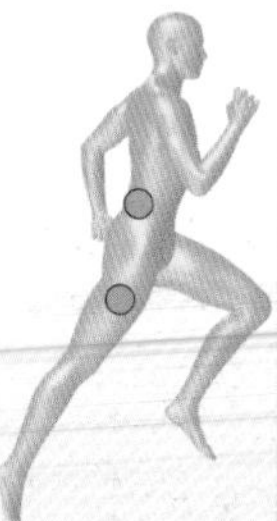

Back pain is extremely common in runners. Poor biomechanical factors especially can subject the lower back to an increased and uneven load. Muscle imbalance, poor running technique, regular training on hard and uneven surfaces, and running in ill-fitting or worn-out footwear can compress the intervertebral discs (jelly-like structures with a tough outer membrane). As a result discs may become inflamed or bulge (known as a "slipped" disc), and press against the nerves of the lower back (sciatic nerves), causing sciatica. Older runners are more susceptible to disc degeneration and stress fractures of the vertebrae.

WHAT ARE THE SYMPTOMS?

You will usually feel stiffness and pain in the lower back that spreads to your buttocks, back of the thigh, and groin and is worse when running or immediately afterwards. You may also experience symptoms after sitting, walking, standing, or lying down in the same position for long periods. If you have a shooting pain down the back of one leg, especially if you bend sideways, and "pins and needles", numbness, or weakness in your legs, you may also have sciatica.

WHAT IS THE TREATMENT?

Stop training, but continue with your normal activities if pain allows; it is important to remain mobile. If pain is very severe, you may need to rest in bed for one to two days. The affected disc may protrude from your spine initially, but should in most cases eventually shrink back as the inflammation is reduced. Apply ice and take pain-relief medication as necessary. If self-help treatment fails, seek medical advice. Your doctor will consider your medical history and carry out a physical examination. If the symptoms are mild, he or she may refer you to a physiotherapist to treat the spine and help restore normal movement. If pain is more severe, muscle relaxants or stronger pain relief may be prescribed. Blood tests, X-rays, and MRI scans may be recommended to rule out any serious structural damage. Rarely, surgery is required.

WHEN CAN I RETURN TO RUNNING?

Depending on the cause of your lower back pain and how you respond to treatment and rehabilitation, recovery may take from a few weeks to a few months. If surgery is required, you will not be able to run for up to six months.

SLIPPED DISC

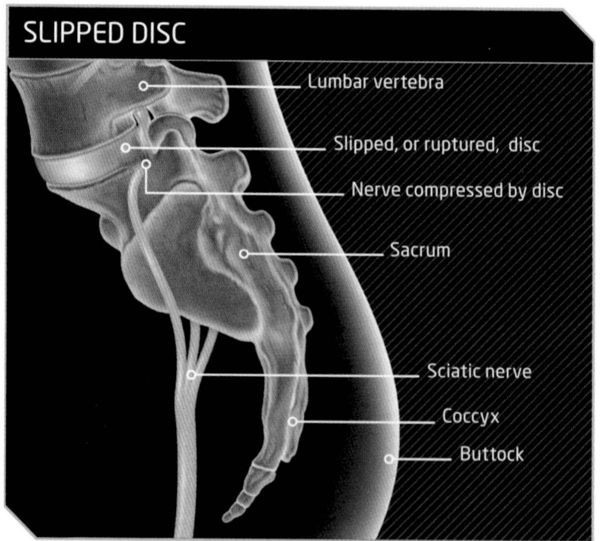

SCIATIA

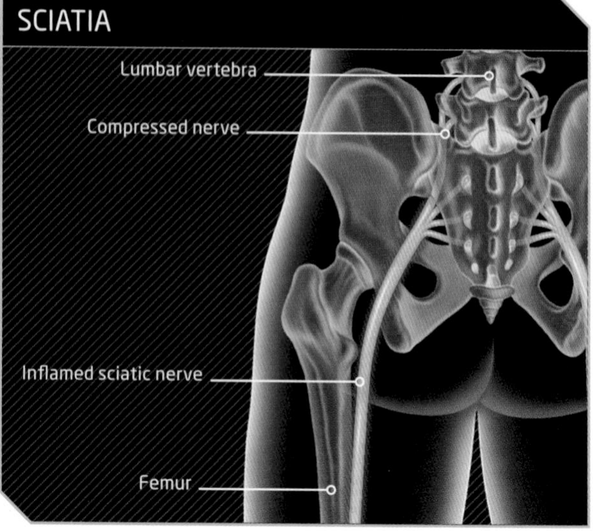

ILIOTIBIAL BAND SYNDROME

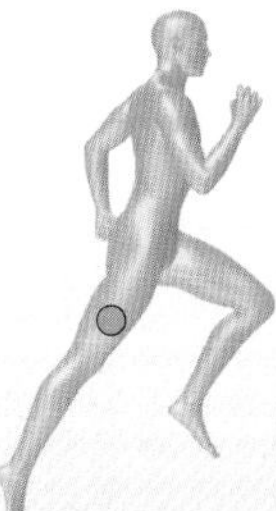

The iliotibial band (ITB) is a long tendon-like structure that extends from the pelvis to just below the knee. It helps straighten the knee, move the hip sideways, and stabilize the leg. Overuse of the ITB is common in runners because the running action causes repeated bending of the knee and rubs the tendon against the outer side of the femur, near the knee. The friction can result in inflammation and pain in the tendon, or iliotibial band syndrome, which can also lead to bursitis (see p.175). ITB syndrome can result from overtraining, muscular imbalances, poor running technique, biomechanical abnormality, and/or sudden changes to training routine.

WHAT ARE THE SYMPTOMS?

The first sign may be pain on the outside of your knee, particularly when walking down stairs. Running, especially downhill, may make the pain worse. You may also notice swelling and/or tightness, and a thickening of tissue along the outer side of your upper leg. Your knee may also be painful when you try to bend or straighten it and you may experience weakness when you move your hips sideways.

WHAT IS THE TREATMENT?

Stop any activity that causes or increases pain. Follow the RICE procedure (see p.173) and seek medical attention. If iliotibial band syndrome is left untreated you can experience long-term pain in the knee and hip. Your doctor will assess your symptoms, and may suggest an ultrasound or a MRI scan to confirm the diagnosis. You will be advised to rest, continue applying ice to the injury for a few days and take pain-relief medication. Your doctor will refer you to a physiotherapist for treatment and exercises that stretch the ITB, correct any muscle imbalance, and improve muscle strength. If your physiotherapist detects any biomechanical abnormality, you should be prescribed insoles or orthotics to wear in your running shoes.

WHEN CAN I RETURN TO RUNNING?

With rest and pain-relief medication, you should recover fully within two months and be able to return to training. On the rare occasion that surgery is necessary, most people recover fully within two months of the operation after a programme of rehabilitation.

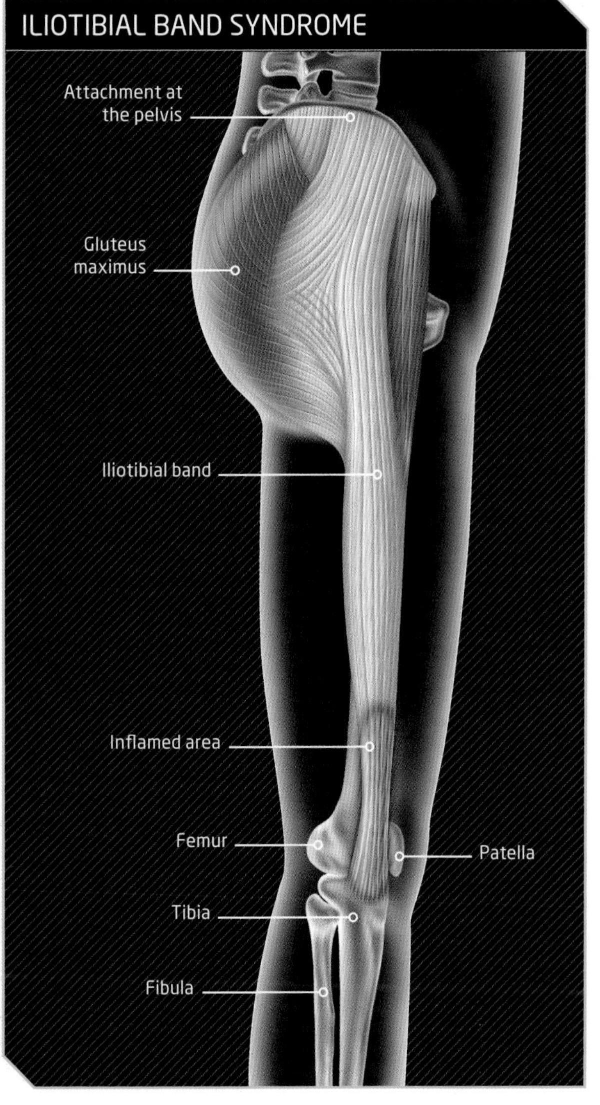

KNEE LIGAMENT INJURY

Four main ligaments work together to strengthen and stabilize the knee joint – the anterior and posterior cruciate ligaments (ACL and PCL), and the medial and lateral collateral ligaments (MCL and LCL). These ligaments can be sprained or ruptured by a sudden twisting movement. In runners, injury can be the result of repeated abnormal strain, twisting as a result of poor technique, or slipping and twisting the knee when you change direction. Often ligament injury is complicated by damage to the cartilage that cushions the knee joint – the menisci. Untreated knee ligament injury can lead to long-term pain and permanent instability.

WHAT ARE THE SYMPTOMS?

There will be severe pain and swelling around your knee if you have strained one or more ligaments – you may even have heard a "pop" at the time of the injury if the ligament is ruptured. Your knee is likely to feel unstable and you may not be able to move or straighten it or put any weight on it.

WHAT IS THE TREATMENT?

Stop training and immobilize your knee. If possible, follow the RICE procedure (see p.173). Do not apply a compression bandage or raise the leg if it causes discomfort. Seek urgent medical help. Your doctor will usually make a diagnosis from a physical examination, but may recommend an X-ray or MRI scan to confirm the ligament injury or establish whether any other part of the joint is damaged, for example the cartilage. If you have a mid-to-moderate sprain, you may need to wear a knee brace and use crutches for two to three weeks. You will be prescribed pain relief medication and will need to undergo an extensive physiotherapy rehabilitation programme. If you have ruptured a ligament, you will need surgery and probably be advised to wear a knee brace for up to six weeks afterwards to stabilize the joint while it heals. Once the brace is removed you can begin physiotherapy.

WHEN CAN I RETURN TO RUNNING?

For a mid-to-moderate sprain, you should be able to return to training within two to 12 weeks, depending on the severity of the injury. If you have had surgery, then eight to 12 months of recovery may be required after the operation. However, if your injury is severe, for example you have a complex injury that damaged more than one ligament, or other parts of your knee, such as the menisci, are injured you may not be able to return to running again.

COLLATERAL CRUCIATE LIGAMENT INJURIES

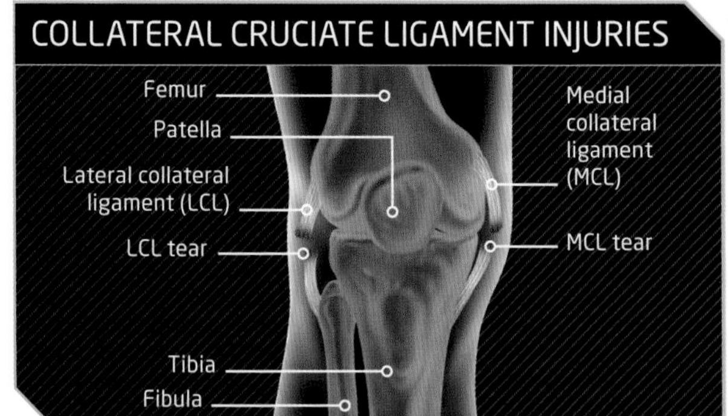

ANTERIOR CRUCIATE LIGAMENT INJURY

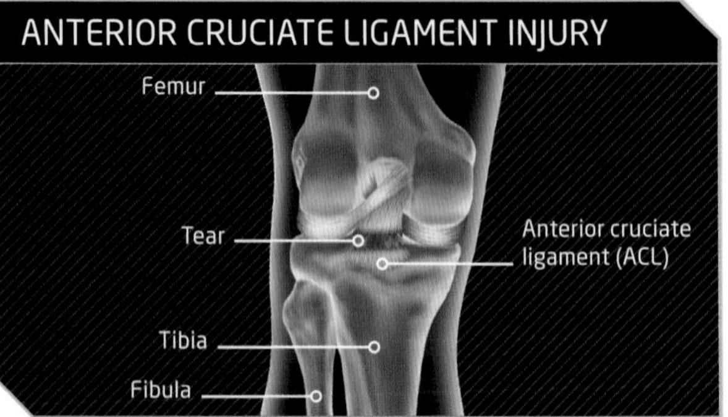

MENISCUS TEAR

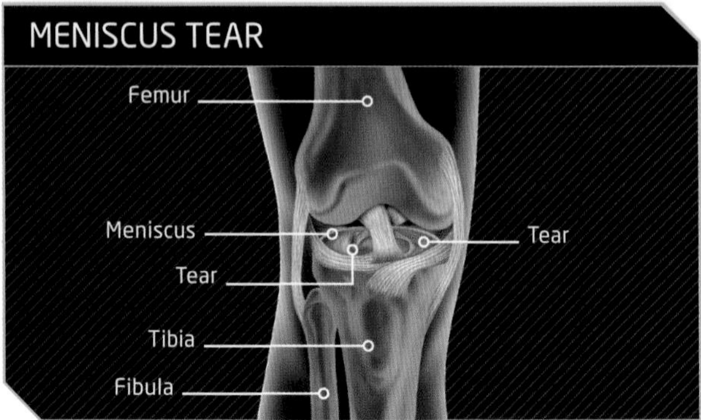

RUNNER'S KNEE

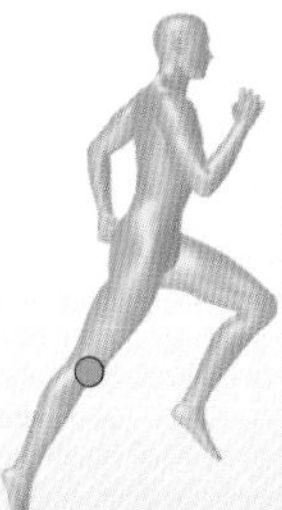

Also known as patellofemoral pain, this develops when the movement of the patella over the bottom of the femur causes pain in the front of the knee. Runner's knee can occur if muscles are weak or unbalanced, tendons are tight, or following abnormal movement of the kneecap.

PATELLOFEMORAL PAIN SYNDROME

Femur

Inflammation around patella

Tibia

WHAT ARE THE SYMPTOMS?

You will feel a general ache at the front of your knee, or behind or around your kneecap. The pain may be triggered by pressing on your knee, walking up or down stairs, or running (especially downhill). Strenuous exercise, squats, and weight-bearing movements that involve bending may worsen the pain. There may be swelling around the kneecap and you may hear a grating sound (crepitus) in the joint.

WHAT IS THE TREATMENT?

Stop your training and follow the RICE procedure (see p.173). If your symptoms have not improved after two weeks of self-help treatment, seek medical advice. A variety of tests may be needed to confirm a diagnosis. You will be advised to rest until the pain subsides, continue treating your knee with ice for four weeks, and take pain-relief medication. Physiotherapy will be needed to prevent permanent damage. Rarely, the injury does not respond to treatment and surgery may be required.

WHEN CAN I RETURN TO RUNNING?

You should see a substantial improvement in three to four weeks, and will have made a full recovery within four to six months. If you have had surgery, your recovery period is likely to be three months from the time of the operation.

STRESS FRACTURES

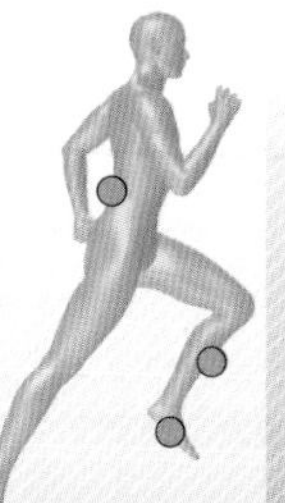

These are small cracks in the surface of a bone that can result from stress and overuse. Stress fractures most commonly occur in the weight-bearing bones such as the vertebrae, tibia, femur, pelvis, and the bones in the feet. If untreated, the cracks can develop into more serious fractures.

STRESS FRACTURES OF FOOT

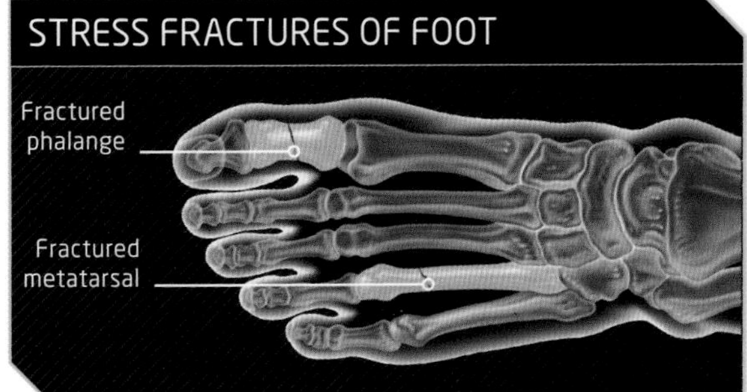

WHAT ARE THE SYMPTOMS?

Stress fractures tend to occur on one side of the body and result from muscle weakness or imbalance, poor running technique, and/or uneven loading. The area around the fracture may be swollen and sore and feel hot to the touch. There will be localized tenderness over the site of the fracture. Walking on the affected leg may be very painful.

WHAT IS THE TREATMENT?

Stop your training, follow the RICE procedure (see pp.172-73), and seek medical advice. An X-ray will be needed to confirm the diagnosis – sometimes the stress fracture does not show up immediately and an MRI scan may be needed. Rest and pain relief will be recommended, followed by a structured rehabilitation programme with a physiotherapist. If a biomechanical abnormality is found to be a likely cause, you may be advised to wear orthotics in one or both shoes.

WHEN CAN I RETURN TO RUNNING?

You should be able to restart your training programme within six to eight weeks, depending on the injury site and likely cause of the fracture, but it can be up to three months. Start with gentle exercise, but stop if it causes pain. Resuming the activity that caused the fracture too soon can cause a more severe break, which will take longer to heal.

SHIN SPLINTS

Also called medial tibial periostitis, this is exercise-induced pain at the front of the lower leg. Shin splints can result from not warming up properly, the stress of a sudden increase in training volume, running on hard surfaces, poor technique, or biomechanical abnormality.

SHIN SPLINT

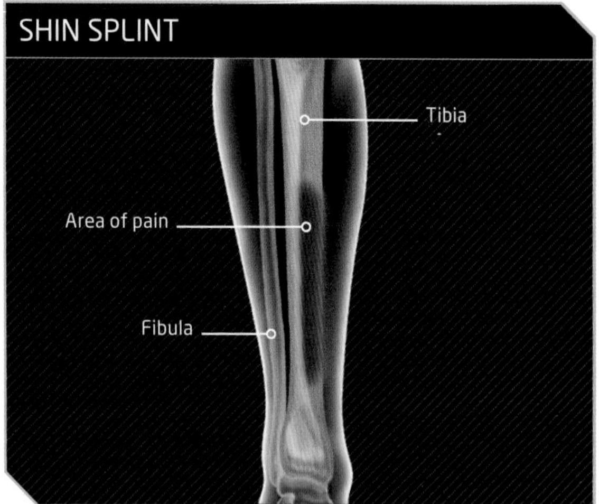

WHAT ARE THE SYMPTOMS?

You may feel a dull ache on the inner side of your shin that intensifies when you begin exercise. There may also be swelling. Shin splints can be caused by compartment syndrome (see right), or result in stress fracture (see p.179).

WHAT IS THE TREATMENT?

Stop your training programme and follow the RICE procedure (see p.173). If there is no improvement after two to three weeks of self-help, seek medical advice. Your doctor will carry out a physical examination, and may suggest an ultrasound or MRI scan. Stronger pain relief may be recommended and you will be referred to a physiotherapist for strengthening exercises. Rarely, surgery is needed.

WHEN CAN I RETURN TO RUNNING?

You should be fully fit again within three to six months, or three months after an operation.

COMPARTMENT SYNDROME

Muscles are contained within "compartments", of connective tissue and bone. Swelling within a compartment following injury or long-term overuse may cause compression of blood vessels and nerves inside it, and is known as compartment syndrome.

COMPARTMENT SYNDROME

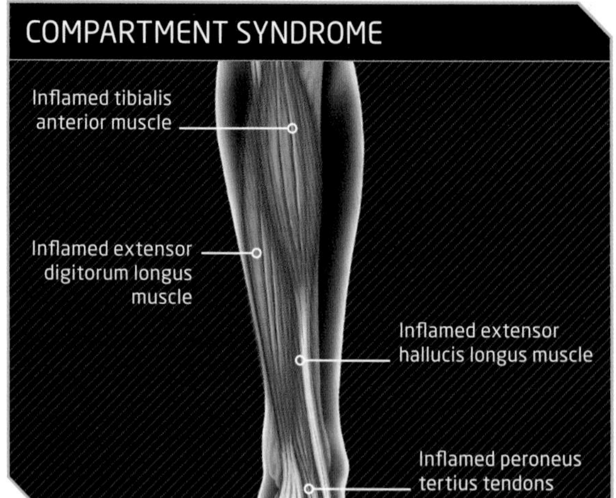

WHAT ARE THE SYMPTOMS?

You will feel intense pain that persists both while resting and when you are active. You may experience weakness, tingling, or reduced sensation in the affected limb.

WHAT IS THE TREATMENT?

Stop your activity, follow the RICE procedure (see p.173), and seek medical advice. If left untreated, compartment syndrome can cause long-term nerve and muscle damage. Your doctor will carry out a physical examination, and you may need a MRI scan. Pain-relief medication will be prescribed and you will need compartment pressure testing. Surgery may be required.

WHEN CAN I RETURN TO RUNNING?

If it is diagnosed early, recovery rates for this condition are good and you should be training within four to six weeks. Recovery may take up to three months after surgery.

ANKLE INJURY

Ankle sprains are among the most common of all sports-related injuries. The ankle joint is designed to adapt to uneven terrain, but a sudden twisting motion can tear the ligaments that support it. With a severe sprain, the ligaments may be ruptured and the ankle bones can be dislocated. In some cases, the bones may be broken. The most common injury occurs when the ankle rolls outwards so that the sole of the foot faces inwards, which stretches the ligaments on the outer side of the ankle (an inversion sprain). More rarely, the foot is forced outwards, which damages the inner ligaments (an eversion sprain).

WHAT ARE THE SYMPTOMS?

There will be pain, stiffness, and swelling around your ankle joint and you may not be able to bear weight on it. Bruising that moves down your foot towards your toes may appear in the days following the injury. If there is a fracture, the ankle will be extremely painful to touch and it may look deformed compared to the other leg if a bone has moved out of place.

WHAT IS THE TREATMENT?

Stop your activity, follow the RICE procedure (see p.173), and seek medical advice. If pain is severe and you cannot bear weight on the leg, suspect a broken bone and don't apply a compression bandage. Immobilize the ankle and seek urgent medical help. Your doctor will examine the ankle and may arrange for an X-ray if a break is suspected. For a mild to moderate sprain you will be advised to take pain relief medication and continue with the ice treatment until the injury has healed; you may need to use crutches for a couple of weeks. Surgery may be required for a severe sprain. If the ankle is broken, your leg will be put in a splint until the swelling has reduced, then in a cast for up to six weeks. You will have to use crutches as you will not be able to walk on the injured leg. Surgery will be required if the break is complex and/or the bone ends have moved out of place.

WHEN CAN I RETURN TO RUNNING?

With rest and treatment, a mild or moderate sprain should heal in a few weeks. With a severe sprain, you will need a supervised period of rehabilitation of up to three months. If you do not undergo proper rehabilitation, you may suffer from chronic pain and permanent instability. If you sprain your ankle repeatedly, you may need surgery to tighten the ligaments around the joint before you can consider running again. If you have surgery, you will need to learn to walk properly after the cast is removed, then depending on the severity of the injury, you may have to wait six months after the injury is healed before you can resume running.

ANKLE SPRAIN

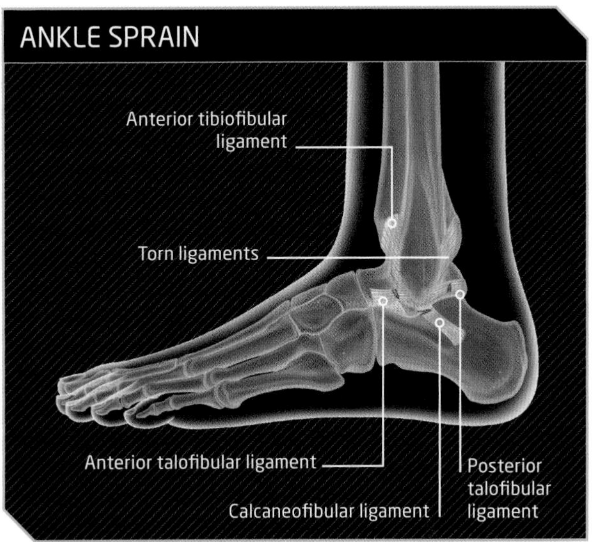

ANKLE FRACTURE

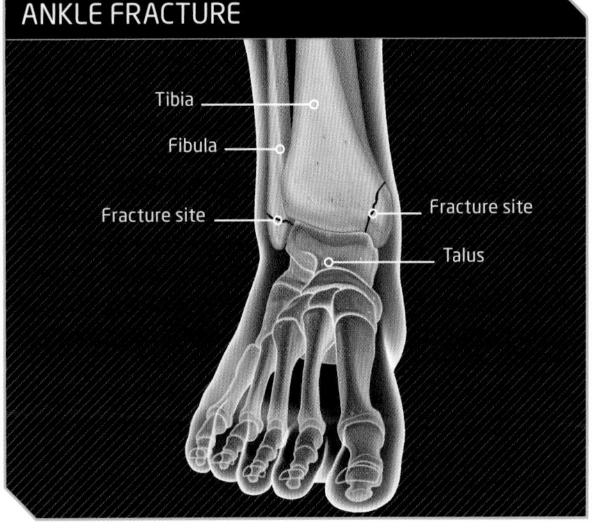

ACHILLES TENDINOPATHY

This is a degenerative condition characterized by pain and swelling in and around the Achilles tendon. An overuse injury that results from repetitive and excessive stress on the leg, it is more likely in middle-aged runners as it is linked to a degeneration of the tendon.

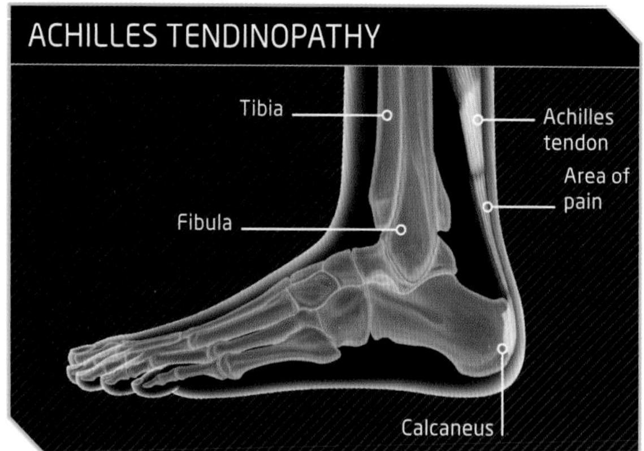

WHAT ARE THE SYMPTOMS?

The main symptom is pain, which ranges from mildly uncomfortable to intense. Some people experience pain only when they are active, others experience it even at rest. The Achilles tendon and lower leg may feel stiff, particularly first thing in the morning. You may also notice swelling and thickening around the tendon.

WHAT IS THE TREATMENT?

Stop your activity, follow the RICE procedure (see p.173), and seek medical advice. The doctor may advise you to rest for five to 10 days, prescribe pain relief, and refer to you a physiotherapist for exercises to strengthen the Achilles tendon. If there is no improvement, your doctor may suggest an ultrasound or MRI scan. Surgery is sometimes needed.

WHEN CAN I RETURN TO RUNNING?

Full recovery takes several weeks at least. With prompt treatment, you are unlikely to require surgery or suffer long-term problems, but even if your symptoms improve, you are at risk of another tendinopathy in the future.

PLANTAR FASCIITIS

The plantar fascia is a thick band of tissue that supports the foot arch. The repetitive action of running puts stress on the underside of the foot, which "bends" the toe joints, putting pressure on the heel end of the plantar fascia. This leads to a chronic condition called plantar fasciitis.

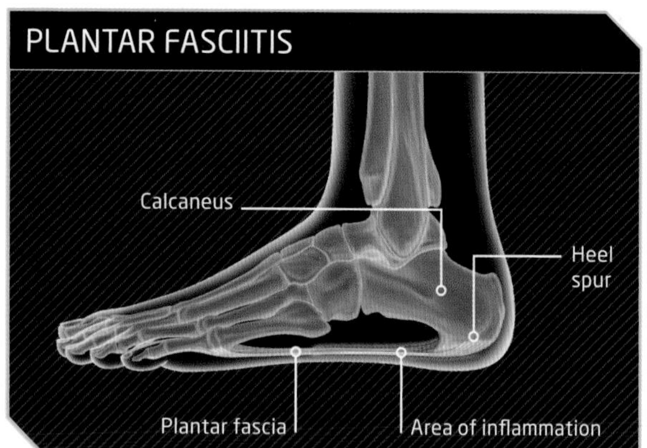

WHAT ARE THE SYMPTOMS?

Pain in the underside of your heel, usually most intense first thing in the morning or after resting, though it can worsen through the day. The pain may stop during running, but will return afterwards. An X-ray may also reveal a calcium deposit known as a heel spur over the calcaneus, which can cause inflammation in the tendons around it.

WHAT IS THE TREATMENT?

Stop your activity, and rest until pain subsides. Apply RICE treatment (see p.173) – the ice reduces swelling – then apply heat to promote healing. Seek medical advice. Your doctor will advise up to a month's rest and pain relief. You may need to have orthotics and/or heel cups for your running shoes, and in severe cases, a cast. Surgery may be required if it persists for more than six to 12 months. Physiotherapy will be required to stretch tight tissues and correct muscle imbalances.

WHEN CAN I RETURN TO RUNNING?

Plantar fasciitis should heal within a few months; if you have to have surgery, you should wait three to six months before returning to running.

TENDON INJURIES IN FOOT AND ANKLE

There are several groups of tendons in the foot and ankle that are susceptible to injury. Persistent overuse of the tibialis anterior (in front of the ankle) and posterior (at the back of the ankle) tendons causes tibialis anterior or posterior tendinopathy. Overuse of the extensor tendons that run along the top of the foot and straighten the toes, and/or the flexor tendons, along the bottom of the foot, causes tendonitis. The peroneal muscles lie on the outer side of the ankle and act to plantar flex (point), evert (point outwards), and stabilize the foot and ankle. Overuse of the peroneal tendons leads to peroneal tendonitis, as can a tendency to roll the foot outwards when running.

WHAT ARE THE SYMPTOMS?

Gradual onset of pain either in the front of your ankle or towards the back of your ankle on the inner side could be tendonitis in the tibialis anterior or posterior tendons. Pain and swelling on the top of your foot can be a symptom of inflamed extensor tendons. Tenderness across the underside of your foot, and a stabbing pain in the arch of your foot, especially when you stand on tiptoe, indicates possible inflamed flexor tendons. Swelling and nodules (small lumps)may appear on your foot. If the arch of your foot collapses completely, you will be unable to bear pressure on the sole of your foot. Pain or soreness on the outer side of the ankle indicates possible inflammation of the peroneal tendons. Peroneal tendonitis commonly worsens with running and eases with rest. Tendon injuries are often accompanied by swelling and the skin around the affected area will feel hot.

WHAT IS THE TREATMENT?

Stop any activity that causes pain, follow the RICE procedure (see p.173) and seek medical advice. Your doctor will diagnose you with a physical examination and possibly an X-ray or ultrasound scan to eliminate stress fracture or other injuries. Initial treatment will be rest and pain-relief medication, followed by referral to a physiotherapist. Persistent (chronic) tendinopathy is a sign that the tendons are failing to heal properly. The condition is difficult to manage and there is a risk that the tendons will eventually rupture. This may require surgery, followed by a longer period of rehabilitation.

WHEN CAN I RETURN TO RUNNING?

Depending on the severity of the injury, you should be able to return to training a few weeks after peroneal tendonitis; it will be six weeks if surgery is required. Recovery from tibialis anterior or posterior tendonitis will take about three months. Extensor or flexor tendonitis will heal in six to 12 weeks. If you have to have surgery, full recovery can take up to a year.

TIBIALIS POSTERIOR TENDINOPATHY

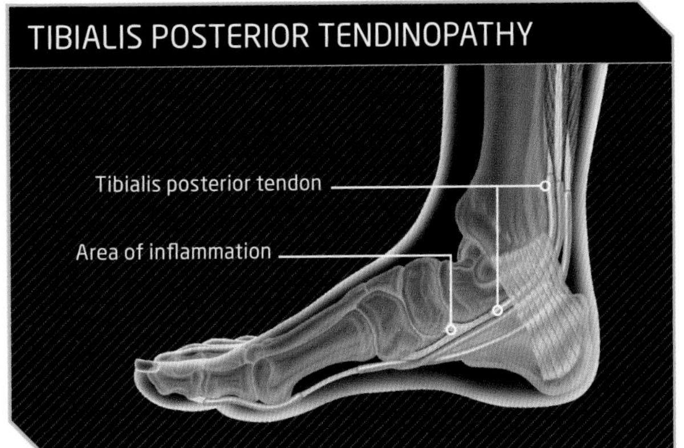

EXTENSOR AND FLEXOR TENDONITIS

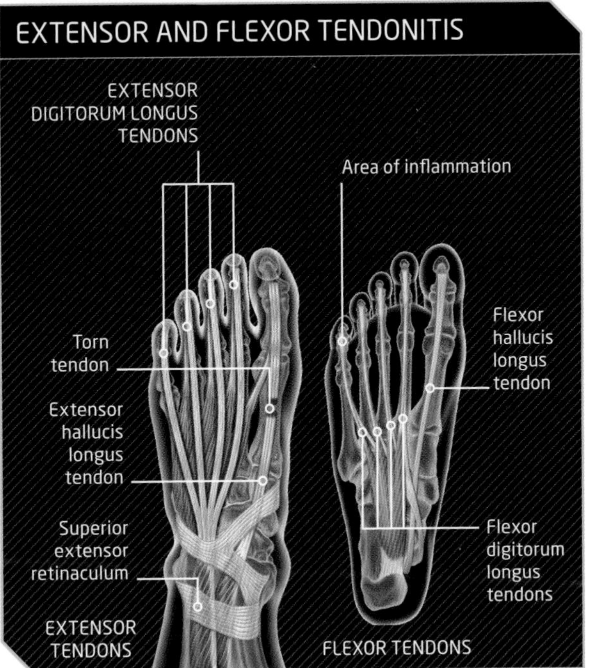

FITNESS CHARTS

Use these charts to assess your fitness levels using the instructions on pp.39-41. The multi-stage fitness test and Cooper 12-minute test (right) are designed to calculate your VO_2 max - your body's maximum capacity for oxygen intake.

NUMBER OF TIMES ITS OWN WEIGHT THAT A MUSCLE FIBRE CAN SUPPORT

RESTING HEART RATE (P.39)

This is the most simple way of measuring your physical fitness - all you need is a watch or clock. Be careful not to move during the test; you can also test yourself at intervals throughout your training programme to see your progress.

RESTING HEART RATES FOR MEN

AGE	18-25	26-35	36-45	46-55	56-65	65+
ATHLETE	49-55	49-54	50-56	50-57	51-56	50-55
EXCELLENT	56-61	55-61	57-62	58-63	57-61	56-61
GOOD	62-65	62-65	63-66	64-67	62-67	62-65
ABOVE AVERAGE	66-69	66-70	67-70	68-71	68-71	66-69
AVERAGE	70-73	71-74	71-75	72-76	72-75	70-73
BELOW AVERAGE	74-81	75-81	76-82	77-83	76-81	74-79
POOR	82+	82+	83+	84+	82+	80+

RESTING HEART RATES FOR WOMEN

AGE	18-25	26-35	36-45	46-55	56-65	65+
ATHLETE	54-60	54-49	54-59	54-60	54-59	54-59
EXCELLENT	61-65	60-64	60-64	61-65	60-64	60-64
GOOD	66-69	65-68	65-69	66-69	65-68	65-68
ABOVE AVERAGE	70-73	69-72	70-73	70-73	69-73	69-72
AVERAGE	74-78	73-76	74-78	74-77	74-77	73-76
BELOW AVERAGE	79-84	77-82	79-84	78-83	78-83	77-84
POOR	85+	83+	85+	84+	84+	84+

MAXIMAL OXYGEN UPTAKE (VO_2 MAX) TESTING (PP.40-41)

VO_2 max is measured here in millilitres per kilogramme of body weight per minute - please note that in this book it is measured in metric units only. Use online calculators for your chosen test for a quick way of finding your score.

RATING FOR MEN (ML/KG/MIN)

AGE	18-25	26-35	36-45	46-55	56-65	65+
EXCELLENT	60	56	51	45	41	37
GOOD	52-60	49-56	43-51	39-45	36-41	33-37
ABOVE AVERAGE	47-51	43-48	39-42	36-38	32-35	29-32
AVERAGE	42-46	40-42	35-38	32-35	30-31	26-28
BELOW AVERAGE	37-41	35-39	31-34	29-31	26-29	22-25
POOR	30-36	30-34	26-30	25-28	22-25	20-21
VERY POOR	30	30	26	25	22	20

RATING FOR WOMEN (ML/KG/MIN)

AGE	18-25	26-35	36-45	46-55	56-65	65+
EXCELLENT	56	52	45	40	37	32
GOOD	47-56	45-52	38-45	34-40	32-37	28-32
ABOVE AVERAGE	42-46	39-44	34-37	31-33	28-31	25-27
AVERAGE	38-41	35-38	31-33	28-30	25-27	22-24
BELOW AVERAGE	33-37	31-34	27-30	25-27	22-24	19-21
POOR	28-32	26-30	22-26	20-24	18-21	17-18
VERY POOR	28	26	22	20	18	17

THE MULTI-STAGE FITNESS TEST (BLEEP TEST, P.40)

This demanding test involves running between two cones 20m (65 feet) apart at an increasingly fast pace until the athlete cannot continue. Typically the test has 21 levels, of which even top athletes will only reach 15 or so. Use an online calculator to find your VO_2 max score.

	MEN'S LEVELS	WOMEN'S LEVELS
TOP FITNESS ATHLETES	15-16	14-16
WORLD CLASS	16+	14+
EXCEPTIONAL	14-15	13
EXCELLENT	13-14	12+
VERY GOOD	11-13	10-12
GOOD	9-11	8-10
AVERAGE	7-9	6-8
POOR	5-7	4-6
VERY POOR	5 OR LESS	4 OR LESS

THE COOPER 12-MINUTE TEST (P.41)

Perform this fitness test either on a running track or with a GPS watch - it simply involves running for 12 minutes and measuring the distance you cover. Correlate the results using the relevant equation on p.41 to find your VO_2 max rating.

RATING FOR MEN					
AGE	VERY GOOD	GOOD	AVERAGE	BAD	VERY BAD
13-14	2,700+m (8,858+ft)	2,400-2,700m (7,874-8,858ft)	2,200-2,399m (7,218-7,873ft)	2,100-2,199m (6,890-7,217ft)	2,100m or less (6,890ft)
15-16	2,800+m (9,186+ft)	2,500-2,800m (8,202-9,186ft)	2,300-2499m (7,545-8201ft)	2,200-2,299m (7,218-7,544ft)	2,200m or less (7,218ft)
17-20	3,000+m (9,843+ft)	2,700-3,000m (8,858-9,843ft)	2,500-2,699m (8,202-8,857ft)	2,300-2,499m (7,545-8,201ft)	2,300m or less (7,545ft)
20-29	2,800+m (9,186+ft)	2,400-2,800m (7,874-9,186ft)	2,200-2,399m (7,218-7,873ft)	1,600-2,199m (5,249-7,217ft)	1,600m or less (5,249ft)
30-39	2,700+m (8,858+ft)	2,300-2,700m (7,545-8,858ft)	1,900-2,299m (6,234-7,544ft)	1,500-1,899m (4,921-6,233ft)	1,500m or less (4,921ft)
40-49	2,500+m (8,202+ft)	2,100-2,500m (6,890-8,202ft)	1,700-2,099m (5,577-6,889ft)	1,400-1,699m (4,593-5,576ft)	1,400m or less (4,593ft)
50+	2,400+m (7,874+ft)	2,000-2,400m (6,562-7,874ft)	1,600-1,999m (5,249-6,561ft)	1,300-1,599m (4,265-5,248ft)	1,300m or less (4,265ft)

PAIN AND THE MIND

It is a good idea to learn to anticipate and work with physical discomfort and even pain. For example, if your legs start "burning" towards the end of a run, use this as a mental cue to aim for the finish line - and if you are feeling sore and exhausted, congratulate yourself on having worked hard. However, don't push yourself to injury.

RATING FOR WOMEN					
AGE	VERY GOOD	GOOD	AVERAGE	BAD	VERY BAD
13-14	2,000+m (6,562+ft)	1,900-2,000m (6,234-6,562ft)	1,600-1,899m (5,249-6,233ft)	1,500-1,599m (4,921-5,248ft)	1,500m or less (4,921ft)
15-16	2,100+m (6,890+ft)	2,000-2,100m (6,562-6,890ft)	1,700-1,999m (5,577-6,561ft)	1,600-1,699m (5,249-5,576ft)	1,600m or less (5,249ft)
17-20	2,300+m (7,545+ft)	2,100-2,300m (6,890-7,545ft)	1,800-2,099m (5,905-6,889ft)	1,700-1,799m (5,577-5,904ft)	1,700m or less (5,577ft)
20-29	2,700+m (8,858+ft)	2,200-2,700m (7,218-8,858ft)	1,800-2,199m (5,905-7,217ft)	1,500-1,799m (4,921-5,904ft)	1,500m or less (4,921ft)
30-39	2,500+m (8,202+ft)	2,000-2,500m (6,562-8,202ft)	1,700-1,999m (5,577-6,561ft	1,400-1,699m (4,593-5,576ft)	1,400m or less (4,593ft)
40-49	2,300+m (7,545+ft)	1,900-2,300m (6,234-7,545ft)	1,500-1,899m (4,921-6,233ft)	1,200-1,499m (3,937-4,920ft)	1,200m or less (3,937ft)
50+	2,200+m (7,218+ft)	1,700-2,200m (5,577-7,218ft)	1,400-1,699m (4,593-5,576ft)	1,100-1,399m (3,609-4,592ft)	1,100m or less (3,609ft)

GLOSSARY

Abductor muscle *Muscle* that facilitates movement away from the body.

Acute injury Injury that happens suddenly, for example a sprained ankle.

Adductor muscle *Muscle* that facilitates movement towards the body.

Aerobic Any process that requires oxygen. Used to refer to low- to moderate-intensity exercise in which the *cardiovascular* and *respiratory* systems deliver all the oxygen the body needs.

Anaerobic Literally means "without oxygen". Used to describe high-intensity exercise in which the body cannot provide all the oxygen the body needs resulting in a build-up of *lactic acid*.

Anterior Located at the front.

Biomechanics Study of the function of the body in relation to movement.

Bones Hard, living tissue that contains calcium and phosphorus. Bones make up the skeleton, which provides the framework for the body.

Bursa Sac of fluid around most joints in the body that helps reduce friction and allows the joint to move freely.

Bursitis Inflammation of the *bursa*, which makes movement painful.

Carbohydrate Substance found in food such as pulses, bread, potatoes, and pasta, and used by your body as fuel to give you energy. See also *glycogen*.

Carbohydrate-loading Eating low *glycaemic index* (or slow energy-release) *carbohydrates* to maximize the *glycogen* levels in *muscles* prior to a competition.

Cardiopulmonary Relating to the circulatory (heart, blood vessels) and *respiratory* (windpipe, lungs) systems and how they work together.

Cardiovascular Relating to the heart and blood vessels (arteries, veins, and capillaries) in the circulatory system.

Cartilage Flexible connective tissue that provides a frame for some parts of the body (ears, windpipe, or *respiratory* tract, for example). Also covers articulating surfaces, where *bones* meet joints.

Chip time Race finish time as recorded by a computer chip, provided by the organisers and worn in running shoes.

Chronic injury One that develops over a long period, and may also be slow to heal.

Cool-down Slow or gentle stretch exercises or running, done after a hard workout or race to help the body recover.

Core Abdomen and central trunk of the body.

Cross-training Low- or no-impact activities such as swimming, cycling, or gym work, which are used to supplement training, or to replace running and maintain fitness when injured.

CT scan X-ray computed tomography. This is a medical diagnostic scan that builds 3-D images of the body by taking two images and combining them digitally.

Dislocation Injury in which the *bones* of a joint are pulled out of their normal position; often accompanied by *ligament* injury.

DOMS Delayed onset of muscle soreness. Pain and stiffness that can develop in the 24–72 hours after beginning a new exercise programme.

Draft To tuck in behind another runner, letting that person set the pace and block the wind.

Electrolytes Essential minerals stored in the body, such as sodium, zinc, and potassium. Electrolytes are lost through sweat.

Energy drinks Nutrient-rich drinks for athletes that replace minerals lost through sweating during hard exercise.

Erector muscle *Muscle* that raises a body part.

Extension Straightening of a joint

Extensor muscle *Muscle* that works to increase, or extend, the angle of a joint, for example when straightening the arm.

Fartlek Swedish word meaning "speedplay". A type of training session that includes faster running alternated with slower running to add variety.

Flexion The bending of a joint.

Flexor muscle *Muscle* that works to decrease the angle of a joint, for example when bending the arm.

Foot strike How the foot makes contact with the ground, specifically which part of the foot first makes contact.

Fracture Break in a bone – anything from a hairline crack to a complete break. Depending on the bone affected, the break can be stable (fixed in position) or unstable (where the bone ends can move).

Glucose Basic form of sugar into which all *carbohydrates* are converted in the body.

Glycaemic index (GI) Ranking of *carbohydrate*-containing foods based on their overall effect on blood *glucose* levels. Foods that are absorbed slowly have a low GI rating, while foods that are more quickly absorbed have a higher rating.

Glycogen The form in which *carbohydrates* are stored in the body, usually in the liver and *muscles*. When glycogen levels fall during *aerobic* exercise, the body begins to feel fatigued and runners may "hit the wall", or feel they are unable to continue.

Heel counter Rigid cup at the heel of a shoe that provides support.

Hill repeats Interval workouts done on hills instead of flat ground. Benefits of hill work can include increased *cardiovascular* strength, as your body learns to deal with the waste product *lactic acid* more efficiently. *Muscle* strength and *turnover* are increased.

Hypertonic drinks Sports drinks that contain a higher concentration of salt and sugar than the human body – useful during marathons as they replace body salts more quickly than *isotonic drinks*.

Insole Inner lining of a shoe.

Isometric training Form of training in which your *muscles* work but do not contract significantly, for example when pushing against a stationary object

Isotonic drinks Drinks that contain contain similar concentrations of salt and sugar to those found in the body.

Isotonic training Form of training in which your *muscles* work against a constant resistance, so the *muscles* contract while the resistance stays the same.

Kinematics Study of classical mechanics in the body. Describes the movements of the different parts of the body and how they relate to each other.

Kinesiology Scientific study of the physiological, mechanical, and psychological mechanisms of human movement.

Kinetic chain Movement system consisting of myofascial (muscular), articular (joints) and neural (motor) components whereby each one is dependent on the others for optimum performance.

Lactate threshold Also known as the *aerobic/anaerobic* threshold, it is the point during high-intensity exercise at which *lactic acid* starts to build up.

Lactic acid A by-product of the body's use of *carbohydrates*, this builds up during *anaerobic* exercise, making the *muscles* feel heavy and tired.

Lateral Located on or extending towards the outer side of the body; also the outer side of a shoe.

Ligament Tough fibrous bands of tissue that hold *bones* together at a joint.

Lumbar Relating to the lower part of the back.

Macronutrients Categories of nutrients (protein, fat, and *carbohydrates*) that you consume in the largest quantities and which provide most of the body's energy.

Medial Located on or extending towards the middle.

Metabolism The sum of your body's chemical processes - it includes anabolism (building up compounds) and catabolism (breaking down compounds).

Metric mile 1500m (1640 yards) - nearest distance to the imperial mile, which equals 1609m (1760 yards).

Microfibre Lightweight, soft woven fabric with very tiny fibres, noted for wind and water resistance and its ability to *wick* (absorb) moisture.

Micronutrients Essential categories of nutrients that you consume in the smallest quantities - minerals and vitamins.

Midsole Central part of a running shoe between the insole and the outsole of the base.

Mobility exercises Exercises that mobilize the joints and *muscles* to prepare them for training (used for *warm-up*).

Moisture wicking Fabric designed to absorb moisture, especially sweat, from the skin's surface.

MRI Magnetic resonance imaging. This is a medical image technique used to visualize internal structures of the body in detail.

Muscle Soft tissue made up of bands of protein filaments that slide past each other to produce a contraction. Muscles work in paired groups, alternately contracting and relaxing to cause movement. There are two main types: *smooth* and *skeletal* muscle.

Muscle force Power generated by *muscle* action.

Neutral spine Position of the spine that is considered good posture, this is the strongest and most balanced position for the spine and needs to be maintained for most exercises. A neutral spine is not completely straight, but has slight curves in its upper and lower regions.

Orthotics Inserts placed in shoes to correct biomechanical problems.

Osteoarthritis Degenerative disease that causes bony growths to develop around the edge of the joints, and damages the *cartilage* that lines the joints.

Overpronation Tendency to roll the foot too far inwards when running.

Oversupination Tendency to roll the foot too far outwards when running.

Overtrain Condition caused by training too much, leading to fatigue, burn-out, and/or injury.

Overuse Repeatedly overusing or exerting too much strain on a particular body part, which often results in injury to *ligaments*, *muscles*, and *tendons*.

Pace Measure of the speed of running, usually described as the number of minutes taken to run a mile.

Plyometrics Exercises that aim to improve the speed and power of movements by training *muscles* to move more quickly and powerfully.

Posterior Located behind.

Pronation Rotational movement of joints such as the ankle and wrist; a pronated foot is one in which the heel bone is angled inward and the arch tends to collapse.

Range of motion Term used by physiotherapists to describe the movement a joint is capable of in any direction.

Recovery A rest period during which the *muscles*, *tendons*, *bones*, nerves and all the different tissues used in sport can recover from their workout.

Rehabilitation The process of recovering fully from injury, often with the assistance of medical professionals.

Resistance training See *strength training*.

Respiratory Relating to the respiratory system - nose, mouth, windpipe (trachea), and lungs.

Running economy Measure of how much oxygen the runner uses for a given, sub-maximal speed. In theory, two runners can have the same maximal capacity for oxygen use (called VO2 max), but the one who is more economical at the sub-maximal speeds is likely to be the better runner.

Rupture A major tear in a *muscle*, *tendon*, or *ligament*.

Scapula Shoulder blade.

Skeletal muscle Skeletal, or striated, muscle is attached to the skeleton, moves the body, and is under voluntary control via the central nervous system.

Smooth muscle Smooth muscle is found in the wall of all the body organs and is controlled by the autonomic nervous system.

Sprain Injury sustained when a *ligament* is overstretched or torn.

Strain Injury sustained when *muscle* fibres are overstretched.

Strength training Using resistance through weights or bodyweight to build muscular strength and stamina.

Strike See *footstrike*.

Supination Tendency to bear weight mainly on the foot's outer side (fifth metatarsal).

Tapering Reducing training prior to an event while maintaining *carbohydrate* intake to build up *glycogen* stores in *muscles*.

Tendinopathy Pain and stiffness felt in the *tendons*, normally as a result of overuse .

Tendon Bands of strong, fibrous tissue that attach *skeletal muscles* to bones.

Tendonitis Inflammation of *tendons*.

Thoracic Relating to the chest area.

Turnover Also called stride frequency, this is the number of steps you take during a minute of running.

Ultrasound Ultrasound imaging (sonography) is used as diagnostic tool. Therapeutic ultrasound can also be used to speed up healing process after injury: it increases blood flow to the injury, reduces swelling, and massages the affected area.

VO_2 max Maximum capacity of an individual's body to transport and use oxygen during exercise, which reflects the physical fitness of the individual. V - volume, O2 - oxygen, max - maximum.

Warm-up Essential mobility exercises that loosen joints and *muscles* and prepare them for exercise. A runner should complete 10-20 minutes of warm-up before setting out.

Wicking See *moisture wicking*.

INDEX

A

B

C

D

G

H

I